FROM
NATIVE SON
TO
KING'S MEN

Contemporary American Literature
Series Editor: Bob Batchelor

Gatsby: The Cultural History of the Great American Novel, by Bob Batchelor, 2013.

Michael Chabon's America: Magical Words, Secret Worlds, and Sacred Spaces, edited by Jesse Kavadlo and Bob Batchelor, 2014.

Hypermasculinities in the Contemporary Novel: Cormac McCarthy, Toni Morrison, and James Baldwin, by Josef Benson, 2014.

Stephen King's Contemporary Classics: Reflections on the Modern Master of Horror, edited by Philip L. Simpson and Patrick McAleer, 2015.

Beyond Gatsby: How Fitzgerald, Hemingway, and Writers of the 1920s Shaped American Culture, by Robert McParland, 2015.

Aging Masculinity in the American Novel, by Alex Hobbs, 2016.

James Jones: The Limits of Eternity, by Tony J. Williams, 2016.

Citizen Steinbeck: Giving Voice to the People, by Robert McParland, 2016.

From Native Son *to* King's Men: *The Literary Landscape of the 1940s*, by Robert McParland, 2018.

FROM
NATIVE SON
TO
KING'S MEN

The Literary Landscape of 1940s America

Robert McParland

ROWMAN & LITTLEFIELD
Lanham • Boulder • New York • London

Published by Rowman & Littlefield
A wholly owned subsidiary of The Rowman & Littlefield Publishing Group,
Inc.
4501 Forbes Boulevard, Suite 200, Lanham, Maryland 20706
www.rowman.com

Unit A, Whitacre Mews, 26-34 Stannary Street, London SE11 4AB

British Library Cataloguing in Publication Information Available

Library of Congress Cataloging-in-Publication Data

Names: McParland, Robert, author.
Title: From Native Son to King's Men : the literary landscape of 1940s America / Robert McPar-
    land.
Description: Lanham, Maryland : Rowman & Littlefield, 2017. | Series: Contemporary American
    literature | Includes bibliographical references and index.
Identifiers: LCCN 2017017288 (print) | LCCN 2017032535 (ebook) | ISBN 9781538105542 (elec-
    tronic) | ISBN 9781538105535 (cloth : alk. paper)
Subjects: LCSH: American literature—20th century—History and criticism. | Literature and soci-
    ety—United States—History—20th century. | Books and reading—Social aspects—United
    States—History—20th century.
Classification: LCC PS223 (ebook) | LCC PS223 .M37 2017 (print) | DDC 810.9/0052—dc23 LC
    record available at https://lccn.loc.gov/2017017288

Printed in the United States of America

CONTENTS

INTRODUCTION

Like waves on the beach at Normandy, memories of World War II slip in and then begin to recede. From a distance of more than seventy years, people may look back, telling stories, recalling a generation who lived, fought, and endured. Soon we will be left with only their stories, with diaries and letters, images and newsreels, pictures in photo albums, and flights of the imagination. Literature, film, and history provide a grand repository of stories that echo among our own. They are a mirror in whose reflection live lessons for our time.

Amid the winds of war, the generation who experienced the 1940s held strong. Told that they would have to endure hardship and fight for their freedom, they did. They chased their dreams; they lived their lives. They held on to hope. And they left us stories.

Stories make inquiries into our human condition. They offer dramatizations of our psychological and social issues, or provide expressions of our vitality, our dreams, or our spiritual malaise. The books that a culture's stories appear in may be symbols of national identity, and they are retainers of memory. Jonathan Rose writes: "For any nation . . . the printed word is essential for survival and identity."[1] In his introduction to *Realms of Memory*, French historian Pierre Nora suggests that "history is needed when people no longer live in memory but recall the past through the assistance of documents that help them to recall it."[2]

Books bear the thoughts and aspirations of one generation into the future to another. The generation that encountered the Second World War met the world through stories, through newspapers, periodicals, radio, films, and photographs. Historical memory is preserved in their stories, reports, images, and documents. American literature during that time continued to absorb the influence of the modernists, who generally held that a post–World War I wasteland could be redeemed through art. This idea informed writers of the 1940s. However, these writers began to take fiction in new directions. The tone and spirit of their time resides in the popular fiction that they wrote: in middlebrow stories, as well as in modernist literary art. The creative works of popular authors enable us to take the temperature of American culture in the 1940s. The fiction of this decade offers us suggestions about the dreams, hopes, anxieties, and cultural imagination of the times. These stories preserve a heritage and legacy that may contribute to our reflection on our dreams, goals, and values in our contemporary situation. They speak to the human condition, and continue to stir our imaginations and entertain us.

"For anyone looking at the history of the twentieth century, the war is in the way," writes literary critic David Wyatt. It separates the century into a "before" and an "after."[3] The Second World War period was a crucible in which much of our world was transformed. Historian William H. Chafe recognizes the 1940s and the 1950s as "[d]ecades that have shaped our lives," and he suggests that most Americans "have little sense of the underlying patterns that have produced the world we live in." Like many other historians, he views the Second World War as "a turning point in our history" which led to America's expanded role internationally in the postwar period.[4]

A patriotic perspective on this era emerges in the personal stories collected by former NBC News anchor Tom Brokaw in his 1998 book, *The Greatest Generation.* Brokaw assembled a series of portraits, a people's history of some interesting and dedicated individuals whose lives provide witness to this period. In contrast, historian Michael Kammen has suggested that there was a diminishment of altruistic goals after the war.[5] The literary critic Paul Fussell regarded "the Allies part of the war" as "sanitized and romanticized" by sentiment, and pointed out that our memory of the past changes and evolves across the years.[6] He added that "the real war is unlikely to be found in novels," for what happened cannot be easily represented. Fussell wrote: "It was a savage, insensate affair, barely conceivable to the well-conducted imagination."[7] Yet, novels do capture the flavor of the 1940s. They suggest the hopes as well as the anguish, the romance as well as the harsh facts of a critical and decisive time.

During the 1940s, that imagination was fed with entertainment, escapism, realism, the novel of manners, and social inquiry. The decade began with the searing examination of race and identity in Richard Wright's *Native Son* (1940) and the engaging southern stories of Carson McCullers and William Faulkner. Upon America's entry into the war after December 7, 1941, fiction in America remained concerned with life on the home front and with many aspects of experience besides the war. Stories appeared that illustrated the wide variety of American life, or brought characters and settings from abroad that enlarged readers' increasing awareness of the world. The 1940s brought changes in concerns and perception. Postwar fiction began to reflect these changes and to appeal to this audience. A veritable industry of fiction set in the World War II period emerged in the postwar years, along with history books and film.

This book offers an introduction to American fiction of the 1940s, and asks whether a kind of guidance for today can be obtained by looking back at the concerns of that decade. Brief synopses of some of the works of the era are provided as an invitation to reading. (With most of these stories, it seemed best to not give away the ending.) This is by no means a comprehensive account. This is an overview of a selection of significant books and writers from an important time in the history of American culture. They are books worth encountering, preserving, and enjoying. Like all good stories, they bring fresh perspectives on human experience.

Tom Brokaw has called America's citizens of the 1940s "the greatest generation." He articulates how those people's lives made a difference. When Donald J. Trump proclaimed "Make America Great Again" as his presidential campaign slogan, the roots of his triumphal assertion lay, in part, in the greatness of people's commitment in that Second World War era. The memory of what they believed in and the world they fought for is a legacy that can be sustained among us. That time of the 1940s was pivotal for the world that we have now. The concerns of that time parallel our circumstances today. The stories of that generation can continue to entertain and inform us. These are the stories that they lived and the stories that they read. The realities, the myths, and the dreams they lived by are reflected in the pages of imaginative literature.

In his book, Brokaw offered us portraits of men and women whose lives and values were shaped by the rigors of the Great Depression and the perils of the Second World War. Our attention here will be given to their imaginative lives: the books and films and music that lightened the burden of those times, or were entangled with it. As an introduction to America's fiction of the forties, this is also a glimpse at our cultural history. It is not so much an analysis as an invitation to reading that can help us to better appreciate our predecessors: our fathers and mothers, grandfathers and grandmothers, aunts and uncles, and the world they lived in and passed along to us. In another sense, this is an inquiry into the consciousness of that generation. It affirms that myth and stories are central to who we are as a nation and as individuals.

In the 1940s, the human imagination wrestled with war, the problem of racism, the struggles and dreams of daily life in a changing world. Imaginative literature assisted with inquiry into these issues, or provided escape and entertainment. As Thomas Freidman has put it, we need "peaceful imaginations" that serve to minimize alienation and celebrate independence rather than self-sufficiency, inclusion rather than exclusion, openness, opportunity and hope rather than limits, suspicion, and grievance."[8] An imagination that is inventive can bring us not only new technologies, economic enterprise, and political savvy in a globalized future; it can be inventive of peace, of workable solutions. It can build social relationships and spaces where we can meet in our politics and concerns and enter a dialogue about our life stories.

The human imagination has prospered from the literary creations and the personal stories of people who lived heroically through the war years. We can only wonder what a difference in our world the young people whose lives were lost in that war might have made. What we do have left from the 1940s are the personal stories of those who lived through that era. Many of those stories have been shared in families and neighborhoods, but may "remain unknown to the larger world," as Brokaw recognized in writing *The Greatest Generation*. However, he observed that "it's so important to hear these stories now, to know what an exceptional time that was for so many and how much they sacrificed to give us the world we have today."[9] The novels, plays, and films that are discussed here were part of their imaginative world. Their efforts and sacrifices have left us a legacy. The literature of that turbulent time is a valuable treasure chest waiting to be opened by today's readers.

In his essay "Writers and Critics of the 1940s," Gore Vidal writes: "To consider the writing of any period, including the present, it is perhaps of some importance to examine the climate in which the work is done, to chart if possible the prevailing winds, the weather of the day."[10] Vidal is interested in literary critics who chart the impact of books, rather than newspaper reviewers who write about them. The latter, he says, tend to reflect "the aspirations and prejudices of the middle class for whom they write." The critic brings scrutiny and analysis "to the private vision of another."[11] Vidal acknowledges the dedication of the "New Critic," who closely examines the text to determine its strategies. Yet, he concludes that the quarterlies in which their work often appears are "largely house organs for the academic world," and are often "more interested in commentaries on writing than in the writing itself."[12] Rather than literary critics writing for critics alone, we need to recognize that critics might also write democratically, for everyone concerned. That is the goal of this book: to invite everyone concerned to reconsider America's literature of the 1940s.

Writing in 1956, Vidal laments that the literary critics of his time do not spend more time with contemporary literature. If they did, he concludes, they would recognize that Carson McCullers, Paul Bowles, and Tennessee Williams are three of the most interesting literary artists currently writing. Vidal writes: "The interior drama at its most bitterly human comes into sharp focus in the writing of Williams and McCullers."[13] For Vidal, their writing is significant in another sense, for they are creative forces who stand free from authoritarian society and conformity. Vidal makes a case for the importance of contemporary literary art. The individual faces a new era in which one stands alone. Yet, "those who most clearly remember the secure authority of other times, the ordered universe, the immutable moral hierarchies, are the ones who most protest the black pit."[14]

McCullers, Bowles, and Williams each seek a "human universe," Vidal points out. It is one of love and compassion that can be "illuminated" by art. They do work "which a machine could not imitate." Vidal suggests that we respond to contemporary art and that we need it, for we are each alone. Stories and plays remind us that we can "communicate with others, touch and be touched." Writing and reading are a form of action, a means of communication in which one can "act and in the act forget his fate."[15] Gore Vidal was just one of many writers whose first works appeared in the 1940s to remind us of how, through interpersonal communication, reading, and imagination, we can touch life.

◦ ◦ ◦

An eruption of the magnitude of the Second World War is beyond the scope of any individual, and every perspective is a partial view. Fiction can be used to explore historical experience. A novel or film that looks back on history offers people a way to seek understanding.[16] Works of fiction are cultural artifacts that may express the spirit of their time. They are not fact-driven documentary history. Historians work against myth, and insist that their stories, or narratives, be grounded in historical fact. However, they also recognize that facts may be interpreted. An analytic history generally does not reach the wide audience that popular novels and films do. Narrative history, like the novel, seeks drama and strives for a narrative arc. The historical novel imagines history. The film re-creates history visually in a dramatic reconstruction. The history study offers an interpretation.

The impact of the Second World War on the novel was considerable. Americans Norman Mailer, James Jones, Joseph Heller, Kurt Vonnegut, William Styron, Paul Fussell, Shelby Foote, and William Manchester all served in the military during World War II. Ernest Hemingway, John Hersey, John Steinbeck, and others were engaged as war correspondents. Much also occurred on the home front, and the extraordinary inventiveness of writers like Eudora Welty, Richard Wright, Robert Penn Warren, Katherine Anne Porter, John Marquand, and Saul Bellow gave readers stories rich in art, insight, and the human drama.

The literature that these authors created was, in part, a response to the times in which they lived. The imaginative writing of the 1940s in America emerged from creative writers working amid a variety of social contexts. They were affected by the Depression era and by the Second World War, which dominated these years. The war consumed human energy; it prompted many changes and generated many stories. The writers of the 1940s were concerned with human behavior, issues of race, politics, faith, and the art of language use. They witnessed the further expansion of a large popular reading audience.

The art of the novel developed in the first half of the twentieth century with modernist innovation. In the 1940s and 1950s, the

American novel broadened its popular appeal through the introduction of the paperback. Americans were reading a wide variety of books, and the middlebrow audience expanded. When the Lynds studied Muncie, Indiana, in the 1930s, the sociologists observed that reading increased during difficult economic times. They noted an expansion of social clubs in Muncie, and an increase in radio listening by 1935.[17] Life was changing in Middletown. In a 1929 Muncie newspaper we can read: "The American citizen's firm importance to his country is no longer that of citizen but that of consumer."[18] Yet, the Depression imposed limits to consumption, and the new pressures of war from 1941 to 1945 compelled Americans to become active citizens. They were informed by print newspapers even when the war introduced paper shortages. People read for entertainment and for escape. They read for knowledge and understanding. A powerful nexus of communications in print, broadcasting, and film was steadily growing.

By midcentury, the American novel was poised on the edge of change. The questions we ask today about canon, class, race, identity, and gender were possible for readers of stories by writers like Carson McCullers, Richard Wright, Ernest Hemingway, William Faulkner, and Eudora Welty. In the forties, the close reading of the New Critics dominated discussion of these novels. Today we may read and re-read the writers of the forties from a variety of perspectives. We ask questions about narrative, the relationship between fiction and history, authorship, and interpretation by readers. This volume surveys a decade of the work of American writers with the intention of introducing you to some of the texts that emerged during those years. The emphasis here is more on cultural history than literary analysis. You are welcomed to explore the rich variety of storytellers who were at work just before mid-century. This is an invitation to read the young Norman Mailer and James Jones, who brought stark, graphic realism and iconoclasm. It is a plea for the reclamation of authors like James Gould Cozzens, John P. Marquand, John Hersey, and middlebrow popular authors like Irwin Shaw, whose star may have diminished across time. The 1940s book market featured Nobel Prize–winning authors like Pearl S. Buck, who drew upon her experiences in China, and John Steinbeck, who ventured an account of travel and investigation into marine biology, books of wartime propaganda, and a comic novel. Certainly, the writers of the American novel in the 1940s were the inheritors of a realist legacy. With their vision and revisions, narrative fiction began to reach toward new horizons and became influenced by popular culture, postwar existentialism, film, and the other arts. The novel, in its grand variety and its adaptations to film, theater, radio, and television, captured the rhythms and images of American life. It spoke the voice of America.

TRENDS AND CHANGES

Our lives have been affected by the aftermath of the Second World War, by Cold War tensions, the atom bomb, racial conflict, school segregation, women's liberation, the economy, and our "culture wars." The international arrangements and technological advancements of the 1940s continue to be part of our world today. The North Atlantic Treaty Organization (NATO) continues to be engaged with security, and the International Monetary Fund and World Bank are involved with a global economy. The GI Bill likewise had considerable postwar impact and contributed to the spread of suburban housing and the increased availability of both college and technical training. Some 5.6 million people became involved in civil defense programs on the home front. Women and African Americans were mobilized in the workforce during the war, and this led to changes the social and economic texture of the United States. World War II ended the Great Depression.

The idea of personal sacrifice "characterized the world of the Great Depression and World War II."[19] Tom Brokaw reminds us that the World War II generation was "a generation of joiners" who belonged to organizations like the Rotary, the Knights of Columbus, the Veterans of Foreign Wars, Elks, or Kiwanis. Generally speaking, moderation in spending was important to them, as was family, "marriage, well-behaved children and church."[20] Sociologists Robert Bellah (*Habits of the Heart*) and Robert Putnam (*Bowling Alone*) have lamented the passing of American community. One might argue today that statistics show far less millennial participation in mainline churches, greater consumer spending on credit, and less civic commitment expressed through the organizations that typified the previous era.

The war took many young men and some young women overseas, and left some families in suspended animation: separate, never knowing how their loved ones were doing.[21] It brought families together in living rooms where big cabinet radios sounded not only the news but the music of Glenn Miller and Artie Shaw's big band, Duke Ellington, Jimmy and Tommy Dorsey, and popular songs sung by vocalists like Frank Sinatra and Bing Crosby. The war brought people together, as veterans formed lasting associations and couples reunited and began families in a time that has come to be known as the baby boom. Marriage was a commitment, and preservation of the family and working together toward a common good were values held deeply as a nation's collective goals.[22]

In 1941, there were no supermarkets. There was no fast food. Apartments lacked air conditioners. The 1940s brought electric razors, tape recorders, 33 1/3 LP albums, and power lawn mowers. Around 350,000 American women were in uniform in World War II, and an estimated 6.5 million at work.[23] American industry buzzed, hammered, and sang in the factories. Music was in the air: big band jazz, swing, musical theater, and pop songs were on the radio. Benny Goodman's 1938 Carnegie Hall concert performance provided a high point for the growing respectability of jazz. Kate Smith's recording of "God Bless America" (1938) became a patriotic theme song in the years immediately before America's entry into the war. The radio was an important medium for news, popular music, and radio drama. In some homes, next to the radio was the phonograph. On October 30, 1938, Orson Welles's *War of the Worlds* radio broadcast frightened some listeners. In 1942, Bing Crosby's voice singing "White Christmas" evoked nostalgia and soothed his listeners. Awakening to the harsh reality of a global war after more than a decade of economic depression, Americans certainly needed some music, light entertainment, and wholesome nostalgia.

American writing lent itself to the visual medium of film. You can see plumes of cigarette and cigar smoke rising in those 1930s and 1940s Hollywood films. Cigarette smoke was in the air, and that made cigarette manufacturers like John C. Reynolds wealthy. The president of the company that made Camel cigarettes donated substantial sums of money to the 1940 Roosevelt campaign. Franklin Delano Roosevelt, for better or worse, was an icon of American government, smiling broadly, puffing away at his cigarette in a long holder. He sought to free the nation from the miasmic mist of the Great Depression. Perhaps American fiction made a contribution to the human spirit by offering the power of story and the freedom of imagination.

The New Deal

For Americans during the war years, Franklin Roosevelt was their president. To some it seemed like he had been their president forever. On March 4, 1933, the gray and overcast day that Roosevelt first assumed office, about 15 million people in the United States were unemployed. On the platform, Roosevelt took the oath of office and then spoke, assuring the nation that there was "nothing to fear but fear itself." In the presidential election, Franklin Delano Roosevelt had received 22.8 million votes to Herbert Hoover's 15.75 million. For more than three years the American economy had struggled through an increasingly troubling Depression. American citizens seemed to hope for a miracle from Roosevelt. In the months before the inauguration some four hundred more banks had failed. With the "New Deal," Roosevelt's administration followed up on his inaugural pledge. "Our greatest primary task is to put people to work," Roosevelt declared. "I shall ask Congress for . . . broad executive power to wage a war against the emergency as great as if we were . . . invaded by a foreign foe."[24]

President Roosevelt brought consolation and encouragement to the American people by radio with each of his twenty-eight "fireside chats." His dramatic performances on radio offered a sense of intimacy as families gathered near the radio, as if around a hearth. "Together we cannot fail," he insisted in his first broadcast. It was an assertion of persistence and unity that would be often repeated during the war years.[25]

Roosevelt suggested that the New Deal was part of a heroic struggle.[26] He sent young people to work on reforestation and conservation in the Civilian Conservation Corps. In May 1933, the Agricultural Adjustment Administration was set in motion. The Federal Emergency Relief Administration (FERA) followed. Harry Hopkins oversaw the social policy of the relief agencies. Most conspicuous was the Tennessee Valley Authority, which concerned itself with controlling the water supply of the Tennessee River through a series of nine dams. The National Recovery Administration of June 1933 was instituted to create fair wages and prices, to overcoming unfair trading practices, and to increase productivity. Harold Ickes was given charge of the Public Works Administration. A righteous public servant of Calvinist background, Ickes was a morally minded thorn in the side of some bureaucrats, and a vital advocate of FDR's New Deal. Ickes was said to have caught ten members of his department slacking off by including phrases from *Alice in Wonderland* in their WPA application. They claimed to have read it but, if so, none of them noticed the anomaly of Lewis Carroll's story in the document.[27]

Some Americans during those difficult years likely felt as if they had gone down the rabbit hole with Alice and entered a difficult and puzzling world. In 1933, Henry A. Wallace urged the U.S. Treasury to add the symbol of the great pyramid to the back of the dollar bill. Under that pyramid is written the words "In God We Trust." This was a society that held fast to that trust, that hope that things would one day be better. Trust and unity seemed crucial to Ma Joad in John Ford's 1940 film version *The Grapes of Wrath*. She evokes the phrase "In God We Trust" on the dollar, expressing concern for the future of the youngest Joad children who "got nothing to trust." However, at the end of the film this tenacious woman appears to reemphasize Roosevelt's comment that "together we cannot fail" when she asserts unity and resilience, echoing the first phrase of the U.S. Constitution as she declares that "we're the people."

This "greatest generation," as Tom Brokaw calls these men and women, faced hard times with tenacity and courage. Both rural and urban areas were affected by the Depression. Some areas of the United States were particularly in need. In the mining region of Kentucky and the coal districts of Pennsylvania there was impoverishment and there were difficult working conditions. The sharecroppers of Arkansas faced poverty. The dry cycles in Oklahoma, northern Arkansas, and Texas brought the disaster of the Dust Bowl. Men and women stood on soup lines in American cities. The children who would one day become the husband and wives, the soldiers, the workers, the future leaders of America looked on like the unnamed characters in the first chapter of John Steinbeck's *The Grapes of Wrath*, drawing circles in the dust, wondering if the men would break. And they did not.

Two years into his first term, Roosevelt was already broadcasting warnings about the dictators who were rearming in Germany and Italy.[28] In October 1937, Roosevelt addressed concerns about Nazi Germany and imperial Japan with his "quarantine" speech. The 1930s brought ominous social, political, and economic changes. The Depression exhausted America, and it was felt throughout Europe. France was beset by civil strife.[29] People turned toward fascist alternatives for hope. Franco took over Spain. Italy captured Ethiopia and looked toward the Mediterranean. Germany, amid intense inflation, set aside the Treaty of Versailles and the Locarno Pact and began rearmament. In the United States, the mid-1930s saw fierce labor disputes in several areas of the country. Roosevelt sought a balanced budget. However, a cut in federal expenditure of more than $2 billion affected the economy. In 1937, with a recession affecting manufacturing and farm prices, nearly 5 million American workers went on strike. John Steinbeck's *In Dubious Battle* (1936) offers perhaps the most convincing fictional portrayal how these economic impacts prompted a worker's agricultural strike in California.

Roosevelt took no action and voiced no formal opposition when Germany absorbed Austria in March 1938. While concerned about Nazi designs on Czechoslovakia, he remained quiet, again making no public statements. Neville Chamberlain's appeasement of Hitler was disastrous. Roosevelt proposed to allocate $300 million for rearmament. When Kristallnacht, the attack on German Jews, occurred in November 1938 the United States withdrew Hugh Wilson, the American ambassador to Berlin. While there were plans to return him to his post, Hitler's occupation of Czechoslovakia changed that.[30] Harold Ickes, anticipating Germany's movement toward war, rejected the sale of helium to Germany, which would be used for zeppelins.[31]

The European nations looked on as Hitler annexed Austria. Britain and France again responded with inaction to the German absorption of the Sudetenland. Neville Chamberlain had returned from the Munich Conference claiming that an agreement with Hitler marked "peace for our time." Then Hitler insisted on annexing the port of Danzig (now Gdansk), in Poland, firmly claiming rights to it. Obviously, these events presented a pattern of territorial ambition, a signal of future aggression. However, few anticipated the magnitude of the conflict that was to come. Further tensions developed in Europe when Poland refused Hitler's demands for Danzig and the Polish Corridor. Hitler knew that some of his generals did not want war, and that there was a plot to overthrow him.

Rumors of war caused the Roosevelt administration to shift their attention from domestic concerns prompted by the Great Depression to foreign policy. In 1939, Roosevelt urged the U.S. Congress to repeal the Neutrality Act. On January 4, 1939, Roosevelt cited a change in the international picture that he believed called the United States to a response other than strict isolationism: "The world has grown so small and weapons of attack so swift, that no nation can be safe," he said. "There are methods short of war but stronger and more effective than mere words, of bringing home to aggressor governments the aggregate sentiments of our own people."[32]

Roosevelt faced opposition from the isolationist wing of Congress and from notable public voices like famed aviator Charles Lindbergh and the staff of the *Chicago Tribune*. The president had to work to persuade Congress and appeal to the conscience of the American people. On Friday, September 2, 1939, the day after the German invasion of Poland, Roosevelt was asked by reporters at a press conference if the United States could stay out of the war. "I not only sincerely hope so, but I believe we can," he said, "and . . . every effort will be made by the administration to do so." In one of his fireside chats, days later, he said: "This nation will remain a neutral nation but I cannot ask that every American remain neutral in thought as well."[33]

In 1940, Wendell Willkie was nominated by the Republican Party to face Franklin Roosevelt in the general election. He was a businessman and the only nonpolitician to run for the presidency on a major party ticket prior to Donald Trump's candidacy in 2016. In the 1940 campaign, Roosevelt overcame a primary challenge from Henry Wallace, and won in the general election over Wendell Willkie. He received 27,244,160 votes to Willkie's 22,305,198, and 449 of the electoral votes compared to only 82 for Willkie. As Roosevelt prepared for another term, many in the U.S. Congress continued to reflect the stance of neutrality, a desire to remain apart from conflict in Europe. The America First Committee asserted its isolationist stance opposing intervention. However, new legislation was implemented to build American defenses. The Selective Service Act of 1940 allowed for a military draft of up to 900,000 new recruits for one year. This legislation would hold fast except in the event of a national emergency. The Selective Service Act specified that draftees had to serve in the Western Hemisphere. Then amendments to the act came on July 10, extending the range of military service beyond the hemisphere and raising the draft limit beyond 900,000. This action created some concern about the powers of the president as commander-in-chief to send troops overseas. However, the strength of the U.S. military would have been greatly diminished if the Selective Service Act had not passed and been extended.[34]

President Roosevelt addressed a joint session of Congress on January 6, 1941, and called for support for the European nations. America, he said, must resolve to uphold freedom of speech, freedom of religion, freedom from want, and freedom from fear. Within days came his proposal for lend-lease aid to Britain, which would supply the British with armaments. Senator Robert Taft insisted that agreeing to the appropriations for military aid was a movement in the direction of war. Arthur Vandenberg, Burton K. Wheeler, Gerald P. Nye, and Bennett Clark also vociferously opposed lend-lease. For these national leaders, nationalism, domestic concerns, and isolationism were more important than internationalism; America must protect its own borders and not be drawn into global conflict. Franklin Roosevelt had other ideas. While he repeatedly asserted that the United States would avoid war at all costs, he asserted that the country must back Britain and the European nations in their opposition to the present threat. The United States, meanwhile, began to build up its military with allocations of $10 billion in defense contracts.[35]

In the United States, Harold Ickes, Secretary of the Interior, wrote to Roosevelt on June 23, 1941: "It may be difficult to get into this war right away, but if we do not do it now, we will be, when our time comes, without any ally anywhere in the world."[36] Roosevelt sought aid for Russia to support resistance to Hitler's Germany. In July 1941, when Harry Hopkins arrived in Moscow as the U.S. ambassador, he was dealing with his own battle with cancer. On October 10, the isolationists in Congress proposed an amendment to prevent aid to the Soviet Union. This was defeated in both the House and in the Senate. On November 7, the Soviet Union began to receive lend-lease aid, as the German army was approaching Moscow. This commitment of aid drew America closer to war. Roosevelt, of course, had no crystal ball to see into the future of U.S.-Soviet relations.

Talks between Franklin Roosevelt and Winston Churchill took place on board the American cruiser *Augusta* and the British battleship *Prince of Wales*. On Sunday, August 10, British sailors sung hymns at a religious service that took place under American flags and British guns. The Atlantic Charter emerged as a statement of principles on August 12, and was made public on August 14. During this time, shipping on the Atlantic was a grave concern. There were several encounters be-tween American ships and German U-boats that could have drawn the United States into the European war. On September 4, a German U-boat was sighted south of Iceland on the edge of the American security zone. The USS *Greer* followed the submarine, reading its position with sonar. Four hours later the U-boat fired torpedoes on it. The *Greer* responded with eight depth charges. The next day, the *New York Times* advanced a claim in its headline: "Roosevelt Orders Navy to Shoot First."[37]

The Navy did not adopt a first strike policy. However, it did continue to face the threat at sea. While responding to a Canadian escorted convoy, the USS *Kearny*, a destroyer, was engaged by German U-boats on October 17. The ship sank, and 11 crewmen died and 124 were injured. The United States did not respond with any declaration of war or reprisal. However, when Roosevelt addressed the nation about the incident in a speech on October 27, he asserted: "Hitler's torpedo was directed at every American."[38] The USS *Reuben James* was attacked by a U-boat west of Ireland days later, on October 31. The ship went down, and 115 lives were lost. This again seemed to be a provocation that would lead the United States into the European conflict. However, Roosevelt did not seek a declaration of war. He was not certain that Congress would support this; a strong isolationist sentiment persisted in Washington. Meanwhile, intercepts of Japanese communications indi-cated growing Japanese aggression in the Pacific and Asia.

America was ill-prepared for war as the new decade began. There would soon be an extraordinarily vigorous arms program. American industry would go into overdrive. There was migration to the cities for work. The movement of black families from the South into northern cities like Chicago, Cleveland, and Detroit increased. Meanwhile, with the unsettling eruption of the Second World War, many women on the home front went to work for their families and for the war effort. This shift from the domestic sphere toward the economic somewhat altered gender roles, although prevailing attitudes remained. Rationing, shop-ping, food preparation, and domestic work was complemented by vol-unteer activity and by work in a variety of occupations. The marriage rate increased in 1942, with couples sealing their vows to each other before men went off to war. The baby boom was beginning.

Pearl Harbor: "A Day That Will Live in Infamy"

Everything changed on December 7, 1941. The Japanese attack on the military installation at Pearl Harbor catapulted America into a global war. The Second World War would change the United States, moving it from its neutral posture as a relatively isolated country between the Atlantic Ocean and the Pacific Ocean into a world power and an indispensable player on the world stage.

The concentration of the American fleet at Pearl Harbor was no secret. The presence of the fleet at Pearl Harbor was boldly announced by the *New York Times* on May 27, 1935. The headline that day was "160 Ships Berthed at Pearl Harbor: Most of United States Fleet Rests in Quiet Water in Hawaii." A *Boston Globe* reporter wrote on September 6, 1941: "A Japanese attack on Hawaii is regarded as the most unlikely thing in the world." Japan's fierce and carefully planned surprise assault upon the U.S. military installation at Pearl Harbor was a daring, almost insanely dedicated, raid that shook America and pulled the nation into the global war. The "day that will live in infamy" is captured well in the accounts gathered by Gordon W. Prange in *At Dawn We Slept: The Untold Story of Pearl Harbor*. The tragic drama is also capably portrayed in the film *Tora! Tora! Tora!*, which is far more convincing than Hollywood's later film, *Pearl Harbor*, which is a romance. Both the book and the earlier film recognize American heroism and express regard for Japanese military strategy. They restate the obvious: the morning of December 7, 1941, marked a momentous turn in history.

As 1940 began, Japanese agents were involved in espionage in Hawaii. The consulate in Oahu was targeted for this spying, and agents scouted the fleet at Pearl Harbor.[39] The United States had broken the Japanese diplomatic code, named "Magic." William F. Friedman achieved this in his work with the Signal Intelligence Service by August 1940, decrypting the Japanese "Purple" code system.[40] Some historians have claimed that naval messages were more difficult to decrypt. However, by 1941 the United States had become aware of Japanese intentions in the Pacific through the breaking of these codes. Intercepted messages between Tokyo and Honolulu suggested that a military move was being planned. Critics have asked what Washington might have known in advance of the invasion. In their view, it is certain that officials must have been aware of the Pearl Harbor fleet's vulnerability. "We were in a state of preparedness instead of a state of alertness," congressman Hamilton Fish of New York later said.[41]

In the days before the attack, Japanese envoys in Washington were negotiating the withdrawal of troops from Indochina. In stark contradiction to this, a convoy of Japanese ships out of Shanghai was sailing toward Indochina. Roosevelt met with the Japanese envoys on November 27. Magic traffic between Tokyo and Honolulu increased during this time. On Sunday, December 7, a Japanese carrier force paused about 180 miles off Oahu's shores. Into the dawn 350 planes climbed toward Pearl Harbor, eyeing its beaches and palm groves and rows of barracks. At 7:53 a.m. Hawaii time, the cry went out: "Tora! Tora! Tora!" Then the bombs began to fall.

A William Faulkner story, "Two Soldiers," suggests the shock of the event for Americans in the Deep South. A family is listening to the radio on their farm on December 8. A young boy from rural Mississippi and his older brother hear the news that will change their lives. In Washington, the president approaches the rostrum of the House of Representatives. He delivers his famous lines to a joint session of Congress: "Yesterday—December 7, 1941—a day that will live in infamy— the United States was suddenly and deliberately attacked by naval and air forces of the Empire of Japan." The elder brother enters military service. The much younger brother tries to find him in Memphis, and insists that he too wants to sign up and join the army.

The attack on Pearl Harbor that precipitated America's entry into the Second World War was a violent surprise aerial assault in a location that seemed to some almost impregnable. The harbor was well defended. Its shallow waters resisted torpedo attacks. Yet, evidence suggests that Pearl Harbor was caught by surprise. Pearl Harbor became a sign of vulnerability, but it also became a call to action. The United States declared war on Japan; Nazi Germany declared war on the United States days later. The United States had entered a war on two fronts—a cataclysmic conflict of global scope.

Nine hours after Pearl Harbor, the Japanese attacked the Philippines, destroying more than half of General Douglas MacArthur's air force while it was still on the ground. At 12:15 on December 8, Clark Field was obliterated. MacArthur would depart from Corregidor with the famous words: "I shall return."[42] Before December 1941, some of the fleet at Pearl Harbor had been sent to the Atlantic. Now the Navy had to recover from the shock of the attack and rebuild. Admiral Husband Kimmel, commander since February 1941, was relieved of command, and Admiral Chester Nimitz was named Commander in Chief of the Pacific fleet on December 31, 1941.

Commemoration of Pearl Harbor Day began the year after the attack. On December 7, 1942, the *New York Times* attempted to sound upbeat: "Pearl Harbor Day Finds Nation Sure: Time for Surprise is Past and America is Taking the Offensive, Officials Note." Some ten thousand people marched in a parade in Brooklyn. Admiral Nimitz asserted that Japan could not hope to achieve victory, and Secretary Frank Knox talked of a war of attrition against Japan's navy. The newspaper reported: "The Boy Scouts of Manhattan will start a daily ceremony of raising the flag each morning and lowering it in the afternoon in twelve parks and public squares of the city." In a note tucked away on the inside pages, we can read that fifty women's organizations in the Bronx planned to meet at 8 p.m. at the High School of Science on 184th Street and Creston Avenue. On December 8, 1942, the Red Cross New York Chapter held a service on the steps of the Subtreasury Building in the Wall Street area of the city. There was a moment of silence in the New York City schools. That evening, the American Bar Association hosted a dinner as a rededication to the war effort. [43]

Controversy has swirled for years about the Pearl Harbor attack. There were calls for an inquiry into how prepared the military was for the attack. A congressional investigation was approved on June 13, 1944. However, it was asserted that the secret classified status of the record must continue as long as the war was in progress. Military leaders at Pearl Harbor were later censured. Secretary of War Henry Stimson stated that General Short had the facts of an impending threat by Japan. The report read: "A war with Japan is threatening. Hostile action by Japan is possible at any moment." Stimson's statement asserted that "the outpost commander should have been on the alert."

John Toland, in *Infamy: Pearl Harbor and Its Aftermath*, argued that President Roosevelt had knowledge of imminent attack. Cinematographer Gregg Toland developed a film begun by John Ford that focused on asking why America was not better prepared for the invasion. Gordon Prange, in *At Dawn We Slept*, offers a balanced view and concludes that mistakes in judgment led to the catastrophe; he does not place any blame on FDR. But the theories have persisted to this day. James Perloff claims that research shows that "Washington knew in advance" and "deliberately withheld its foreknowledge" from the Pearl Harbor base commanders.[44] Robert B. Stinnett is equally strong in his criticism of Roosevelt. He notes a provocation strategy outlined by Lieutenant Commander Arthur H. McCollum, an officer with Naval Intelligence, in a report that indicates steps through which Japan could be prompted to instigate an act of war. Stinnett asserted that FDR engineered an attack on Pearl Harbor to get America into the war. Gore Vidal claimed that Stinnett, who served on the same aircraft carrier as President George H. W. Bush, had found a "smoking gun." But this claim must be qualified. It was argued that the United States could only crack Japan's diplomatic codes; Stinnett claimed that the United States could crack military codes as well as diplomatic ones. He asserts that Japan did not keep radio silence on their approach to Pearl Harbor.[45]

Japan's "Purple" code was cracked by 1940, and "Magic" was broken before the United States entered the war. A Navy cryptographer decoded what appeared to be a potential attack days before Pearl Harbor—a message asking for U.S. positions and information on torpedo netting. This codebreaking could not have prevented the attack, some historians argue; Japan never sent a clear message. Japanese ambassadors in Washington were not informed of their nation's plans for a military strike.

For the Pearl Harbor fiftieth anniversary commemoration, ABC News televised a special, "Pearl Harbor as Both Sides Saw It: Two Hours That Changed the World." This was presented by David Brinkley and written by Brinkley with Lionel Chapman and Yugi Hashimoto. The *Today Show* broadcast on location in Hawaii. CNN carried live each moment of the commemoration ceremonies. PBS broadcast "American Experience: Pearl Harbor, Surprise and Remembrance." CBS offered "Remember Pearl Harbor" with Charles Kuralt and General Norman Schwartzkopf. The Survivors Association gathered for their last memorial. People stood in line to see the USS *Arizona* Memorial at Pearl Harbor. The film *Pearl Harbor* was called by one critic "the movie that changes history as it sees fit."[46]

World War II did change the world. It set American manufacturing and the U.S. economy into high gear. The Gross National Product (GNP) grew from $91.1 billion in 1939 to $213.6 billion in 1945. The

U.S. war budget totaled $321 billion from 1941 to 1943. The nation showed an increase in research and development. The view that money was never to be wasted had come out of the Depression. The year 1940 brought an emphasis on savings bonds. With the war, these became "Victory Bonds." Taxes were withheld from salaries beginning in 1943.

The war also underscored service and patriotism. If "old soldiers never die, they just fade away," as Douglas MacArthur once said, many of today's patriots hold that it is our responsibility to sustain their memory and honor their contribution. Robert Dole was the last World War II veteran to head a major-party presidential ticket. On Memorial Day weekend 2016, Dole spoke of the World War II Memorial, saying that "veterans are so proud of it."[47] Dole's comment on observing Memorial Day was, "I know for some people it's just a day to go fishing but take a few minutes to remember."

So, we do remember: through memorials, through historical records, and through imaginative re-creation. Novels and films have an impact on how we remember events. They are imaginative re-creations that entertain us. They are works of art, or popular forms of storytelling, that appealed to readers and viewers in a particular context, at a particular moment in history. Stories may reflect everyday life, or imagine alternatives. Read with an eye to the culture in which they were produced, they can tell us something about the concerns and cultural habits of a period. The Second World War shaped the modern era. Not all novels of the 1940s concern themselves with the war, although that reality is often a shadow in the background of the stories they have to tell. These fictional narratives are works of unique, individual creators, each with his or her idiosyncratic artistic vision. However, these novels and films also speak of the culture in which they were created. In the interest of gaining a better understanding of our own period in light of the 1940s, it is to the imaginative creations of that culture that we turn.

SIGNALS FROM THE FIELD

Ernest Hemingway, John Steinbeck, and the
War Correspondents

ERNEST HEMINGWAY, *FOR WHOM THE BELL TOLLS*

One of the most popular books of 1940, Ernest Hemingway's *For Whom the Bell Tolls*, was written between March 1939 and July 1940. Hemingway was in Cuba then, chasing adventure. His story, set during the Spanish Civil War, takes place across three days in late May 1937 in the Sierra de Guadarrama, mountains northwest of Madrid. Perhaps the three days suggest a symbolic time frame: the three days in which, the New Testament holds, the events of the crucifixion and resurrection of Jesus Christ occurred. However, while Hemingway's character Robert Jordan suffers war, he is never clearly a Christ figure. Rather, he is a questioner. We hear from him resistance to religious solutions to the anguish, struggle, and mystery of life: no God, he says, would ever have permitted what he had seen.

Robert Jordan has taken on a cause and has become the leader of a guerilla group that enters boldly into enemy territory. His objective is to blow up an enemy bridge. However, he must wait until the enemy attack begins, and then destroy the bridge to prevent fascist forces from using the road. The novel is filled with drama and with love scenes between Jordan and Maria. Pilar, leader of the guerillas, offers a prophecy, plans strategy, and comments on the scent of death. The guerilla band becomes our community as we follow them and Jordan through the action of the story. There are comparisons between bullfighting and battle. The mission is filled with complications. Jordan's relationship with Maria draws the attention of Pilar, and creates some tension among his comrades. We see Pablo's opposition to Maria's love for Jordan. Enemy planes fly threateningly overhead. Jordan, a man of reflection, encourages himself to be a man of action. He says, "Turn off the thinking now . . . you're a bridge blower now. Not a thinker."[1]

The introductory caption to the novel draws the reader's attention to the poet John Donne. We are all part of the same continent entire and, thus, we are implicated in each other's lives, wrote Donne: "Ask not for whom the bell tolls, it tolls for thee."[2] For Whom the Bell Tolls proceeds to give us Ernest Hemingway's imaginative presentation of the Spanish Civil War. Hemingway was a news reporter and spectator in this war, rather than a soldier and participant. However, in going to Spain, he did face danger and expose himself to considerable risk. With his novel, he wrote a romance. George Orwell's Homage to Catalonia, in contrast, offers political analysis and concern about both fascism and totalitarianism.

In the early 1930s, Spain split into two powerful political groups. There were the conservative Nationalists, which included landowners, businessmen, the army, and the Catholic Church in Spain. There were the Republicans on the left: industrial workers, peasants, farmers, socialists, and communists. The mining industry had faltered and the agricultural sector was struggling, as perhaps as many as 3 million itinerant peasant farmworkers drifted across the country in search of work. Economic issues were severe, and unemployment rose. In 1934, there were general strikes in Valencia and Zaragoza, and street fighting broke out in the major cities of Madrid and Barcelona. Miners protested and villages were seized, Civil Guards were killed, and churches burned. Franco's army suppressed the revolt.

In Spain, on February 16, 1936, the leftist Loyalist Popular Front received the most votes in a close election. The nation then tumbled into the calamity that led to their fratricidal civil war. There were attacks on churches and convents, street gang violence, and general chaos. Franco responded to the unrest with a revolt, taking western Spain and lands north of the Guadarrama Mountains. His actions were supported by weaponry from Nazi Germany and from Italy, which supported a Nationalist victory in Spain. Franco's army took Cadiz, Granada, Malaga, and much of the southern coast of Spain by October 1937. The next year, his Nationalist armies pushed eastward, overcoming forces in Barcelona in January 1939 and in Madrid in March. Picasso captured the chaos of the bombing of Guernica in his memorable painting. The city lost one thousand people, and about 70 percent of its buildings were turned into rubble.[3]

Can novels influence or support action in the world and affect history? Fidel Castro, the Cuban revolutionary turned dictator who died in November 2016, once told Kenneth Tynan: "We took *For Whom the Bell Tolls* to the hills with us and it taught us about guerilla warfare."[4] In January 1959, Castro seized power in Cuba, and Fulgencio Batista fled to the Dominican Republic. However, in the view of critic Edmund Wilson in 1940, Hemingway's novel had little to do with politics but everything to do with a man taking a moral stance in the world. He wrote: "What Hemingway presents us with in this study of the Spanish war is not so much a social analysis as a criticism of moral qualities." Hemingway was an individualist, literary critic Lionel Trilling asserted; as a writer, "he is wholly at the service of the cult of experience and the result is a novel which, undertaking to celebrate the community of men, actually glorifies the isolation of the individual ego." Of Hemingway's *For Whom the Bell Tolls*, Robert Spiller writes: "It is hardly likely that this novel represented an awakened social consciousness." He adds: "The critics who saw in this book merely a tract for the loyalist cause were not reading Hemingway."[5]

Hemingway's novel was scheduled for publication in October 1940. It became a Book of the Month Club selection and sold a half million copies in the first five months. The novel was a best seller. In April 1941, the Pulitzer Prize committee voted it the best novel of the year. However, Nicholas Murray Butler, the conservative president of Columbia University from which the prizes are issued, opposed this and no prize was awarded. Hemingway's sympathy with the Loyalists came through in his novel, and this political edge was enough to persuade the committee to not award it the prize. The novel was critically well received; Edmund Wilson wrote in *The New Republic*, "What Hemingway presents us with in this study of the Spanish war is not so much a social analysis as a criticism of moral qualities."[6] Film rights to the novel were sold by agent Donald Friede to Paramount Pictures for $100,000, a hefty sum in those days. The novel gained a further boost in sales when the film appeared. Hemingway was not happy with the subsequent film.

During his lifetime, Ernest Hemingway made more income from the film adaptations of his novels than from his books. Paramount gave him $150,000 for *For Whom the Bell Tolls*, which was adapted for the screen in 1943 by Dudley Nichols. The dialogue and action in Hemingway's story made this story readily adaptable. So did its romance, and the clear objective of trying to blow up a bridge to hamper the enemy. Gary Cooper, a friend of Hemingway, was cast as Robert Jordan. Nichols diluted Hemingway's support for the Loyalist cause in Spain and made his script more neutral ideologically. Viewer interest would be held by the love story, not the politics. When Ingrid Bergman played Maria, her troubling experience of abuse by the fascists would not be shown; she would tell of it in words. Robert Jordan's interior monologues in the novel were eliminated, so that there would be less psychological depth and probing into the main character's consciousness. Even so, the film was three hours long. It was dramatic and strongly acted, and drew an enthusiastic popular audience. Gary Cooper, Ingrid Bergman, and Akim Tamiroff, as Pablo, were nominated for Oscars. Katina Paxinou, as Pilar, won the Academy Award for best supporting actress. The film was one of the box office hits of 1943.

In the film adaptation of *For Whom the Bell Tolls*, director Sam Wood focuses on the romance between Maria and Robert Jordan, and much of the novel gets swallowed up in the process. Hemingway took a hard look at the Spanish Civil War and was straightforward in his criticisms. The film provides period detail in wardrobe and weapons, Spanish saddles and horses. It considers moral issues of the war while implying support for the Republican cause. Yet, it does not enter the war as well as Hemingway's novel, or George Orwell's *Homage to Catalonia*.

Hemingway's Women and Marriages

When Hemingway returned to Key West in December 1939, he was dealing with his marital break from Pauline Pfeiffer Hemingway. Years before, he had left his wife Hadley and child Bumby for a relationship with Pauline. The affair had persisted through 1926, and he divorced Hadley in January 1927. In December 1939, he was now saying farewell to Pauline. He packed his things at Sloppy Joe's Bar, and drove to the Key West–Havana ferry the day after Christmas. Hemingway's sons Jack and Patrick returned from Cuba to be with Pauline. (Jack would live with his mother and spend vacation time with his father.) Hemingway planned another marriage, this time with Martha Gellhorn. She was also a writer and, at thirty-two, was nine years younger than Hemingway. Hadley had been eight years older; Pauline was four years older.

Hemingway's new wife-to-be was a war correspondent and she had been covering the war in Finland from November 1939 to January 1940. Martha Gellhorn was writing a novel, *A Stricken Field* (1940), which appeared later in the year under her maiden name. On September 1, 1940, the couple left for Sun Valley, Idaho. They married in Cheyenne, Wyoming, on November 21, after Hemingway's divorce was finalized. Gellhorn's short stories were published the next year as *The Heart of Another* (1941). The collection includes her well-regarded story "Ruby"; "Good Will Toward Men," which is set in France on the edge of war; and "Luigi's House," in which a woman returning from the Spanish Civil War tangles with a Corsican peasant. One of the highlights of the story collection is "Slow Train to Garmisch," in which a young woman, brokenhearted from a love affair, travels through Germany during the tense time of the early 1930s.

The Hemingways were a peripatetic couple whose journalism kept their lives in restless motion. The marriage was not without conflict; it was as though they didn't want to be apart, but couldn't live well together. Photographer Robert Capa celebrated them in a January 1941 photo essay, "The Novelist Takes a Wife," in *Life* magazine. However, the war and their careers affected the difficult balance of the marriage. Jeffrey Meyers tells us that Hemingway was drinking more after 1940, and that surely placed some strain on the relationship.[7] They took a trip to China in January 1941, just months after they were married, as Martha had an assignment for *Collier's* magazine. Chiang Kai-shek's war against Japan was not going particularly well. On the China trip, Martha Gellhorn went on the Burma Road, a dusty dirt path through the mountains from Chungking to Lashio, and Hemingway sent "Dispatches from the Far East." On June 9, an interview with Hemingway by Ralph Ingersoll appeared in the newspaper *PM*, and Hemingway wrote a series of articles for *PM* from June 10 to June 16. On June 10, he commented on

Russia's aid to China; the next day, June 11, an article on rubber supplies in the Dutch Indies appeared. Hemingway tells Americans that they should be concerned because their daily transportation relies upon rubber tires. He is clearly conscious of the moves of the Chinese communists. On June 15, he discusses these moves, and on June 16, he affirms that "Japan can never conquer China."[8]

Martha collected her articles on China in a volume titled *Travels with Myself and Another* (1941). Martha met and interviewed Chou En-Lai, whom she regarded positively, and predicted that, after the war, there would be a communist takeover of China. While Hemingway wrote his pieces for *PM*, he was not especially interested in China, observes biographer Jeffrey Meyers.[9] Meyers points out that travel and relationships often stimulated Hemingway toward writing; this time they didn't. He returned to Cuba and wrote no stories, instead writing intelligence reports.

For *Collier's* in 1942, Martha Gellhorn Hemingway investigated U-boat activities in the Caribbean. In Europe from 1943 to 1945, she turned her attention to reports of deaths of Jews in the Warsaw Ghetto and refugees fleeing Poland. During Ernest Hemingway's time in Cuba during World War II she was often away. In the midst of her work as a correspondent, she wrote a novel, *Liana* (1944), which was published by Scribner's. Hemingway found other pursuits to keep him occupied: writing, fishing, and spying on German U-boat activity. He also increased his involvement in his other favorite habit: drinking. Scotch and soda, whiskey, vodka, and wine became staples of his daily diet. He knew well that drinking "blunted the edge of his perceptions," as he writes about a character in *The Snows of Kilimanjaro*.

Cuba

In the first years of the Second World War, Hemingway lived in Cuba and organized a spy network that he called the "crook factory." Its goal was to collect information on Nazi sympathizers. He investigated the Spanish Falange on the island, gathering information through contact with local fishermen and other townspeople. In October 1942, Hemingway recruited Gustavo Duran, an artist who had fought in the Spanish Civil War. The undercover operation was approved by Spruille Braden, the American ambassador to Cuba, and Robert Joyce, who coordinated intelligence. The U.S. Navy at Guantanamo Bay provided support for the operation. Some agents in the FBI viewed this as a dangerous amateur activity, and something best accomplished by the FBI itself. Hemingway appears to have romanticized this mission. He prepared his boat to conduct surveillance, sailing out on the water to watch for U-boats. The U.S. ambassador approved his request to patrol "certain areas where German sub activity has been reported." Hemingway's boat, the *Pilar*, was armed with guns but looked like a fishing boat. He gained information on the location of German subs, although he never directly encountered one.

Finca Vigia, in San Francisco de Paula, was twelve miles southeast of Havana. Hemingway lived there on a hill in a Spanish colonial house with high ceilings and tile floors. He bought it in December 1940 with $12,500 from his earnings from *For Whom the Bell Tolls*. One may ask how Cuba, as a culture of artistic experimentation, affected Hemingway's art with its impressionism and African Cuban influences. Hemingway placed cubist paintings on his walls at Finca Vigia: Juan Gris's *The Guitarist* and *Le Torero*, Joan Miro's *The Farm*, and works by Paul Klee and Georges Braques. The place was maintained by gardeners, maids, and a carpenter. Hemingway employed a driver, a Chinese cook, and Rene Villared, the butler. Hemingway noted that the highway that ran downhill to Finca Vigia had trees on either side, bringing friends like Elicio Arguelles, Mario (Mayito) Menocal, and Thorwald Sanchez to his door.

Hemingway met Arguelles, a lawyer, in 1945. Arguelles owned a ranch and was a fisherman and a hunter. His father had been a fund-raiser for Franco in Spain, to whom Hemingway's own politics were opposed. Elicio read books from Hemingway's library. Sometimes they could be seen at Finca Vigia with Mario (Mayito) Menocal, a man Hemingway had met in 1935. Menocal was the son of an engineer trained at Cornell University, who was a general in the Cuban war against Spain. His father had been president of Cuba from 1913 to 1921. Menocal managed the sugar mills. Arguelles and Hemingway went hunting and fishing together; Menocal and Hemingway mostly drank together. Thorwald Sanchez was a relative of the writer Anaïs Nin, and the grandson of the Dutch consul in Havana and heir to a sugar fortune. Sanchez had many real estate holdings in Cuba. He also went hunting and fishing with Hemingway. He owned a yacht, where he mixed martinis and smoked cigars. Hemingway, intoxicated by more than martinis, threw Sanchez's clothes out the window of his home during his fortieth birthday party.

Hemingway as a War Correspondent

Ernest Hemingway, as a correspondent for *Collier's*, arrived on the seventh wave at Omaha Beach in the attack in the 1944 D-Day invasion. On June 5, he was aboard the USS *Dorothea L. Dix*; he was transferred to a landing craft on June 6. He heard the USS *Texas* firing its guns and watched infantry struggling up the shore. Like the other news correspondents, he was not permitted to follow the invading force onto land. His cover story appeared in *Collier's* on July 22. Hemingway wrote: "The beach had been defended as stubbornly and as intelligently as any troops could defend it."[10] However, despite mines and other obstacles, the Allies took the beach. On D-Day, Martha Gellhorn was on a 422-bed, white hospital ship marked with a red cross. It brought the wounded of both the Allies and the Germans on board for treatment.

Hemingway met Charles T. "Buck" Lanham, commander of the 22nd Infantry, on July 28, 1944. On September 4, he left Paris to join the regiment in Belgium on the Siegfried Line. On November 4, his article, "The GI and the General," appeared in *Collier's*. His report begins with a description of the land, much like we find in *A Farewell to Arms*. On November 18, he reported that "the infantry crashed the Siegfried Line."[11] Hemingway's Frederic Henry in *A Farewell to Arms* insisted on concrete language rather than platitudes or abstract words like *glory, honor,* and *courage.*[12] He recognized that words affect each generation's thoughts and imagination. When Hemingway became a correspondent for *Collier's*, he again had to provide words that would help his readers to see and construct their responses to the war raging in Europe.

Hemingway was not a soldier, except in spirit. Michael Reynolds points out that the author was more like a spectator at a bullfight.[13] Hemingway was an ambulance driver in the Great War. He saw some of the Spanish Civil War firsthand, and was briefly a correspondent during the Second World War. He was injured by a mortar fired by the Austrians. He experienced the impact of war. Reynolds points to "residual nightmares" and Hemingway's frequent tests of nerve.[14] Hemingway was an artillery casualty; he had been with the infantry, he told Colonel Charles "Buck" Lanham.[15] His short story, "Big Two-Hearted River," never mentions the First World War, but the story is shadowed by it. Nick wants to simply go fishing, forget the war, and return to how his life was before it. He dips down into the waters of memory as he fishes to restore and refocus his life.

Hemingway's private struggle with "residual nightmares" came even as publicly he was highly regarded. Malcolm Cowley, in his introduction to *The Portable Hemingway* (1944), placed the author with Poe, Hawthorne, and Melville. In the coming years, critics offered psychological insights into Hemingway's art. Philip Young (1952) provided a psychoanalytic approach, and saw Hemingway as covering a painful wound, "as a defense against reopening it."[16] One could also look at earlier evidence; for example, in a 1938 letter to Maxwell Perkins, Hemingway blames his depressed mood on having lived in a war zone while trying to write stories about the Spanish Civil War.[17]

War was at the center of his art because it evoked a life lived intensely. War called on a moral code that included courage and discipline. Hemingway wrote an introduction to the anthology *Men at War*, which he dedicated to his sons. Beginning in May 1944, he spent seven months in war-torn Europe, which enhanced his image of fearlessness. In France, in the months after the invasion at Normandy, he met with photographer Robert Capa and soldier-writer Irwin Shaw. Hemingway evidently wanted to fight; as a correspondent, he carried a gun, although he was not supposed to. He went on patrols, carried maps, and kept the gun in his room. Captain Marcus O. Stevenson, the public relations officer for the Fourth Division in the liberation of Paris, would vouch that Hemingway had not entered the fighting.

In September, Hemingway scribbled a long poem across eight pages in tribute to the men who had fallen in battle on the Siegfried Line on September 13 and 14. He carried it in his pocket while he was in Paris.[18] He was involved with the fighting in the Hurtgenwald, between Aachen and Bonn, with the 22nd Infantry regiment. He was engaged there for more than eighteen days, from November 15 to December 4. These weeks included some of the most intense fighting he witnessed during the war. One incident forced him to join the combatants. On November 22, a German platoon hunkered down in a bunker near their camp at a forest clearing. Two days later they came storming out, attacking and killing the commander, Captain Mitchell. Hemingway, in the thick of it, had to fire back at the enemy with a machine gun. The Germans were then captured and held prisoner. But German artillery barrages in the next several days did not let up, and Hemingway was a witness to that destruction as well. He was also present when the 22nd Regiment cleared out the village of Grosshau in hand-to-hand combat. The regiment was "virtually decimated," Hemingway biographer Carlos Baker tells us: "Between November 16 and December 3 it sustained 2,678 casualties."[19]

Retiring from this field of battle, Hemingway soon was witness to another one. Despite being ill with pneumonia and preparing for his return to the United States, he responded to the news that a German mechanized onslaught had begun in Luxembourg against the First Army Division's defenses. He evidently wanted again to be near the action, but by the time he reached the area, the most intense fighting had already passed. He gathered information on the conflict. This participation as a war correspondent took place in what later came to be known as the Battle of the Bulge.

During his time as a war correspondent for *Collier's* in 1944–1945, Ernest Hemingway established a relationship with Mary Welsh, who was from Minnesota. Welsh was a news correspondent who had recently been married to Noel Monks, an Australian who worked for the *Daily Mail* in London. Welsh was a *Time* London correspondent who had worked for the *London Daily Express*. She had reported from Munich on Neville Chamberlain's meeting with Adolph Hitler in September 1938, and had reported from London on the Blitz in 1940. Hemingway asked Irwin Shaw to introduce him to Walsh, and they met on December 24, the day before Christmas. He engaged in an affair with her at the Ritz Hotel in Paris. Tensions between Ernest and Martha Gellhorn remained, and the marriage was nearly over. Carlos Baker tells the story of how Hemingway met with Mary Welsh at the Paris Ritz with officers Buck Lanham and Bob Chance of the 22nd Infantry Regiment, who were back from their military command posts. Hemingway took a photograph of Mary's husband with him into the men's room and shot it to pieces. He also destroyed the toilet.[20]

Hemingway returned to the United States and to Cuba with Mary as his fourth wife. His son John H. Hemingway (called Bumby as a child and now known as Jack) remained a prisoner of war. On May 28 Jack had parachuted with an Office of Strategic Services (OSS) force into La Bosquet d'Orb, north of Montpelier, to train partisans of the French underground. However, he and Captain Justin Green were captured in the forest along with one of those partisans. Remarkably, the captain in charge of the unit that captured them was an Austrian who had known Ernest Hemingway and had met Jack as a child. He sent Jack to a hospital in Alsace, and he was freed from a POW camp near Hammel-burg. Unfortunately, Jack was captured again and placed in Stalag Luft III at Nuremberg. He did not see freedom until the spring of 1945.

One would think that Ernest Hemingway would follow through with a full-length novel based upon his 1944 experiences. There might have been a rousing story of action from D-Day to his involvement at Hurt-genwald. But Hemingway chose a different approach. He returned to the United States with the thought of bringing his experiences to bear on a new novel about the Second World War. Instead, he began writing *Garden of Eden*, a story that emerged spontaneously and was not about the war. He later created the story of an aging military man, *Across the River and Into the Trees* (1950), which fell short of any monumental ambitions to write a World War II novel.

Ernest Hemingway traveled with his newly pregnant wife Mary Welsh Hemingway toward Sun Valley, Idaho. While in Casper, Wyo-ming, she complained of pain. Mary had an ectopic pregnancy and her left fallopian tube had burst. In critical condition, she was rushed to the hospital and survived the ordeal. The writer who had once created the fatal demise of Catherine Barkley in *A Farewell to Arms* was spared the reality of the death of his pregnant wife.

Hemingway wrote *Garden of Eden* by hand; the story was typed later. He began the story in a seaport village, Le Grau-de-Roi. David Bourne, a novelist, enjoys his time with his wife, Catherine. Other char-acters, Nick and Barbara Sheldon, live on the rue du Cardinal Lemoine. These couples have been considered reflections of Hemingway's life with his previous wives.[21] Carlos Baker notes that by 1947, about a hundred pages of this novel were typed and more than nine hundred pages had been written by hand. This was a long, unwieldy work that would later need to be edited. Hemingway told Buck Lanham that he wrote it spontaneously, or as Carlos Baker put it, "invented it minute to minute."[22] This approach to writing *Garden of Eden* reveals a Hemingway who, as a writer, is quite different from the young man who once painstakingly crafted his stories in Paris in the 1920s.

Hemingway was a good reader of the national character and America's limitations, Walter Lippmann once pointed out.[23] Hemingway moved away from European culture and found new places to live and work: Cuba, Key West, Sun Valley, and Ketchum, Idaho. By the mid-1940s, his writing had begun to change to something less laconic, more expansive. His white beard had gown full on his face. It would become the image Hemingway would be identified by in the 1950s. Meanwhile, there were other changes. In June 1947, his longtime editor, Maxwell Perkins, died. In August, Hemingway suffered from headaches and hypertension. He spent some time at Sun Valley. In 1948, interviews with critic Malcolm Cowley were turned into articles that built the Hemingway legend: that of a sturdily masculine heroic man. Hemingway read *The Young Lions* by Irwin Shaw and *In Sicily* by Elio Vitorini.[24] He was convinced that Shaw had portrayed Mary Welsh as his character Louise, and had created a character from his brother Leicester. He did not like the book, which was intended for a popular audience. Vitorini's book he liked better, and commented on the specific images of Sicily. Cowley's first article, "A Portrait of Mister Papa," appeared in *Life* magazine. Hemingway had rejected the idea of a full-length biography. Meanwhile, he had turned his attention to writing a new novel, eventually deciding on the title *Across the River and Into the Trees*.

Across the River and Into the Trees (1950) was not as strong a novel as *For Whom the Bell Tolls*. John O'Hara responded with a review on the first page of the *New York Times Book Review*, in which he called Hemingway the best writer since Shakespeare.[25] Subsequent critical evaluations were more modest. Jackson Benson groups *Across the River and Into the Trees* with "dark laughter" and calls it a "novel of pity and irony."[26] In the novel Richard Cantwell, a professional soldier, is growing older and is interested in a woman half his age. Perhaps he is unable to let go of his lost youth. He appears to be a man who is caught up in romantic illusions, but takes himself quite seriously. Cantwell believes in honor and heroism. Cantwell's driver thinks that his eccentricity comes from being frequently injured.

Hemingway, likewise, took blows. He suffered several concussions, which surely could have contributed to his times of depression. There were airplane accidents, three car wrecks, and the injuries he sustained in Italy in World War I. He was a man both strong and broken, with nightmares, insomnia, depression, and likely post-traumatic stress disorder. Hemingway made gestures toward danger, and ritualized courage and honor. Carl Van Doren saw a sensitive man, "subtle and articulate beneath his swaggering surfaces."[27] He faced danger, had an impressive will, and exhibited bravery.

Once he was finished with the novel, Hemingway expected to see it serialized in *Cosmopolitan* magazine. Aaron Hotchner had arrived in Cuba for a vacation with his wife in September and was given the first chapters. (There was little derring-do in this venture, as there might be in an episode of *Criminal Minds*, in which the television show's FBI team leader is Aaron Hotchner's namesake.) Hotchner became Hemingway's agent with *Cosmopolitan*.

THE WAR CORRESPONDENT IN EUROPE

Hemingway's work as a war correspondent during the Second World War was a relatively brief episode in his career. For others, reporting on the war was a formative experience in the lives of many young men and women who had an impact upon journalism and popular writing. News media reporters in the 1940s included John Hersey, novelist and journalist. William Shirer was stationed in Berlin for CBS. Joseph Mitchell was a *New Yorker* staff writer from 1938. Gordon Parks in 1948 became the first African American photographer for *Life*. Ernie Pyle, the folksy, poetic journalist, was killed toward the end of the war. George Polk died covering the Greek Civil War in 1948. Walter Winchell was a gossip columnist who had a radio show in 1948.

Several news corporations and networks that remain important in our era were significant players in 1940s media, CBS and Time/Life among them. News reporters of the 1940s included Edward R. Murrow, who would become the voice of CBS and public affairs director for the network. Murrow gave details of the European war and London reports to radio listeners. William Shirer, a CBS correspondent stationed in Berlin, later wrote riveting recollections of his experiences in *The Berlin Diary* and *The Rise and Fall of the Third Reich*. Eric Sevareid, who reported on the war from Europe and other parts of the world, became national correspondent for the CBS Evening News and a mainstay of broadcast journalism through the 1970s. He reported on the fall of Paris in 1940 and the D-Day invasion at Omaha Beach. In Burma, his plane had engine trouble, and he was forced to parachute to safety. Charles Collingwood was a Murrow protégé who reported on Operation Torch in North Africa and opposed criticism of broadcasters in the 1950s. Larry Lessneur covered the London bombings for CBS on *London After Dark*. He also covered news at the front in the Soviet Union, reported on the liberation of Paris, and saw firsthand the liberation of the Dachau concentration camp. He later worked with CBS and Voice of America. Howard K. Smith started his long career as a foreign correspondent with United Press International (UPI) in London. He joined the Murrow team in 1941 and was assigned to Berlin. He became CBS bureau chief after the war and later became the anchor for ABC News and the moderator for *Face the Nation*. Walter Cronkite also began work with UPI and covered action in North Africa and Europe. Cronkite stayed with UPI despite an offer from the Murrow organization. He was selected as one of eight journalists on B-17 bombing missions, flying with the 101st Airborne, and he covered the Battle of the Bulge. From 1946 to 1948, Cronkite was UPI's lead reporter in Moscow. Another offer from Murrow in 1950 led to his work with a CBS affiliate in Washington, DC. He was the CBS anchor for the presidential conventions in 1952, 1956, and 1960. This developed into his distinguished career as the CBS television news anchor.

Time magazine brought news and feature articles on personalities and events to millions of readers. *Life* magazine emerged as a popular periodical with striking photography and award-winning photojournalism. It was no secret that Franklin Roosevelt disliked Henry Luce, owner of both *Time* and *Life* magazines. Clare Booth Luce, who was elected to the House of Representatives in 1942, was an opponent of Roosevelt's policies. In 1943, Roosevelt, likely out of distaste for *Time* magazine, rejected a proposal to give *Time* war correspondent John Hersey the Silver Star for his assistance of the wounded while under fire. Hersey had written the novel *A Bell for Adano* and would write *Hiroshima*, a vivid account of the experience of survivors of the nuclear blast over the city of Hiroshima on August 6, 1945.

The growth of new media outlets also brought opportunities for female journalists. Women made strong contributions to both print and photojournalism. Mary Marvin Breckenridge, a photographer and videographer, was the first female correspondent for CBS. When she married diplomat Jefferson Patterson, she retired from broadcasting. Margaret Bourke-White was raised in a family that heavily supported female equality and her personal development. She became a leader in the field of photojournalism, and many of her photos graced the cover of *Life* from 1936 on. Marguerite Higgins earned a degree from the Columbia School of Journalism and joined the *New York Tribune*. She was allowed to go to London in 1944, and reported on the war from France. She later traveled with troops that liberated the Dachau and Buchenwald concentration camps.

American writers covering the war overseas reached an audience at home. Ernie Pyle was perhaps the most famous of World War II correspondents, writing on military action and soldier life in North Africa, Italy, and in the Pacific. He received the Pulitzer Prize in 1944 for his reporting. Pyle connected with the troops and brought colorful human-interest stories to the attention of his readers. He died in the war, in service to his profession, his readers, and his vision of freedom.

A. J. Liebling

The ordinary American engaged in an extraordinary undertaking was at the center of journalist A. J. Liebling's reports and stories of the war. In dozens of vignettes, he recorded voices and images that bring us to the places and situations about which he wrote. He recalled one British mother who protected her children during a London air raid: "I remember one woman throwing her children on the ground and covering them with her body. I was never to see people so frightened during a real bombing."[28]

Liebling observed people in Paris the year before the city was invaded by the German army. German planes were flying reconnaissance missions overhead, and he wrote that the people of Paris were "tentatively picking up the threads of existence."[29] In May 1940 he saw that Paris was in grave danger. Holland had fallen, and Belgium surrendered on May 21. He pointed out that "an individual soldier had no chance to understand the military situation as a whole."[30] He was in a bar of the Hotel Cotti "for the aperitif" when he heard "a tremendous noise of motors in airplanes too high to be seen."[31] The sound was met by the pulse of antiaircraft guns. Waiters in the restaurant lowered the shades. The bombardment lasted for about forty-five minutes. On June 5, there was a second attack, and by Monday, June 10, he was at the Spanish consulate requesting a visa to leave France. "The roads leading south from Paris were gorged with what was possibly the strangest assortment of vehicles in history," he wrote.[32] In Bordeaux the streets were filled with anxious people, several of them refugees. They crossed to the Spanish frontier.

Liebling concluded that German industry would support the German army's military victories, and wrote: "The French strategy had been amorphous, the tactics bad, and the material woefully and unexpectedly deficient."[33] He added that this was not a deficiency of the people. Liebling went on to Lisbon, a city that he said was "not easy in its mind" and wanted to stay free from "the Spanish yoke."[34] In a wine bar, he met a man who claimed that Hitler had "absolutely no designs on Canada or the United States." The man said of Hitler: "He is a fair man and wants only his rights."[35]

The New Yorker arranged for Liebling's journey home to the United States. In New York, he and his colleague Dick Boyer, who had returned from Berlin, walked in Rockefeller Plaza, watching the skaters on the rink who were moving to the music of a waltz. Boyer said, "That girl skates as if thousands of other girls weren't cold or hungry or cowering from bombs."[36] On October 14, 1940, Liebling registered in an elementary school for compulsory military service. He squeezed into a child's desk, thinking not about the war, but about school and math classes in long division.[37] He remained in the United States until July 1941. *McCall's* magazine had him write in a propaganda campaign to "make the subjects as clear as a dress pattern," and he observed that the isolationist *Chicago Tribune* had a cartoon of Lady Liberty "loaded with chains," beaten as if by "a sort of ape man."[38] Concerned about isolationism and "para-fascists" like Charles Lindbergh, he declared: "I think democracy a most precious thing, not because any democratic state is perfect, but because it's perfectible."[39]

War came to civilian populations. The dividing line between soldier and civilian dissolved. Liebling reported that he and an acquaintance entered an establishment in London that felt like an American club. Some women sat down with them. One of the women "was clearly distraught" and was "not making too much sense." She was affected by the London bombings and seeing people dead or badly injured. "Why didn't you get out of this bloody awful London?" he asked her. "Every time the blitz came I'd get blind drunk," she said. The bombings continued and she repeated this behavior. "I thought I'd go mad," she said.[40] Liebling pointed out that there had been no blitz for two months. This woman's nervous system was disturbed by the shock of war. Other people seem more resilient. We hear in Liebling's missives the voices of people who have been displaced and are staying at a hotel; it is a model of English propriety, he noted, but outside "there resounded pretty continually the cheerful click of the Picadilly tarts' high heels."[41] In summer 1941, "the Germans had knocked the world about," Liebling wrote, but "Britain was getting stronger by the minute."[42] He also saw the movements of espionage around him: "Operatives shadowed each other, until lunch at Claridge's or the Ritz Grill resembled a traffic jam of characters out of an Alfred Hitchcock film."[43]

The war correspondent went to North Africa on November 9, 1942, about twenty-four hours after the first landings there. Also with him was Ernie Pyle, who would become perhaps the best-known correspondent of the war. Pyle was writing for Scripps-Howard; Bill Lang of Time-Life, Red Mueller of *Newsweek,* Ollie Stewart of the *Baltimore Afro-American*, and Bob Neville for *Yank*, an army magazine, also had come aboard. There was an air raid on Oran the night Liebling arrived.[44] He stayed in Algeria at the Hotel Leon and he wrote about "Photo Freddie," a German air reconnaissance pilot who would fly overhead.[45] Nobody wanted to hurt Freddie, he tells us. Freddie had become a familiar sight, like the hands on the farm that "popped into slit trenches when the bombs began to fall."[46] Libeling wrote about Brigadier General Teddy Roosevelt, the assistant division commander, who with his staccato walk, short cane, and head down in a determined stride, always visited the men. The namesake of his relative, the former president, memorized verse and read detective stories, according to Liebling.[47]

Liebling provided us with narratives, stories of experiences, vivid images of people, and rich descriptions of battle. He gave us pictures with words, images of "geysers" of black smoke that are shell bursts, and "a dozen dots" of tanks seen from a distance; the tanks were described as "clumsy black bodies, belching dark smoke."[48]

The correspondent's portraits of infantry include one of an individual who might be called a common reader, a private from the Bensonhurst section of Brooklyn who was captured at the end of the North African campaign. Liebling observed that he was reading a copy of *Candide*. "These little books are a great thing," the soldier said. "They take you away. I think the fellow that wrote it, Voltaire, used the same gag too often though."[49] Fassy was also from Brooklyn, and Liebling introduced these two men. One of them asked the other: "So, do you know Sidney Wetzelbaum?"[50] Liebling acknowledged the great changes that they had all experienced. "The past didn't look like Sheepshead Bay now," he wrote.[51] There is a man from Louisiana wearing a tin helmet, who had spent a year at Tulane. A big college football player named Vaghi is from Danbury, Connecticut. Frankel, a signalman, is from East 18th Street in Brooklyn. He had played in dance bands. Sergeant Angelatti, from Cleveland, is glad he has been "saved." Lieutenant Miller appears nervous. Liebling gave us portraits of men who are about to enter battles far from home. Much like Ernie Pyle, he wrote with a storytelling quality that brought the humanity of soldiers at war home to his readers.

Propaganda and Public Opinion

Wartime needs propelled media outlets to enlist American writers in the business of propaganda. The government reached out to filmmakers like Frank Capra and William Wyler, playwrights like Robert Sherwood and Irwin Shaw, comic book creators like Stan Lee, and clever artists like Theodore Geisel, later known as Dr. Seuss. Their job was to encourage patriotism and sway public opinion. John Steinbeck became a part-time propagandist, writing an Army Air Force recruiting book, *Bombs Away*, and the script for Alfred Hitchcock's film *Lifeboat*. The goal of news media was not only objective reporting; it was to stir public opinion.

John Dewey and Walter Lippmann engaged in intellectual debate about the American public in the 1920s. In the 1930s, John Dewey advocated scholarly communication, which he believed would benefit community and support democracy. Dewey emphasized the "ethical idea of humanity," and insisted on public intellectual engagement that would reduce barriers between academics and the broad public. A few years after the First World War, Dewey debated Walter Lippmann in his review of Lippmann's *Public Opinion* (1922). Harold D. Lasswell and Walter Lippmann both stated that democratic government was "safer" in the hands of a well-educated elite: the few, rather than the many. Dewey challenged Lippmann's perspectives on public irrationality and managing public opinion, or the public mind, which Lippmann shared with several social scientists of the period. They advocated social engineering models and believed that social-political institutions should be rationalized. Lippmann advocated "the manipulation of the masses through symbols."[52] Dewey rejected technocratic realism, and asserted that democracy required a humanizing approach to the public.

Dewey used the term "Great Society" to describe the new communications era. He saw clearly that social and political institutions had to be responsive to the changes in American culture. In *The Public and Its Problems*, Dewey noted that "men feel that they are caught in the sweep of forces too vast to understand or master."[53] Concerned about democracy in a "machine age" of growing mass communications, Dewey reflected on a "new age of human relationships."[54] Dewey and Lippmann maintained different values in their assessments of the public capacities of America's citizens; Dewey believed in a public-centered view of participation, while Lippmann sought scientifically trained experts. Dewey focused upon public dialogue; Lippmann focused upon manufacturing public consent, commenting that "the pictures inside people's heads do not automatically correspond with the world outside."[55] Both Dewey and Lippmann looked to social science for evidence. Social scientists often offered a language of control and mastery, a discourse of power.[56] Dewey insisted on education, democratic participation, and a focus on enlightening the public.

Dewey called Lippmann's position an "effective indictment of democracy" and its limitations. He argued that democracy requires "a more thoroughgoing education," exceeding the goals of officials. In his 1946 introduction to *The Public and Its Problems*, Dewey encouraged the application of scientific method to social problems. He continued to oppose Lippmann's rule by experts and asserted that the public ought to be able to express "common interests"; public intellectuals ought to strive to improve dialogue and discussion.[57] An informed society was threatened by mass-produced ideas, by consumerism, and by declining interest in public affairs.[58] Citizens ought not to be replaced by consumers. Entertainment and communications technologies could be a distraction rather than vehicles for public renewal. The positions of Dewey and Lippmann were influential in the 1940s and, perhaps, they ought to be reconsidered now.

JOHN STEINBECK

The government assigned John Steinbeck to write propaganda during the war. He wrote fiction, film scripts, and an account of a bomber squad. He was also a war correspondent who created essays on the personalities and events that he experienced in Europe. In that role, Steinbeck arrived in London on June 8, 1943. On August 23, he was in North Africa, and he arrived with the Allied forces in Algiers on August 28. Steinbeck describes the GIs in North Africa as "collectors [who] have home in mind" and "machinery in their souls." They must leave some of the memorabilia of battle behind: gun shells, pistols, helmets, baskets, and shawls. French and Arabic are spoken in the streets. Steinbeck says that to communicate with the local people, a soldier will gesture with his hands and toss in "a French word here and there." In the Allied landing at Salerno on September 3, Steinbeck joined the commando unit led by Douglas Fairbanks Jr. He wrote home to his wife Gwyn: "I've done the things I had to do."[59]

There were fires in the Sicilian fields from the barrage of bombers that prepared for the landing. Along a 105-mile coastline, there were sixty-seven assault battalions comprised of eight hundred men in each. Commander Hewitt's group split into three near Malta, and would land Patton's Seventh Army across an area on the Gulf of Gela. The Italian campaign went on for many months, into 1944. The battle of Anzio was fought on January 22, 1944, thirty miles south of Rome.; it has been described as a battle of attrition.

The Moon Is Down

The war had been on John Steinbeck's mind since before the U.S. entry. In *The Moon Is Down* (1942), Steinbeck imagined an occupying force in a European town. The novel had come to mind as he speculated on what might happen if a small American community was occupied by an invading army. Steinbeck's publishers believed that the suggestion of this would trouble Americans, and diminish their morale. Steinbeck rewrote the story and set the action in an unnamed occupied country in Europe. Some readers believed that his story reflected the situation in Norway. The book was censored in occupied Europe, but copies of it were circulated by members of underground resistance movements, who embraced its message. Steinbeck's *The Moon Is Down* declares: "A free, brave people is unconquerable."[60]

Steinbeck's character Mayor Orden is a heroic man of integrity. His opposite is Colonel Lanser, the well-educated leader of the invading force that has swept into the town. The novel opposes those who use violence to gain power over others. The occupation soldiers are less than complete men, and Major Hunter is "a haunted little man of figures, a little man." He sets his men in rows, diminishing their humanity. There is in him no humor, music, or mysticism of mathematics; he lives by an arithmetic that counts men like beans. Captain Bentick is a family man who imitates the English and has no ambition and is too old to fight. He is a man of pipes and sticks, a patriarch for the Freudian-minded reader. Captain Loft is his opposite: too young and overly ambitious. Loft is a sycophant: "He knew every kind of military courtesy and insisted on using it all."[61] He clicks his heels, in fine military deportment, and believes that women fall in love with a man in a uniform. He imagines, says the narrator, that if there is a God, he is an old man in a sharp uniform putting wreaths on the graves of valiant soldiers.

Steinbeck's satire continues with a description of the lieutenants, Prackle and Tonder, whose very names convey ridicule. These emotional young men have been indoctrinated to hate "degenerate art," like the modernist creations so reviled by Hitler. Prackle draws pencil sketches and spends his time seducing Tonder's sister. Tonder is "a bitter poet"; he is "a dark romantic," perhaps the troubled side of the German Romantic tradition that historians have considered. He dreams of honor by death on the battlefield and mythological glories "lighted by the setting sun": Valkyries, big-breasted women, "Wagnerian thunder." These men have followed the orders of Colonel Lanser. Steinbeck portrays the colonel as a man who is not so deluded about the course of war. Lanser has fought in the First World War and seen its horror: he tries to convince himself that this war will be different.

The humanity of these men, as much as their vulgarity, is brought into focus. The second chapter of the novel introduces them with sharp satire, but gradually begins to round out their characters with the quality of a play, portraying them as they take over and settle into the mayor's "little palace." The narrator suggests that their minds have been fogged by parades and crowds and triumphal nationalism. This celebration of military vitality brings a "gray dream in which real things become unreal." Tension and excitement, weariness, movement—all merge in one great gray dream," and one forgets how one has killed and ordered men to be killed. The conquerors are men a long way from home, bound up in a situation, caught up in a nightmare.

Steinbeck's short novel had a mixed reception in the United States. His approach to *The Moon Is Down* was debated, with some American readers thinking that he was too soft on the enemy. Steinbeck drew portraits of his German characters suggesting that, while they were misled, they were also fully human. *The Moon Is Down* presented the enemy as people with lives, just as the novel presented the people of the occupied village as heroic. When critics complained that the invaders, obviously Nazis, were not portrayed more negatively as the enemy, Steinbeck responded that he was writing a novel, not wartime propaganda. *The Moon Is Down*, although sometimes classified as propaganda, is certainly more a story of moral integrity than a propaganda piece. The novel continues the emphasis of *The Grapes of Wrath* on focusing on a community beset by power-seekers and bullies, like the camp guards and California vigilantes.

When we turn to the resistance fighters of *The Moon Is Down*, the question becomes whether people who love freedom and are willing to fight for their homeland can become an effective group of resisters. Mayor Orden becomes a hero and a martyr to the cause. Facing execution, Mayor Orden sets the case before Doctor Winter by recalling his reference to Socrates in *The Apology* during a graduation speech, forty-six years before. The mayor says that "a man who is good for anything ought not to calculate the chance for living or dying; he ought only to consider whether he is doing right or wrong." The town's resistance forces have been told that the mayor will die if they persist in their actions. Mayor Orden stands firm. He tells Colonel Lanser that he and his men will be "driven out": "The people don't like to be conquered, sir, and so they will not be."[62]

Following the war, Steinbeck was honored with a medal by the king of Norway for his contribution, through his novel, to the Norwegian resistance to Nazi occupation. This may have contributed to his later nomination for the Nobel Prize. Although *The Moon Is Down* has not been regarded highly among Steinbeck's novels, it was, in practical terms, one of his most important.

Bombs Away

In 1940, Steinbeck was concerned about the possibility of German espionage in Mexico. On June 26 of that year, Steinbeck encouraged President Roosevelt to maintain a watchful eye on the southern border of the United States. Steinbeck also dreamed up a plan to flood the economy of the enemy power with thousands of bills that would inflate its economy, but U.S. Treasurer Henry Morganthau deemed this idea impractical. Once American participation in the war began, Steinbeck was anxious to contribute to the war effort and sought to be a war correspondent overseas. He was drawn into the network of the Foreign Information Services, which was connected with the OSS (later transformed into the CIA). In the Office of War Information, Steinbeck assisted with propaganda.

Steinbeck wrote quickly to create *Bombs Away: The Story of a Bomber Team* (1942). Steinbeck donated all of the proceeds to the Air Force Society Trust Fund. His book was a service to the government, but this heroic portrayal of the training of a bomber crew has "flat" characters, like those drawn for a comic book. It is Steinbeck's weakest book. *Bombs Away* was a product of Steinbeck's role as a consultant to the Secretary of War assigned to Army Air Force Headquarters. General Henry "Hap" Arnold had traced out the plan for the book, and Steinbeck's friend, the actor Burgess Meredith, had supported the idea. The author states that his purpose is to "set down the nature and mission of a bomber crew and the technique and training of each member of it."[63] Steinbeck was hesitant to engage in the project because he did not want the enthusiasm and patriotism aroused in young men reading this book to lead to their deaths in combat. However, it is possible that it may have attracted men to bomber squads, since this was the volume's purpose.

Bombs Away presents the image of a democratic team effort. Steinbeck does not discuss the pilot first but, rather, places the pilot within the context of the group. Steinbeck called this bomber squad the greatest team in the world. His theme is the heroism of the common man.

Photographs accompany the text and help to bring together the information and message. Steinbeck shows that heroism in a group can uphold the principles of democracy with integrity in the midst of war.

Once There Was a War: Steinbeck in World War II Europe

When Steinbeck was permitted to report on the war in Europe, he had to leave his wife Gwen Conger to do so. In 1943, he wrote eighty-five articles while in Europe as a wartime correspondent. Steinbeck's dispatches during his four-and-a-half months overseas were published in the *Herald Tribune* (June 21–December 15, 1943), and twenty-three of these pieces appeared in the London *Daily Express*. They can be read in *Once There Was a War*, published in 1958. Steinbeck wrote feature stories: sketches, travel pieces, observations, and war stories he was told as he traveled with the troops. He gives us the image of rows of helmets of soldiers, lined up along the deck of a ship bound for England. He reports on their trip across an Atlantic, threatened by German U-boats. In London, he wrote from a bomber base. "A Plane's Name" is about giving names to planes, like they are given to ships. In "Superstition," the tailgunner on a bomber has lost his "medallion," or good-luck charm. Steinbeck writes about personalities he had met, or heard of, like Private Big Train Mulligan, who drives officers to important meetings. As in his fiction at this time, his writing focused on characters and observations. He wrote seeking objective details. Steinbeck was a participant observing the Allied beach landings in Italy, but he wrote with detachment. His writing brings us images and characters, brief stories of life in action far away.

2

SOUTHERN VOICES

Carson McCullers, Thomas Wolfe, William Faulkner,
Eudora Welty, and Others

The South chased a memory—a myth, some have said. Their
American dream lay in the past, in a time unfettered by modernity.
Southern writers were repeatedly drawn to expression in fiction
through a deep interest in history. They developed an imagined myth of
a well-ordered, bygone time. We see this in the work of Robert Penn
Warren, William Faulkner, and Eudora Welty. History in their work
intersects with home, a sense of the South that the Agrarian critics
greatly valued. Home, in the novels of Faulkner, Warren, and Welty,
has a specifically Southern setting. These writers sought a usable past.
As Louis D. Rubin Jr. has pointed out, Southern literature deals with an
experience, and it "mirrors a community."[1]

From the writings of Wilbur Cash to the songs of Johnny Cash,
home is at the center of Southern consciousness. Southern literature is
suffused with the attempt to go home, to assert a regional identity that
can endure through change and time. Southern novelists and short-
story writers sought a language, a tradition, and a myth. Underlying the
attempt to sustain the myth of an Edenic home lay the *unheimlich*, or
the uncanny, and the eccentricities that Southern writers so capably
highlighted in their works. The myth conceals the grotesque, the problems of racism, and those elements in Southern fiction that bear an
inverse relationship with the concept of home.

In *The Mind of the South*, Wilbur Cash theorized about the essential continuity of the Southern mind from the antebellum era to after Reconstruction. Home, family, land, and a domestic and agrarian attitude are central to that continuity. The critic Allen Tate once observed that Robert E. Lee fought not for an abstract principle, but for his homeland. This concern with home and the traditions of a locale repeat throughout the southern fiction of the 1940s. The mythic home is an Edenic place where Adam maintains his ideals. Home holds a hope, a wish that the family and the community may have been unscathed by sin and the fall, or by the passage of time and the encroachments of modernity. Home is the land of the South on which the family home is built. It is the yeoman's farm, familiar fields, hickory wind in the pines. It is the rural world that, by the 1940s, was diminishing. This theme of memory echoes in *You Can't Go Home Again* (1940) by Thomas Wolfe. There, the Southern traveler is looking backward with the desire to recover something lost. Even so, the central subject in Wolfe's work may be, as C. Hugh Holman has recognized, "the American self," grounded in the South but ever expanding outward "to realize the promise of America."[2] For America, in all its variety, is home too.

Margaret Mitchell's *Gone with the Wind* (1936), a popular best seller, lamented a lost world and urged the tenacious survival demonstrated by its protagonist, Scarlett O'Hara. Its popular appeal was enhanced by that novel's adaptation to the classic 1939 film that was still playing in movie theaters in 1940. Mitchell's book and the film underscored the myth of an idyllic antebellum home that had vanished with the War between the States. Something had been lost, and a tenuous wistfulness seemed to be all that was left. Romance attempted to endure. Mitchell's novel was more broadly popular than the well-crafted works of female writers like Ellen Glasgow, who was of a previous generation, or those of Caroline Gordon, a writer of careful technique whose novels are concerned with families, agrarian life, and the Southern region. Gordon's novel, *Green Centuries* (1941), tells the story of a family and three careers in the army. *The Women on the Porch* (1944) is a story of alienation and infidelity that draws on the Greek myth of Iphigenia. In that novel, Jim has been uprooted to a city life. Catherine has come home to the South, and finds her return home to be uncomfortable. Three women, her relatives, sit there, and her Southern home, having encountered modernity, has changed.

Historian C. Vann Woodward dated the "Southern renaissance" in the literary arts from 1929. The flourishing of Southern literature emerged, he suggested, from the tension between tradition and the modern world. As Richard King points out, Woodward recognized that this emergence of inquiry and expression was more than just a literary movement. It extended to history, sociology, politics, and journalism.[3] Lewis Simpson claimed that this Southern flourishing was about "memory and history." Louis D. Rubin Jr., and Richard M. Weaver each drew their critiques of this Southern renaissance from their sense of Southern history, even when New Critics were moving away from it. Richard King viewed Southern writers as "working through," in a Freudian sense, the family romance and the burden of the past.[4]

Carson McCullers once said that she returned to the South to be reminded of horror. She was not speaking of the horror of the war, but that of racism and the burden of historical consciousness. The American South's inclination toward historical fiction and experimental fiction came not from the horror of the war, but from its entanglement with the past. It arose, according to novelist John Gardner, "as an expression of disorientation and the collapse of values." In his view, the attempts of Southern intellectuals to understand the South in the modern era came from "conservative thought and feeling," and he added: "What passion this movement had come from, authentic concern about the moral issues and about the survival of southern aristocratic attitudes . . . became more Gothic."[5] Gardner saw some of the stories of Southern writers as "distinctly products of their time—the sort of thing one wishes were planted in time capsules."[6]

CARSON MCCULLERS

The Heart Is a Lonely Hunter (1940), one of the first literary successes of the 1940s, embraces the society of a Southern mill town. McCullers brings us into the lives of townspeople like Singer, a deaf-mute, who cares for another mute. We meet Dr. Copeland, an African American doctor; Biff, the owner of a café; and Jake, who is always on the move and dreams of social change. The protagonist in the midst of all these characters is Mick. This is a story of her growth and development, as well as a story about this group of people. This isolated town hears of distant events in Europe over the radio. However, local events are also significant. McCullers addresses the economic issues and racial issues that are encountered by the poor whites and blacks in the community. McCullers's portrayal of African Americans was complimented by Richard Wright in the *New Republic*, when he wrote of her skill in being able to "embrace white and black humanity in one sweep of apprehension and tenderness."[7] In the novel, Dr. Copeland believes that education can help to change things in the future for his sons and his daughter. However, they fall into behavioral patterns that are not going to help them to advance or improve their situation. The doctor's daughter Portia is a sympathetic and good-natured person who is not inclined to fight for what she needs.

In considering McCullers's novel, A. S. Knowles points out "the sentimental reforming spirit of the early forties," which we also see in Steinbeck's *The Grapes of Wrath* (1939).[8] Sympathy and social criticism move vigorously through McCullers's novel. Loneliness and alienation seem to plague the characters. Mick is seduced by Harry Minowitz, and sexuality becomes fearful. She works through a variety of approaches to her relationships.

Following McCullers, 1940s fiction was filled with the work of other Southern writers: Robert Penn Warren, Eudora Welty, Katherine Anne Porter, William Faulkner, Truman Capote, and Tennessee Williams among them. Much fiction by Southerners made a literary impact before the U.S. entry into the Second World War, including Caroline Gordon's *Green Centuries*, Andrew Lytle's *At the Moon's End*, and William Faulkner's stories in *The Hamlet*. Gordon was associated with the Southern Agrarians at Vanderbilt University, and she married the poet Allen Tate. They divorced in 1945, but then tried to make their marriage work again. Lytle was also involved with the Agrarian group with Tate and Robert Penn Warren. Lytle's 1941 novel, *At the Moon's Inn*, develops from reflections on the Spanish explorer De Soto's expedition in Florida. Lytle wrote several more novels and later became the editor of the *Sewanee Review*.

McCullers's second novel, *Reflections in a Golden Eye* (1941), was published in New York during the cold month of February. This novel is set on a Southern army base. Mrs. Alison Langdon and her all-too-sensitive houseboy are affronted by the insensitivity of others. Major Langdon runs off with Leonora Pendleton in an extramarital relationship. Captain Pendleton appears interested in Private Williams, who rides naked on horseback. *The Member of the Wedding* (1946), McCullers's masterful work that followed, has sometimes been characterized as a *bildungsroman*, a story of growth and development. More than this, however, *The Member of the Wedding* is an investigation of relationships, gender, modern alienation, sexual and racial identity, and issues of social exclusion. Frances "Frankie" Addams, age twelve, will attend her brother's wedding. However, the thrust of the novel unfolds in an exploration of her developing identity. She feels like an alienated person—an "unjoined person," she calls herself, one without human connection. She talks to her Negro servant Berenice Sadie Brown, and spends time with her cousin John Henry West, who is six years old. A soldier mistakes her interest in him as sexual. She goes to the wedding and doesn't act well there. Later she chooses to be wedded to life itself, and grows into womanhood and her identity.

THOMAS WOLFE

Thomas Wolfe was an intense, lyrical, verbose novelist who left the world too soon. His novel *Look Homeward, Angel* (1929) was a stunning debut. Its success, observed Louis D. Rubin, "is based on the rich, emotion-laden concreteness of the characterization of the Gant family and especially of Eugene" and his recollections.[9] Wolfe's longer novel, *Of Time and the River* (1935), followed; critic Bernard DeVoto remarked that it was filled with "long, whirling discharges of words, unabsorbed in the novel . . . raw gobs of emotion, aimless and quite meaningless jabber, claptrap, belches, grunts, and Tarzanlike screams."[10] The lengthy novel was culled from reams of written pages, and edited by Maxwell Perkins at Scribner's. *The Web and the Rock* (1939), *You Can't Go Home Again* (1940), and *The Hills Beyond* (1941) were published after Wolfe's death. So, we might say that Wolfe is primarily a writer of the late 1920s and 1930s. He merits mention here for the distinguishing features of his work published posthumously. His images of American characters and experience had a lasting impact. Wolfe's writing, much of which is set in North Carolina, has a quality of expressing American life. He recognized his life's work as an attempt to creatively articulate this.

In *The Story of a Novel*, Wolfe asserted his role as an American writer: "It is not merely that he must make somehow a new tradition for himself, derived from his own life and from the enormous space and energy of American life . . . it is even more than this: that the labor of a complete language, is the task that lies before him."[11] This artist was surely "self-centered, neurotic, and garrulous," as Richard S. Kennedy has said; his fiction was based in autobiography and has a Southern setting, but it is also American in its "multiplicity and diversity."[12] Wolfe writes that "out of the billion forms of America, out of the savage violence and the dense complexity of all our swarming life, from the unique substance of this land and life of ours, must we draw the power and energy of our own life, the articulation of our speech, the substance of our art."[13]

Wolfe sought American speech in his work. He was an observer of sights and actions, and was interested in the diversity of humanity. In *Of Time and the River*, he wrote of "the intolerable desire to fix eternally in the patterns of an indestructible form a single moment of life's beauty, passion, and unutterable eloquence, that passes, flames, and goes."[14] Wolfe's fiction flickers with passion and eloquence.

At the end of *You Can't Go Home Again*, George Webber has gone back to Germany. Aachen is the last stop before the border. There a nervous passenger has been taken by the authorities. The rumor is that he is a Jew who is trying to escape. He urges them to let him go. He will not betray his companions as he passes by them. He is left on the platform, a man with "terror stricken eyes." Wolfe writes that in his gaze "was all the unmeasured weight of man's mortal anguish."[15] They all felt that they were saying farewell to humanity. There is a prescient quality to this scene of a view from a train of a man left isolated on the platform.

Jude Law's magnificent portrayal of Thomas Wolfe in the film *Genius* (2016) reminds us of the conflict between Wolfe and his most necessary partner in publication, his editor Maxwell Perkins, who is played by Colin Firth in the film. As many critics have pointed out, Wolfe's final illness tends to overshadow this conflict between Wolfe and Perkins, in which Wolfe decides to bring his manuscripts to Harper's editor, Edward C. Aswell. *The Web and the Rock* (1939), *You Can't Go Home Again* (1940), and *The Hills Beyond* (1941) concluded Wolfe's prolific work. *The Web and the Rock* begins as George Webber disembarks from a boat and begins his work as a teacher in New York and Brooklyn. This character is a revision of Eugene Gant, the protagonist of Wolfe's novels *Look Homeward, Angel* (1929) and *Of Time and the River* (1935). He is also Wolfe's autobiographical self. George Webber teaches English composition at the fictional Washington Square College while working on his novel about a young person's life in North Carolina. He has a tumultuous affair with Esther Jack, the wife of a businessman. Esther, a scene designer in the theater, represents the city, the magnetizing draw of a mature life that he never quite realizes. The relationship is one of fitful love. The novel wanders across George Webber's inner life and experiences. *You Can't Go Home Again* announces, in that most famous and lasting phrase from Wolfe, that one must let go of the past. In his unquenchable lust for life, he sets forth a mystical-sounding goal: "To find a land more kind than home, more large than earth." [16]

WILLIAM FAULKNER

"He has the most talent of anybody," Ernest Hemingway wrote of William Faulkner in a letter to critic Malcolm Cowley; "he just needs a sort of conscience that isn't there." [17] Perhaps some of Faulkner's characters—Jason Compson, Popeye, Flem Snopes, Ike McCaslin—needed to develop a conscience. In the 1940s, Faulkner pondered family, race, and memory. Among the ancestral ghosts, the patterns of violence, prejudice, and bigotry that haunt some of his stories, he surely raised the matter of conscience.

William Faulkner's *Go Down Moses*, like *The Hamlet* (1940), was a series of interlocked short stories. In each case, his stories were reworked into a new narrative design. Throughout the 1930s, Faulkner had written stories about a cunning fellow named Flem Snopes. *The Hamlet* follows Snopes's attempts to become a respected member of his society. He starts out as a clerk in a general store in a little town called Frenchman's Bend; this is the hamlet of the story's title. Will Varner owns the store. He is a local businessman, a Southern landowner. Flem Snopes gradually becomes his business partner, marrying Will Varner's daughter.

Years later, *The Hamlet* was adapted to film as *The Long Hot Summer* (1958) with Paul Newman as the Snopes character, who is now named Ben Quick. Will Varner is played by Orson Welles. Eula is no longer Varner's daughter, but has become his daughter-in-law. Instead, Ben Quick pursues Will's daughter Clara (Joanne Woodward), and he is a lot nicer than Faulkner's seedy Flem Snopes. The technique that Faulkner used in *The Hamlet*, that of bringing together his short stories, was one that he turned to again in 1943 in *Go Down Moses*. There Faulkner is "moving further away from his own early modernism," notes Eric Sundquist, who sees him looking back to the traditions of the nineteenth-century novel.[18] Like other Faulkner critics, he points out that the ritual of the hunt is present in all the stories. The stories obviously highlight racial conflict and issues of human intimacy and relationships.

Go Down Moses

William Faulkner's fiction tends to elude summarization. He was a remarkable stylist and his fiction moves fluidly across time, incorporating perspectives past and present. Faulkner once commented, "There is no such thing as was because the past is. It is part of every man, every woman, and every moment. All of his and her ancestry, background, is all a part of himself or herself at every moment."[19] Faulkner's *Go Down Moses* explores this lingering claim of the past on our lives. Through interlocked stories, he focuses upon a family line that includes the McCaslins, the Edmondses, and the Beauchamps. *Go Down Moses* explores their mixed-race lineage across six generations. Ten stories are brought together into a novel drifting across time in which the parts echo and inform each other. The plantation world is the creation of Carothers McCaslin, whose vanity, pride, and miscegenation traps his ancestors. Carothers has moved slaves and family and bought his land from Ikkemottube, the Chickasaw chief. His dominance turns to the control of Cass Edmonds. The motif of a ritual hunt appears early in the story cycle and repeats in "The Bear," providing a kind of thematic unity across the stories.

In the stories that comprise Faulkner's *Go Down Moses*, chronology is scrambled.[20] The narrative moves between present and past. Faulkner wrote these stories between 1935 and 1941. The first of the stories is "Was," a story comically rendered, which initiates the serious theme of race relations within an entangled family. "Was" is told from a boy's perception and understanding, and thus carries young Cass Edmonds's innocence about the events that he sees and hears around him. We meet his Uncle Buck and Uncle Buddy, who are about sixty years old. Tomey's Turl, who is black, is Carothers's son by his daughter and slave, Tomasina. We are told that Tomey's Turl is forever escaping to look for his beloved. For Uncle Buck and Uncle Buddy he "became quarry . . . that received the same respect as the deer or the bear would."[21] As we read this story we see that Tomey's Turl is running away again, and Uncle Buck is searching for him again. He is pursued in a game of hide-and-seek. The hunters know the rules, and so does Tomey's Turl. That does not stop him from continually escaping to be with Tennie Beauchamp, his love. We see that "Was" also presents a series of bets between Uncle Buddy and Hubert Beauchamp that have to do with Tennie. The poker players ironically call on Tomey's Turl to deal the cards.

"Was" introduces us to the mixed racial relationships. In "Was," life is turned into a ritual hunt and into card games. The hunting of Tomey's Turl is a game. The bet between Uncle Buck and Hubert is also a game. So too is Miss Sophonsiba's hunt for a husband. It is absurd that Turl is repeatedly running away and followed. It is ridiculous that Uncle Buck inadvertently ends up in Miss Sophonsiba's bed. Uncle Buck is able to get away from Miss Sophonsiba, although he later succumbs. It is odd how a fox is regularly released in the house to be pursued by the dogs. On the other hand, it is a perverse game to have the fate of Tomey's Turl and his girl Tennie to be determined by a turn of the cards. The randomness and general disregard of their humanity are likewise absurd. However, Tomey's Turl does not truly suffer within this pattern of life. Uncle Buddy continues to play his ritual card game. A change from the first person to the third person brings changes of diction. The folksiness and ungrammatical sentences disappear, and standard grammar reports a child's viewpoint.

Ike McCaslin's life is at the center of this composition. In reading the stories, the reader gradually accumulates knowledge about him. Our first glimpses of Ike come to us in "The Old People," which originally appeared as a short story in *Harper's*. The story moves back and forth in time, and provides us with an account of the initiation of Ike McCaslin in the wilderness. We are introduced to his mentor, Sam

Fathers, who is part Native American, and part African American; his father was Ikkemottube. Sam has lived much of his life in an African American context, yet he also has a deep connection with the wilderness. His perspective has a lasting impact on Ike McCaslin, who is told of the eternal circle of life. The deer that he is coached to track is a sign of this eternity. Ike learns a sense of honor from his mentor, and carries with him a view that the land is not owned. His hunting initiation as a boy supports his later view of life.

Ike McCaslin has been educated in the ways of the plantation by his father, and in the ways of the wilderness by Sam Fathers, who was a surrogate father to him. For Ike, the past is forever present. There is a lost tradition, an innocence that may be associated with his youth. The hunting stories recall this innocence, an unaffected natural world, and the young Ike McCaslin is something like the American Adam. However, the family legacy of old Carothers has cast a pall of doom that extends into the future, as "the old world's corrupt and worthless twilight" has come to the new world of the American South.[22]

Across the stories of *Go Down Moses* is the central image of the hunt. We see the chase after Tomey's Turl, the finding and lynching of Rider, and Gavin Stevens's search for Lucas Beauchamp. We witness Lucas Beauchamp's search for gold and Ike McCaslin's pursuit of the bear. There is a sharp difference between the ritual of the search for Tomey's Turl and the very serious search for Rider, who is tracked down like an animal. Faulkner focuses on the relationship of the family of whites and blacks, the world of the McCaslins and Beauchamps and Edmondses. He draws us toward a recognition that the control of Carothers McCaslin has set things in motion across time. The story tells of time and changes within a culture, and the gradual disintegration of some of that culture. In "Was," Uncle Buddy and Uncle Buck are the second generation between old Carothers and Ike McCaslin. They will free whichever slaves may be freed through their game. These are the cultural moves expected of the McCaslins. Cass Edmonds will become the future guardian of the McCaslin tradition when he becomes older. He will pass that on to Isaac McCaslin.[23]

"Pantaloon in Black" shifts the tone of the narrative to an objective perspective, and provides a contrast with the opening story and the story that follows. Following an omniscient narrative opening, "Pantaloon in Black" introduces us to the character Rider, whose tragedy stems from grief and the loss of someone close to him. We also meet the mischievous and cunning Lucas Beauchamp, who seeks his fortune. This story is about race relations, but it is not about the McCaslin family line. In Rider's tragic story we see his isolation after his wife's death. He returns home, sees her ghost, has a conflict with the moonshine dealer, and kills the gambler, Birdsong. He is pursued and lynched by Birdsong's men. Rider's tragedy is caused by his grief and passion. However, the sheriff is unable to understand Rider's behavior or comprehend his grief.

The dehumanization of Joe Christmas that we see in *Light in August* repeats in *Go Down Moses*. The situation of Tomey's Turl is simply ludicrous, but that of Rider, in "Pantaloon in Black," is deadly. The murder that Rider commits in his grief leads to his hanging and the deputy's incomprehension of Rider's motives. "The Fire and the Hearth" brings us the tussle between Lucas and Zack in Zack's bedroom, which Sundquist recognizes as "ritual combat."[24] Ike McCaslin's ritual hunting of the deer and then of the bear follow this story. Irving Howe observes that there is "a moral history" and growth in Faulkner's work with respect to racial concerns: "Faulkner is not . . . a systematic thinker; he has no strictly formulated views on the 'Negro question' but he has been involved in 'a painful journey of self-education' which began with an almost uncritical acceptance of the more benevolent southern notions and ending with a brooding sympathy and humane respect for the Negroes."[25]

"The Fire and the Hearth" moves us two generations further. Lucas Beauchamp is facing Zack Edmonds in the bedroom. Then Lucas is seeking gold with a mechanical box. There are no miracles for him in this ritual as he explores the possibility that an old legend might be true. He maintains some distance from believing this altogether, although the salesman with him seems to be easily fooled. Lucas can be mischievous. He can assume a mask of indifference as a black, or he can assert the white McCaslin blood of his ancestors.

The fire on the hearth, a symbol of the home and its holiness, has been disturbed in the past by Carothers's seduction of his own daughter Tomasina. Miscegenation and incest are passed down as a legacy, and this reverberates across the generations. "The Fire and the Hearth" is presented as a counterpoint to Ike McCaslin's initiation in the hunt ritual with "The Old People" and "The Bear." In "Delta Autumn," we see that Ike has repudiated his family past, although to no effect. He wants to renounce his paternal past, the guilt of his forefathers, and to set aside his own responsibilities to the future. For Ike, Cass Edmonds is the plantation tradition of his forefathers; Sam Fathers, the descendant of Indians and blacks, is his teacher of a spiritual wilderness tradition.

The ritual once provided a sense of continuity and wonder, qualities Ike learned from Sam. But the wilderness retreats before modernity and its new roads. The dream Ike once had seems to lose its significance. In "Delta Autumn," he is too old to be involved in a hunt; he is about eighty by now (seventy is an earlier version, but clearly closer to eighty in a latter one). He went into the woods in a hero's quest when he was young. Now he meets Roth's mistress and, upon learning that she is part black, he urges her to go marry a black man. Things may be different in the future: "Maybe in a thousand or two thousand years it will have blended in America. But not now. Not now."

Toward the end of this novel comes the repudiation by Ike McCaslin of his patrimony. His rejection of his responsibility to the plantation does not free him from the ancestral curse. The events in the past have happened, and cannot be changed. Meanwhile, Ike's life and the wilderness are "two spans running out together, not toward oblivion, nothingness, but into a dimension free of both time and space."[26]

"The Bear"

The central story of Go Down Moses is "The Bear." From the time that "The Bear" first appeared as a short story, it has drawn much critical comment. The Saturday Evening Post story focuses upon Ike's initiation, in which he learns of the spirit of the wilderness from Sam Fathers. He learns how to track, sight, and honor Old Ben the bear by saving him. The opening paragraph in the revised version is new to the novel. The story is then set when Ike McCaslin is young and untutored. Sam is identified with the wilderness, and it becomes clear that he is sensitive to the movements of life and nature.

Faulkner's mythmaking is most obvious in this story. Robert Penn Warren and Malcolm Cowley both demonstrated how critical "The Bear" is for our grasp of the South. It underscores the importance of the land, and offers some perspective on the African American people in that region. Ike McCaslin is brought on an annual hunting trip with a group of men, and Sam Fathers teaches him about the wilderness and hunting. This leads to the hunting of the mythic, or legendary, bear.

"The Bear" brings us back to the primal ancestral experience of the human race and the human encounter with natural forces and animal life. The bear of legend and myth is an archetype, a central figure in this encounter. There is the solitude of a place "through which human beings merely passed without altering it, lacking no mark, no scar." It is a place that likely looks the same as when the Chickasaw ancestors of Sam Fathers passed there. Sam teaches young Ike McCaslin how to track the bear, how to see and use his senses in the "immemorial darkness of the woods."[27]

The bear will not be captured. Sam Fathers suggests that they need the help of the dog named Lion. The pursuit resumes when Ike is sixteen years old. Boon, the Indian helper, tries to assist. Lion is wounded, and Sam is exhausted by the effort. Sam teaches Ike to approach the bear and the wilderness with reverence and a sense of dignity and appreciation for the creation. The hunters, in contrast, are sportsmen who do not approach the wilderness in this way. Part 4 of the story drifts off to another time and recalls the McCaslin family, white and black. Ike speaks of the South and of the land. He can do little to change the curse that seems to linger over men like Carothers. Ike wishes to choose noninvolvement, a repudiation of that past, and an impossible neutrality. In part 5, Ike recalls his experience, and visits the graves of Sam and the dog Lion.

In "Delta Autumn," the landscape has changed. We read that once there was cane and cypress, gum and holly, oak and ash. There were cotton fields and deer and bears, paths and streams; "most of that was gone now."[28] People made their quest into the wilderness to conquer it. Now any remaining wilderness "was two hundred miles from Jefferson when once it had been thirty."[29] Ike recalls Sam Fathers as a repository of memory. Reflecting on this past, Ike affirms that while he stands on his land, he has never truly owned any of it: "it belonged to all; they only had to use it well, humbly and with pride."[30] He is brought back to the present by visitors. Maybe in some distant future we will have forgotten about race. He thinks about this as he recognizes that a young man standing near him is black. "Maybe in a thousand or two thousand years it will have blended in America and we will have forgotten it."[31]

In "The Bear" we saw Ike McCaslin's relationship with Sam Fathers, who is part Indian and part black. In "The Fire and the Hearth," Roth Edmonds realizes that Molly Beauchamp, a black woman, is the only mother he ever really had. He and his friend Henry Beauchamp sleep in the same bed, and their houses are interchangeable homes for them. In the title story, "Go Down Moses," Miss Worsham recalls her child-hood relationship with Mollie Beauchamp: "Mollie and I were born in the same month. We grew up together as sisters would."[32] However, there are bitter moments as well: Rider's execution, the broken frater-nity between Roth and Henry, the toying with Tomey's Turl, and the persistent patterns of rituals like the hunt. Yet, Faulkner's views about race are "the least interesting aspect of his work," as Irving Howe once commented.[33] What matters is the shape that racial issues take within his stories. In *Go Down Moses*, Faulkner recognizes an inheritance that has lingering effects on the lives of white and black alike. "Complex and ambiguous responses" have come from Southern writers who have been sensitive to these issues, as Howe observes in his reflections in his essay, "Faulkner and the Negroes."[34] The message of Faulkner, it seems, is a broader one for America. Howe reminds us that the only happy memo-ries for the Compson family in *The Sound and the Fury* (1929) come from the time when white and African American children play together.

Intruder in the Dust

Intruder in the Dust (1948) is the story of Lucas Beauchamp, now elderly, accused of shooting a white man named Vinson Gowrie in the back. A mob is after Lucas, and it is out for blood. Lucas is innocent, and Chick Mallison persuades his uncle Gavin Stevens to defend him. They exhume the body of Vinson Gowrie, intruding the dust of his burial ground. The autopsy and ballistics show that the bullet that killed the man came not from Lucas Beauchamp but from the gun owned by Vinson's brother, Crawford. Evidently, Crawford cheated Vinson out of a lot of money, so he decided to murder him and frame Lucas Beau-champ.

Lucas Beauchamp is an interesting, intelligent individual who is quite resourceful. In "The Fire and the Hearth" he appears to be quite aware of the oppression he experiences as a black man. With his ap-pearance in *Intruder in the Dust*, we see Lucas as a character of self-assurance who has made something of himself. Lucas Beauchamp is "durable, ancestryless."[35] With tenacity, he becomes what David Wyatt has called "a new kind of hero" in Faulkner's fiction.[36] Lucas is a man with "an irascible desire for justice," Irving Howe pointed out.[37] Yet, his "patient endurance" may be a mask that Lucas assumes to deal with a hostile world, and questions about race repeat in later Faulkner novels and sound "with growing urgency," notes Howe. Howe's own questions are interesting; in 1951, he asserts that "Faulkner has not yet presented in his novels an articulate Negro who speaks for his people."[38] For Howe, the "inner logic of his own work" appears to portray a character that is "in serious, if covert, rebellion against the structure of the South."[39]

Faulkner's novel was transformed into a film by director Clarence Brown and screenwriter Ben Maddow in 1949. Faulkner himself added some touches to the script. The film does not hesitate to explore the racial theme. We move from a church spire to the congregation who walk toward the church. The music of hymns sounds near the town square where a lynch mob is assembling. The contradiction between Christian principles and a crowd that is set upon murder and revenge is highlighted. Juano Hernandez plays Lucas Beauchamp, and Will Greer plays Sheriff Hampton. Gavin Stevens, renamed John, is played by David Brian. The spinster Miss Habersham is played by Elizabeth Patterson. Following the scene with the mob gathering near the church, we see Miss Habersham sitting inside the door of the jail with her sewing basket. She seems like a sweet little old lady knitting, but what she is really doing is guarding the path to Lucas Beauchamp's cell, so that Crawford and his mob will not harm him.

Faulkner the Stylist

Faulkner's sentences expand; they range out like the Mississippi River into tributaries, extended by adjectival and participial phrases. They do not so much overflow the banks of his paragraphs as challenge the structure with swift currents or with the meandering accumulation of words. Faulkner's innovation, on all levels, seems to contest the sleepy towns, the inbred families, the locked patterns of history. The two worlds of the plantation and the wilderness are given to us in language and structure that distinguishes one from the other. There is the mythical world of the forested region and its legendary bear, and there is the documentary world of the plantation. As critic Susan Willis has pointed out, these are two different ways of experiencing history.[40] "The Bear" can be read in relation to the traditions of folk storytelling. It can be viewed as a nature myth that indicts industrial capitalism's impact on the plantation system. It is a story of Ike's initiation, a boy's introduction to these worlds.

Faulkner's verbal dexterity in his long, unfolding sentence patterns and variations of style are one of the treasures of this text. He introduces verbal rhythms in his storytelling that suggest that he is unraveling an ancient legend. He engages in experimentation, crafting a movement from the omniscient narrator to the boy's point of view. "The Bear" is mythical, legendary, and at times has the feeling of an age-old tale of humanity's confrontation with the wilderness and a mysterious archetypal figure. However, later stories like "Delta Autumn" mark the intrusion of modern life on this natural world, as well as on Ike McCaslin's high ideals of honor. The new roads, the car, the grab for land, suggest a diminished awareness of anything sacred or to be revered. Practicality has burst the dream. Ike, who is now close to eighty, is a man caught in a past he cannot shed as life continues on. When he discovers that the girl who has arrived is black, he suggests that she seek to marry a black man, but she says: "Old man . . . have you lived so long and forgotten so much that you don't remember anything you ever knew or felt or even heard about love?"[41]

The author who created Yoknapatawpha County was a storymaker. He was not using fiction as a platform for any political position. Faulkner explored the ghosts and aberrations of the American South in stories marked by issues of inheritance, isolation, family, community, and guilt. He was an artist who explored consciousness, human psychology, and time. He was a writer who continually experimented in his quest for form, narrative design, and voices that brought his stories to life. *Go Down Moses*, a novel that is a story composite, may suggest that all of Faulkner's varied fiction is like one big book. This book is an intertextual feast of overlapping stories and characters. He is the magnificent creator of a mountain range to be explored path by path, and by scaling one mountain at a time—until at last the reader has experienced an extraordinary vista of burdened, wonderful, troubled, animated humanity and life.

Faulkner's style, his lengthy periodic sentences, may draw a reader's wonder, or perhaps perplexity. His texts compel close reading. The stories emerge in scenes, with many stylistic nuances, and are linked through recurring characters and sometimes remembered incidents. Across these stories emerge several themes. There is the primal encounter of humans with the wilderness, and the loss of the wilderness to the habits and technologies of modern life. There is the struggle and exploitation of black men and women. The stories are units that may stand alone, but they gain further meaning when they are brought together intertextually. The form that Faulkner chose for this work is an expansive stretch across generations: the development of people within a particular setting. As they probe human action, race, and culture, they call for our assessment of the moral awareness of these individuals and the moral consciousness of Ike McCaslin. Yet, much of this novel, this gathering of stories, is not specifically about Ike. It is also about Lucas Beauchamp, McCaslin Edmonds, Uncle Buck and Uncle Buddy, Tomey's Turl, and their game of hunting. Faulkner's families and locales are about a larger world of relationships.

EUDORA WELTY

On a summer evening in Mississippi, the windows are open. Eudora Welty, the daughter of the president of an insurance company, is at her desk writing a story. Maybe it is one of the "beautiful stories" that Katherine Anne Porter commented on in her review of Welty's first story collection. Porter wrote: "Let me admit a deeply personal preference for this kind of story, where external act and the internal voiceless life of the human imagination almost meet and mingle on the mysterious threshold between dream and waking."[42] These comments came from one of the most highly regarded short-story writers of the forties. "She has simply an eye and an ear sharp, shrewd, and true as a tuning fork," Porter added.[43] Porter reflected on Welty's art, and asserted that "the short story is a special and difficult medium."[44] She suggested that one ought not to expect a novel from Welty.

Welty, of course, did write five novels: *The Robber Bridegroom* (1942), *Delta Wedding* (1946), *The Ponder Heart* (1954), *Losing Battles* (1970), and the Pulitzer Prize–winning *The Optimist's Daughter* (1972).

The Golden Apples (1949), a series of interlinked stories with time as a consistent theme, may be read as novel. However, it was her first story collections, *A Curtain of Green* (1941) and *The Wide Net and Other Stories* (1943), that firmly established her as a fine short-story writer. "Eudora Welty can write," Ernest Hemingway wrote to Malcolm Cowley.[45] Eugene Armfield of the *New York Times Book Review* pointed out "the fineness of her descriptive writing." Like other critics, he recognized that specific images, the "casualness" of events, and the ordinariness of several of her characters provide a key to her fiction. Katherine Woods remarked on "a sound folk quality" in Welty's stories. Jean Stafford, in *The Partisan Review*, was critical, saying that the stories were "so vague that not only actual words but syntax itself have the improbable inexactitude of a verbal dream." (One might ask if this sentence is not also inexact.)[46] Diana Trilling, in *The Nation*, said that it was "a book of bullets, not of stories." Responding to this, Robert Penn Warren wrote in "The Love and Separateness in Miss Welty" that what distinguished her writing was "the special tone and mood, the special perspective, the special sensibility." Her characters try to escape their isolation, he pointed out.[47]

Short Stories

Welty's stories must be read and puzzled over, and her rich use of language must be savored. There is much in Welty's stories that cannot be easily retold; these are searches for meaning, probing the minds and lives of characters, mostly women. As David Wyatt points out, "Few American writers more resist plot summary."[48] Diana Trilling pointed out Welty's tendency toward a stylistic focus and "fine" writing. Welty, she said, had "an eye for the Gothic in detail" and effectively grasped "the day to day horrors of actual life, not only the horror of dreams."[49] Trilling compared Welty's second collection of stories with a story in her first collection, "The Petrified Man." In that story, her readers meet a three-year-old amid the bobby pins and sexual confidences of the beauty parlor where odd rumors fly from the mouths of nosy neighbors. They talk about a pregnancy, a couple named the Pikes, and the schemes of the petrified man.

"The Wide Net" is a story that Trilling finds "best fuses content and method."[50] (She also liked "Livvie," which she noted was the only story other than "The Wide Net" that she understood.) In "The Wide Net," Hazel Jamieson has disappeared from her home. William, her husband, has discovered a note from her stating that she is not going to put up with him anymore. Her note says that she is going to the river to drown herself. Fearing the worst, William gathers his friends and brings a wide net to sift through the river water. He is joined by Doc, Brucie, Grady, Virgil, and two African American boys, Robbie and Sam, who dredge the river. The sky threatens with rain and lightning. Later, William goes back home and finds Hazel standing in the bedroom doorway. "I was hiding," she tells him. They step out to the front porch, where she tells him that she will "do it again if I get ready." After warning him that she may again protest sometime in the future, she takes him by the hand and leads him back into the house.

"At the Landing," the final story in the collection, is described by David Wyatt as "perhaps Welty's most radical and disturbing story."[51] Jenny, who lives up the hill from the river landing with her grandfather, sees Billy Floyd, a fisherman, and has a thought about love. Her innocence is gone before trouble begins for her. Yet, she is a person of insight: "She had a knowledge come to her that a fragile mystery was in everyone and in herself."[52] David Wyatt sees this as a recognition of "love and separateness." There is a distance we have from one another: "Something in us cannot be touched. . . . What we love and acknowledge in another is separateness."[53] Saved by Billy Floyd from the rising water of the river, she sleeps, and upon waking is raped in a "shock of love" that reverberates beyond this moment. In her house, which has been damaged by the flood, she busies herself with "an ecstasy of cleaning, to wash the river out," and she remains stunned by the experience.[54]

Eudora Welty elicits our sympathy for some of her characters, and our horror at others. In her first story, Lily Daw seems to be a gentle girl who is perhaps a bit gullible, or bereft of intelligence. Lily surprises the women around her when she declares that she is going to be married. She has met a xylophone player in the traveling show. In "The Key," Ellie and Albert Morgan sit together in a remote little station, waiting for a train. These characters are drawn carefully. Ellie is a large woman with a face described as "as pink and crowded as an old-fashioned rose." She carries a black satchel purse on her wrist. Albert is a shy little man who looks "home-made," or somehow "knitted" and "contrived" into life by his wife.[55] His attention turns to a key that a young man flicks to the floor. To Albert, the key is a wonderful talisman, a key to their future. He seizes it and puts it into his pocket. There is a surrealistic quality to his dream, and an endearing quality to this elderly couple. They seem simple, limited to this place, as they dream of a little vacation in another place. The young man across from them seems immodest and casual. He is more mobile than they are. He seems to toy with them, amusing himself as he passes through this station on his way to somewhere else.

A different narrative voice introduces "Old Mr. Marblehead"—one with a regional accent. Mr. Marblehead is old. His wife is old. She has "a voice that dizzies the other ladies like an organ note and amuses men like a halloo down the well," and she is described as "servile, unde-lighted, sleepy and tortured."[56] He married her when he was sixty and they live in an ancestral home. The river may come up to consume it; the back garden has crumbled away. One imagines that behind the black mahogany door and those red walls is a place that is "dark, with old things about," a room that is "draped and hooded and shaded." Despite this timeworn decay and their sixty years, the couple has a son who is only six years old and attends the Catholic school. Mrs. Marble-head belongs to the Daughters of the Revolution and the United Daughters of the Confederacy.[57] Mr. Marblehead travels in "his ancient fringed carriage with the candle burner like empty eyes in front."[58] Welty's imagery brings us into their neighborhood and its chinaberry trees, flower beds, "screen doors whining, the ice wagons dragging by, the twittering noises of children."[59] Mr. Marblehead stands at the front door of his house, achingly bending over the row of zinnias his wife has planted. Suddenly, we are told that he has another wife, and to her he is "Mr. Bird." He reads *Terror Tales* and *Astonishing Stories* about "things happening to nude women and scientists . . . stories that scare her to death." Beneath common surfaces are currents of the grotesque. He "plays with this double-life" and continues "shuttling, still secretly back and forth" between two lives.[60]

In "Why I Live at the P.O.," Sister refuses to listen to others or accept any responsibility. She appears jealous of Stella-Rondo, who is younger than she. Stella bears the name of a star and a musical form. She is named for that ethereal light in the night sky and intangible music within a form and pattern. The narrator jealously complains that

Stella always had anything in the world she wanted, and "she'd throw it away."[61] Stella is like the prodigal son in the Bible. She has returned home with a blonde child; this is an important event in their lives. Yet the characters in "Why I Live at the P.O." seem to be obsessed with trivia. Sister has a job at the P.O., the "smallest P.O. in the entire state of Mississippi."[62] She lives in the P.O. with her radio, on which she can hear the war news.[63] Sister is in a dysfunctional situation, and seems to judge everyone, while claiming detachment. She is surrounded by some peculiar characters. We meet Uncle Rondo, who is cross-dressing in one of Stella-Rondo's flesh-colored kimonos.[64] He looks foolish in the kimono, and on the Fourth of July he drinks too much and falls over and snores. Here the story moves into dialogue, and proceeds much like a play as we hear Sister and Stella-Rondo and learn of their family tensions. Uncle, who is annoyed at the narrator, tosses a string of firecrackers into her bedroom. Sister appears caught up in her own perspective. She pulls the plug on the fan, pulls the pillow out from behind Papa Daddy, and races upstairs to find "her charm bracelet in her bureau drawer under a picture of Nelson Eddy."[65] Sister can go to the P.O. and she wants to take her things with her, objects that suggest her own eccentricity: a sewing machine motor, a calendar that notes first-aid remedies, watermelon rind preserves, and bluebird wall cases.

The comedy and the family's eccentricity in "Why I Live at the P.O." belies the more serious and problematic conflicts among them. In this story, life is diminished amid trivia. Reality is not turned into fantasy and fable, as Robert Penn Warren saw Welty doing in many of her stories. Rather, Sister is enmeshed in family concerns with the trivial. This reveals more about her attitude, issues, and morals than she may be conscious of. Sister likely recognizes that she is absurd, living at the tiny P.O. Robert Penn Warren sees her as isolated from the world.[66] Charles E. May, in his essay, "Why Sister Lives at the P.O." insists that we cannot simply label her schizophrenic and leave it at that.[67] Sister provides self-justification for her behavior and her attempt to escape from the world. We are led to analyze her perspective and her situation.

In "Death of a Traveling Salesman," Welty brings us immediately into the sensibility of a traveling show salesman. He has been on the dusty roads of Mississippi for years, but after a bout with the flu he is more uncertain of the road. This general disorientation can also be found in Arthur Miller's traveling salesman, Willy Loman. If the wandering salesman is a figure representative of a kind of uprooted cultural drift, this is for Welty a phenomenon of the South. For Miller, the disenfranchised salesman is more a sign of depersonalizing capitalist competition, a changing and displacing of the old guard for the sake of efficiency. Welty's salesman is unnerved by the desolate hill country. He nostalgically recalls his grandmother, who may represent a beckoning, nurturing sense of home, or a vague anticipation of his own passing into eternity: "And he seemed to be going the wrong way—it was as if he were going back, far back."[68]

The salesman, Bowman, is a wanderer, a rambling man for whom home is absent and women are passing memories: "little rooms within little rooms" and reminders of loneliness.[69] He has driven to Beulah before, but his surroundings now seem unfamiliar. He feels as if he may be lost, but he can hardly admit this to himself; nor can he bring himself to ask the strangers that he sees in the fields for directions. Besides, they are locals who hardly know to where the roads go. Welty gives us some fine sentences to describe the countryside. Then, suddenly, Bowman's car tips over into a ravine. He miraculously gets out of it and sees his car caught in grapevines that "rocked it like a grotesque child in a dark cradle." Wondering where he is, he walks uphill to a house. His heart races and he sees a woman in "a formless garment of some gray coarse material." The woman is silent, like some mythical figure holding a lamp. Finally, she says: "Sonny, he ain't here." The hope comes that "Sonny" will arrive to move the car.[70]

The title story in the collection, "A Curtain of Green," seems at first to come like a hint of sunshine. Calm narrative description draws us into Mrs. Larkin's garden. Her neighbors see little order there; "it had the appearance of a jungle, in which the slight heedless form of its owner daily lost itself."[71] A dreamy black boy, Jamey, sometimes assists her there, dragging the hoe through the flower bed as he whistles his tunes. A memory returns occasionally to disturb Mrs. Larkin. A chinaberry tree loosened from its roots once fell on her husband, leaving her a widow tending her garden. "A Curtain of Green" is a sketch that has a meditative quality and a subtle interiority. Life and death are there in Mrs. Larkin's hands. She stares at Jamey, who is stirring the dirt, lost in his daydream. The docility she thinks she sees in him begins to "infuriate her."[72] The boy is carefully described, as if his smile "were a teasing, innocent, flickering and beautiful vision." She could kill him. She could raise the hoe above her head and bring it down on that "clustered, hot, wooly hair, its intricate glistening ears, its small brown branching stream of sweat, the bowed head holding so obviously and so deadly its ridiculous dream."[73] In this woman, who seemed so placid at first, is a disturbing undercurrent of violence. The emotion passes and she lays down the hoe.

A change in Mrs. Larkin's consciousness is marked by a change in the weather. The landscape, touched by gentle rain, takes on a life of its own. The scene dissolves into Mrs. Larkin's impressions: wet fragrance, tenderness, rainfall. She now has "eyes looking without understanding" and she is "sinking down into the flowers, her lips parting," as if dying.[74] The boy runs to her, flowers breaking under his feet, and he calls her name and then, perhaps frightened, he runs away. On the surface, this seems to be a rural setting where nothing much appears to happen. Drawn into this lonely woman's psyche, we enter a nightmare world.

Katherine Anne Porter points out that a *Curtain of Green and Other Stories* (1941) is grounded in ethical universals: "But there is an ancient system of ethics, an unanswerable, indispensable moral law, on which she is grounded firmly." The grotesque is surely present and Welty has "a strong taste for melodrama, and is preoccupied with the demented, the deformed, the queer, the highly spiced."[75] In *The New York Times*, Marianne Hauser saw the stories as "dark, weird, and often unspeakably sad in mood." Yet, critics like Hauser saw "something profound" in them. Kay Boyle called Eudora Welty "one of the most gifted and interesting short story writers of our time." All of these critics recognized the contributions that the Southern settings made to her stories. However, Granville Hicks, in 1952, asserted that Welty was far more than a regional writer. Her stories are concerned with people and how events affect them, he said. Her stories are not driven by plot; they explore character.[76]

The Mythic Core

Welty's novels made explorations of curious characters and Southern families. There is much attention to time in her novel, *Delta Wedding* (1946). The Fairchilds resist time. Like the Renfros in *Losing Battles*, they have togetherness and love, but they "shield themselves from the world." They hold fast to tradition and their family line. Portraits of great grandparents are alive for them, looming over the fireplace. Welty's novels, like many of the stories, have a quality that Diana Trilling saw in Welty's writing: she is a mythologist, a "creator of legend."[77] Welty's short story, "Livvie," recalls Persephone. A young woman discovers a murderer at sunset. She is carried away to a house on Natchez Trace, as in Persephone's abduction by Hades. The interlinked stories of *The Golden Apples* are set in Morgana, named after a figure in the Arthurian myths. In Welty's novels, myth and death, rebirth and revival appear to be similarly linked.

Fairy tale meets with history in *The Robber Bridegroom*. Merrill Skaggs underscored this connection between history, legends, and fairy tales in Welty's fiction, beginning an essay by quoting a comment from Welty to the Mississippi Historical Society: "I made our local history . . . legend and the fairy tale into working equivalents. It was my firm intention to bind them together."[78] Welty cited two fairy tales by the Brothers Grimm as her sources. She drew attention to European fairy tales and folk legends. This merger of fairy tale, legend, and history may raise questions for us about how we view history and how we remember people's lives and events. *The Iliad* is, for example, a legend that is perhaps based on some historical event that has been entwined with myths of heroism and the gods. Our own perspective on World War II history has been affected by stories and films with mythological qualities. Skaggs pointed out that the Natchez Trace in Welty's novel "can be found in Robert Coates' popular history of 1930, *The Outlaw Years*," and also pointed to Bruno Bettelheim's *The Uses of Enchantment* and the view that fairy tales can help "to relieve severe inner pressures" and consider "the promise of success."[79] Skaggs correlated southern tall tales with this use of extravagance and enchantment "to confront basic fears and anxieties." They are stories for adults and the "fears of vulnerability" incited by them are "ageless" and fundamental to human experience.[80]

Lionel Trilling observed that Welty's *The Robber Bridegroom* is indeed a fairy tale that draws the European tradition of fairy tales into the American frontier, and saw in Welty's writing "conscious simplicity."[81] Clement Musgrave, a planter in southern Louisiana, claims innocence. What is this place but a timeless, rural land of woods, trees hung with Spanish moss, and fields. The story takes us back to some ancestral, hidden yesterday. *The Robber Bridegroom*, as Merrill Skaggs observed, provides reassurance, like the fairy tale does. It tells us that, despite our anxieties, things will work out in the end.[82]

Eudora Welty did not write in the shadow of her fellow Mississippi writer William Faulkner, but went in her own direction. Noel Polk begins his book, *Faulkner and Welty and the Southern Literary Tradition* (2008), by saying that writers and readers have often seen the South through Faulkner's eyes and are often "driven by his influence." He reaffirms how "inescapable" Faulkner's works are; his stories often define what can be seen, and Polk recognizes that many Southern writers write in his shadow. However, Eudora Welty is not pulled into this Faulkner circle. Polk writes that "she has not even generally entertained the question of Faulkner's influence on her worth and her time."[83] Faulkner writes large, cosmic themes. The seemingly more domestic work of Eudora Welty likewise addresses these broader themes. We are not prepared to be made uncomfortable by the everyday world of Welty's stories, says Polk.[84] Welty focuses on the domestic *and* the grotesque. She looks at things we might avoid. Polk claims that critical language has kept us from understanding Welty; he writes: "In *Golden Apples* she rewrites southern literature or at least provides an opportunity to erase it and start over."[85]

Welty examined isolation, love, separation, family, and community. Her stories are anchored in a specific place, and the personality of her characters and the region in which they dwell. *Delta Wedding* ponders the lives of the Fairchild family and the meaning of love, separateness, and marital and familial relationships. Her stories seem particularly poignant when she reveals how sympathetic characters who have a curious charm and vitality are isolated, lonely, or outcast. Social structures marginalize and isolate these people, such as the tenant farmers of *A Curtain of Green*. Society appears oblivious to poverty and human need. When Phoenix Jackson in "A Worn Path" enters the clinic after her arduous journey, she is treated condescendingly, with bemused tolerance rather than sympathy. In *The Golden Apples*, Welty explores the outcast, the individual ostracized from the so-called community.

Louis D. Rubin, Jr. wrote in 1949 on *The Golden Apples*: "With Miss Welty, plot is subordinate to character, serving only to develop her people." He added that more than anyone else except Thomas Wolfe's North Carolina, "these people of hers are Southern. . . . This is prime, regional literature," and asserted that there is hardly another book "that more completely gets the feel of the particular texture of Southern life, and its special tone and pattern."[86]

POPULAR FICTION

Southern writing in the 1940s also included other voices. There were writers born in the South who had moved elsewhere, and those who stayed. Edward Kimbrough of Mississippi focused on politics in *From Hell to Breakfast* (1941), which was about a demagogic politician in Mississippi. *Night Fire* (1946) and *Secret Pilgrim* (1949) owe a debt to William Faulkner and Robert Penn Warren in terms of style and subject, for in *Night Fire*, Kimbrough explores racial issues in a way that seems to derive from Faulkner. A farmer tries to save an innocent African American from a lynching. *Secret Pilgrim* involves a soldier's asylum, the search for a father, violence, and experimentation with shifts in time. Robert Ramsey, who wrote *Fire in Summer* (1942), was from Memphis, Tennessee. In his first novel, a boy named Blue recalls the story of a bigoted tenant farmer named Spence Lovell. We see a man who is strict with his family and blames his problems on the blacks. We feel danger around this man that seems to arise in images of burning barns and guns. His daughter gets pregnant and runs off, and his family struggles with this pitiable, destructive man.

History was an important feature of the work of Ben Ames Williams, a Mississippi novelist and short-story writer. His novels *Leave Her to Heaven* (1944) and *House Divided* (1947) were well-regarded best sellers. Perhaps of greater importance to historians was his editing of Mary Boykin Chesnut's *Diary from Dixie* (1949), an insightful and enduring record of observations by Chesnut, a Confederate officer's wife, during the Civil War period. Williams reflected on the years before America's entry into the Second World War in *A Time of Peace* (1942). The next year he wrote *Amateurs at War: American Soldiers in Action* (1943). *The Strange Woman* (1946) followed this. In the 1950s he produced *All the Brothers Were Valiant* (1955).

Perhaps there was history in his blood. His father's name was Daniel Webster Williams. His mother, Sara Marshall Ames, was a niece of Confederate General James Longstreet. She read aloud to him when he was a child. The family moved from Mississippi to Jackson, Ohio, when he was a child, and he later studied in Massachusetts, but the culture and history of the South never left his thoughts and imagination. He went to Wales for a year, when his father was consul in Cardiff. He then attended Dartmouth and worked in Boston as a reporter at the *Boston American*. His stories began to appear in *All Story* magazine, and later in *Collier's* and *The Saturday Evening Post*. He married Florence Traft Taipey, who was from Maine and descended from a long line of sea captains. They had two sons and a daughter, and lived in the suburbs of Newtonville, Massachusetts, and then at Chestnut Hill near Boston. They vacationed by the seacoast of Maine, on a farm where he wrote many of his stories. In all, Ben Ames Williams wrote thirty-five novels. Dartmouth and Colby College in Maine gave him honorary degrees. *House Divided* presents the story of the Currain family in more than a thousand pages. In this novel, Williams examines the causes and effects of the American Civil War.

Lloyd Douglas (1877–1953), a minister, wrote *The Robe* (1942) as a story of the miraculous. He was also the author of the best-selling *The Big Fisherman* (1948), which was filled with biblical characters, including the title character of St. Peter. Ministry occupied Douglas's attention more than fiction writing until he produced *Magnificent Obsession* when he was fifty years old, in 1929. He was immediately seen as a writer of the religious epic, like *Quo Vadis* or *Ben Hur*. *The Robe* sold more than 2 million copies and became a motion picture with Richard Burton in 1953. *The Big Fisherman* was not supposed to be filmed, but it also became a motion picture in 1959.

The Robe is about the crucifixion of Jesus, a historical event that Douglas views through his Christian faith. Douglas began writing the story after Hazel McCann, a clerk at an Ohio department store, wrote him a letter in which she asked what had happened to Jesus' garments. Douglas began sending his chapters to her. They finally met in 1941, and he dedicated the novel to her. The story focuses upon the aftermath of the crucifixion and centers upon the experiences of a Roman centurion, the tribune Marcellus, and his Greek slave, Demetrius. Marcellus has carried out the crucifixion. He later arranges for the robe to be given to Peter, the big fisherman, and this sets up the sequel. Marcellus has been taunted into wearing the robe at a banquet, where Pontius Pilate is a guest, and he has a breakdown. He retreats to Athens to rest. In Athens, Demetrius persuades him to touch the robe, and he is healed.

In *The Big Fisherman*, Peter, a fisherman, becomes an apostle. Douglas focuses on his life story as a journey toward forgiveness and redemption. In the novel, Peter assists an Arab-Jewish girl, Fara. She is a daughter of Herod Antipas, who has cast aside her mother. John the Baptist finds her and encourages her to become a follower of Jesus. That is when Peter begins to protect her. A character named Voldi follows her, and tries to bring her home. Meanwhile, she wants to do away with Herod.

Truman Capote, *Other Voices, Other Rooms*

Truman Capote is best known for *In Cold Blood*, the sensational nonfiction account of a murder. He also wrote *Breakfast at Tiffanys*. However, his Gothicism began with his first novel, *Other Voices, Other Rooms* (1948). Capote became an image, a media celebrity, beginning with the *Life* magazine profile of June 2, 1947. There he was matched with other writers like Jean Stafford, Gore Vidal, and Thomas Heggen, whose *Mister Roberts* was then about to become popular. In the photo, Capote sits on a couch in a checkered waistcoat, a cigarette in his hand. The novel had not yet appeared, and he looks out at us with big eyes and a wistful look on his face.

Other Voices, Other Rooms was published in a cold January to much publicity and fanfare. Yes, it was that odd, slightly decadent-looking man with the big eyes and the glasses again. In the *New Republic*, on January 26, John Farrelly drew attention to all of the advertising that was circulating about Truman Capote. Leslie Fiedler asserted that Capote's novel was like a compendium of Southern literature, and Elizabeth Hardwick in *The Partisan Review* (March 1948) called it a parody of that literature. The next year, *A Tree of Night*, a collection of short stories, followed. The *Saturday Review* (February 12, 1949) offered an interview with Capote in which he offered a curious account of his life. It must have seemed to many readers like an exaggerated, self-created image.

The late 1940s was an era well suited to the Gothic genre. It was a time of trying to reassemble the pieces after war and control the horror that had upended the world. It was a period of film noir, horror films, and recovery from international violence. Joel Knox, the young homo-sexual protagonist of *Other Voices, Other Rooms*, is brought to the remote Gothic mansion of Skully's Landing to meet a father he does not know. He is told very little about the man. His stepmother seems to ignore the question. The black servant with the scar on his throat tells him to not ask about Mister Sansom. Ask cousin Rudolph. Ask Miss Amy. A strange lady looks out at him from an upstairs window. Joel is on edge. A thumping sound he hears is merely a red tennis ball. The mysteries are similarly revealed: his father is a mental invalid whose crippled hand set the tennis ball in motion. The lady in the upstairs window was Rudolph in drag, recalling the love of his life: Pepe Alvarez, a boxer. With its generally rational and reasonable hero, Joel, Capote's novel is a form of parody of the Gothic, and a kind of serious play.

Robert Penn Warren, *All the King's Men*

As *All the King's Men* (1940) begins, Robert Penn Warren's lyricism brings us down the road with Jack Burden. Readers are drawn into this narrating persona by Warren's expansive poetics and are invited into the story by Jack's apparently reliable language and way of looking at the world. Jack is not only a reporter, or a historian; he is an analyst and philosopher of his world. Jack has run off to the West Coast as if for a new frontier, but now has returned to a deeper involvement in his past. He has begun to frame life with a philosophical turn of mind, noting that "all of life is but the dark heave of blood and the twitch of the nerve . . . which is the dream of our age."[87] Jack welcomes the reader to current and past events: to follow the rise of a politician, Willie Stark, to bring together the reports, images, and fragments of his story. Jack insists by the story's end that he will further research his ancestor Cass Mastern's story. However, what he has in effect given us is the story of Willie Stark and the story of himself. In his words, we learn from history that people "are good and bad" and that "good comes out of bad."[88] Even so, when we read Jack's own life story, we may wonder at that final hope of his that some good may have come out of it all.

Jack Burden, as a student of history, learns a useful skill: that of researcher and investigator. He has read history for many years. He tells us that he lay around Judge Irwin's house and read American history, not for school and not because he had to, but because he "had stepped through the thin crackly crust of the present and felt the first pull of the quicksand around my ankles."[89] To read history became a way to, at least partially, secure himself in the present. History enables one to better understand origins, precedents, actions, personalities, and strategies that have set up the framework of the contemporary world. Even so, Jack, who is intrigued by his family's past, is limited as a historian. Nor is he a particularly good reporter. While he pursues the story of Cass Mastern, he is unable to explain the Civil War past and his relative's place within it. Although he reports on the political and social impact of Willie Stark, he generally seems more concerned about himself. That is not to say that Robert Penn Warren is anything other than effective in giving us Jack Burden's narrative voice and perspective. *All the King's Men* is a novel about history and politics and the South, as well as one about family shadows, psychological issues, ancestral history, romance, and dark secrets. In the sense that it is a story of gradual revelation of those secrets, it is like a detective story. Jack Burden is fashioned as a limited consciousness in the process of discovery.

All the King's Men fits with the moral tone of some of the novels of this period, which appear to reflect a desire to set the world right. For example, Larry A. Gray compares Warren's novel with Raymond Chandler's *The Big Sleep* and *Farewell My Lovely*. In these novels, crimes against individuals can be traced to larger criminal organizations.[90] However, morality is also at issue in these story-worlds. The moral code is to be remedied by a detective. Jack Burden is something like a detective, uncovering difficult truths. Gray points out that Jack Burden is an insider who is "disconnected."[91] In his movement from newspaper reporter to political company aide to Stark, he begins to cover for his boss even as he uncovers the moral bankruptcy of Judge Irwin. Willie Stark is a striving ego, a media candidate and public-image maker who has some people believing that he is a great man.

Jack Burden's narration, like that of Nick Carraway in *The Great Gatsby* (1925), is a written testimony. He seeks to understand and communicate his role in events. He writes: "This has been the story of Willie Stark, but it is my story too."[92] He needs to understand the past and connect it with his present. He defines the historian's role as being responsible for the past, as Ben Railton has pointed out. James Perkins points out that the novel ends with irony. By the end of this novel, readers may know more than the narrator does, and we are left to figure out Jack's paternity.[93]

The historical quest, for Jack, is a search for understanding. At the turn of the twentieth century, the conservative and positivist historical approach sought objectivity and the scientific. In the 1920s, James Hervey Robinson, Charles and Mary Beard, and Carl Becker questioned this approach, and sought to use the past to advance society's movement into the future, to contrast formalism with an emphasis on present relevance. Parallel with this was John Dewey's drive to make American culture more democratic. What Robert Penn Warren shows is that history also has a narrative form. A narrative is imposed on experience to dissect or interpret it, to tell how it was. He distinguished his role as a novelist from that of the historian. The historian seeks the facts behind the world; the fiction writer most knows the inside of his world.[94] Jack Burden, within his world, is a historical detective who seeks facts that will elucidate his paternity, his family past, and his place in a complicated, shifting world of change.

The Civil War haunts the American South still. If *All the King's Men* is a novel about politics, one may wonder why fifty pages are devoted to the Civil War and to Cass Mastern's affair with the wife of his friend. Why do we read about a slave, Phebe, who has been sold down the river and his attempt to retrieve her? Robert Penn Warren gives us a story within a story that considers race and integration. His racial politics were gradualist and in the 1940s he had little expectation of a sudden transformation of Southern society beyond its "separate but equal" doctrine to fully recognize racial equality. He was one of the Southern intellectuals and storytellers that Louis D. Rubin has called "mythmakers."[95] The Civil War and the honorable lost cause remained throughout the twentieth century one of the enduring myths of the South. Slavery remained one of its persistent legacies.

Willie Stark, likewise, is mythical. He was originally Willie Strong, or Willie Talos: a Greek mythological figure. Whereas Willie is often criminally unjust, using any means to achieve political power, he forges an effective political machine. Of course, political machines do not care much about people. Willie represents himself as a man of the people who hails from outside the system. He offers the claim that he would take from the rich to make the state great again. A social insurance proposal he makes, however, is flawed. In 1981, Robert Penn Warren introduced a new edition of his novel, with observations on the politics of Willie Stark and Huey Long: "He lived in terms of power, and for him ends seemed to justify means."[96]

The career of Louisiana Governor Huey Long served as a point of origin for this novel. However, the novel is not about Huey Long. Set in 1930, it presents a dark vision of history and politics and provides an interesting window upon the campaign machinations of politics and the appeal of populism. Yet, the novel is about more than politics. In a 1953 essay in the *Sewanee Review*, Warren asserted that he did not plan Willie Stark as a fictional expression of Huey Long. Rather, he suggested that his self-conscious narrator, Jack Burden, was the figure most central to his novel.[97] More than a story of politics, Jack Burden's story is a recollection of the past and a search for meaning. The modern person is faced with a complicated world. In response, Jack first seeks romance, then retreats into solipsism. He then returns home with a shred of idealism and joins the political team of Willie Stark, working as his assistant. His idealism then fades to fatalism, like one of those old films in which the image is swallowed up in a tight circle and fades to black.

Robert Penn Warren had a philosophical orientation. He was a Southerner who essentially remained an Agrarian. Like his character, Jack Burden, he was fascinated by history, writing his first full-length work on the abolitionist John Brown. His novel is far more about American memory than it is about politics per se. His critical grounding undergirds a novel in which there is an encounter with encroaching modernity and a search for a usable past. The forces of modernization that pressed upon individuals in the South, indeed throughout the modern world, included the machine technologies that an Agrarian would have viewed as a potential threat to the traditions of the land and to art, faith, and the person. *All the King's Men* begins with the concern that "you" will be reduced to a statistic. One must not make the mistakes of Jack Burden and be hypnotized and lulled into the Great Sleep. We are going somewhere with Jack Burden as this novel begins, but we know not where. The landscape and voices are of the American South, but we travel and see through time as well. With Jack Burden, we are propelled into motion. With Willy Stark, we are pushed into politics. We are shuttled across ages.

As a reporter, Jack Burden meets Willie Stark in a pool hall. He follows his opposition and then covers his run for governor. After Jack finds that he cannot write according to the slant of the newspaper that employs him, Willie hires him. Jack is essentially still a journalist. He undertakes a quest for the truth, and his narrative takes on the tone of an investigator. He becomes an inquiring historian of the Cass Mastern material. He probes the background of the judge who accepted a bribe. Eventually, he will try to find out why Adam Stanton moved toward an act of assassination.

The politics that Robert Penn Warren portrays in his novel and in his novel's title asks a question that is relevant for our own time: Who will make America whole again? If all the king's horses and men in Washington, or in the statehouse, cannot put together Humpty Dumpty again, who will? When the late Michael J. Meyer addressed this question in 2006, he observed that "Penn Warren represents an almost Godforsaken universe where the significance of a higher power has steadily deteriorated, and where the Cain question is now summarily answered: "No! I have no responsibility for another's well-being. I am not my brother's keeper."[98]

The United States in the Second World War was indeed "my brother's keeper." The nation fought not only for American national security, but for the broader claims of democracy and global security. It engaged with its Allies in a battle against a perceived tyranny. This response was driven by patriotism, courage, and concern, as well as by the necessity of the times. Jack Burden fumbles in his attempt to recover his historical roots. He does not have a faith in which to anchor his trust. Instead, he becomes lost in a whirlwind. He is an empty stage upon which Willie Stark will act out his drama. In a society that seems largely engaged in a game of Monopoly, Willie Stark provides him with a momentary commitment that is almost religious in its fervor. The charismatic Willie may not realize that his power and popularity is fleeting. He is, as Meyer recognized, like a broken egg that "cannot be easily refashioned if broken."[99]

Jack Burden's quest is to know. Early in the novel, the narrator reflects on humanity's drive for knowledge: "The end of man is knowledge, but there is one thing he can't know. He can't know whether the knowledge will save him or kill him."[100] This exploration of consciousness does not emerge in Robert Rossen's 1949 film adaptation of *All the*

King's Men. Rossen's script centers on Willie Stark. Despite a series of well-orchestrated flashbacks, Jack Burden is no longer the center of awareness that moves us through the story. The film medium and its audience call for a more objective approach than Jack's meandering meditations. Jack Burden is played by John Ireland, who portrays a more passive figure than in the novel, one who reacts to events. Jack gradually begins to acknowledge that Willie Stark's means to gain political power are leading him into further corruption. Rossen succeeds in underscoring Willie Stark's idealism as well. Whereas the novel is about Jack Burden's attempt to draw together the pieces of his life into a moral perspective, in the film Jack is left to try to understand what was good in Willie Stark that must somehow be sustained and carried on.

Robert Penn Warren was a poet, a critic, and a novelist of historical revisionism. He affirmed the past and the persistence of tradition, and he rejected industrialism. The quest for the self is central to his novels *All the King's Men* and *Band of Angels* (1955). Warren sought to reaffirm home, family, and community, and free individuals from liberalism, social Darwinism, and the dehumanizing aspects of industry. The individual must earn his or her identity within this world through ongoing struggle within the human condition. Warren argues for moral awareness and community within a tragic world. The individual stands in relation with this community, and no individual is completely isolated. One must accept responsibility for a community of love and law, and recognize a moral significance to life. Humanity is subject to corruption and life can be difficult, but God has not abandoned the world.

3

NATIVE SONS AND DAUGHTERS

Richard Wright, Chester Himes, Ann Petry,
James Baldwin, and Ralph Ellison

RICHARD WRIGHT

Native Son

Black lives matter. Since they do, and because all lives matter, Richard Wright's *Native Son* remains especially powerful today within our present concerns about race in America. We still have Bigger Thomas among us. He is a character that Wright once called "a product of a dislocated society," the rebellious young black man who seeks answers by moving in the wrong direction. Bigger Thomas chases an elusive dream and has no tradition, faith, or sense of belonging to orient or reassure him: "Tense, afraid, nervous, hysterical and restless . . . he is a dispossessed and disinherited man; he is all of this, and he lives amid the greatest plenty on earth and he is looking and feeling for a way out."[1] From the stresses on people in inner cities to the need for fair and equal opportunity, this novel, published in March 1940, is a challenge to readers now, even as it was then.

Native Son is a story of alienation, resistance, and struggle. It begins with Bigger Thomas setting fire to his house. Bigger is repeatedly told to keep quiet, but does not accept being forced to be silent. As he stands before a fireplace, he pushes straws from a broom into it. He reminds us all that anger can be voiced through actions. Richard Wright, in 1940, asked: "Who will be the first to touch off these Bigger Thomases in America, white and black?"[2] The native son, whom he called "a symbolic figure in American life," held within him "the outlines of action and feeling we would encounter on a vast scale in the days to come."[3] America was now like a laboratory in which one could see how the public "would react under stress."[4]

Bigger Thomas could not easily embrace the American dream. He was injured and degraded. "His emotional and intellectual life was never that articulate," says Wright. He was caught in a world where he was trapped in racial tensions, a world that he keenly felt was over and against him. Bigger's response was not that of Martin Luther King Jr., who sought to overcome injustice through dignified, nonviolent action. The protagonist of *Native Son* was angry and demonstrative. He was not part of the black folk culture or of any church. Rather, he was alienated. His material world was one of dreams that he could not attain, and he possessed no higher vision. Wright describes Bigger Thomas as an individual whose subjective life is "clothed in the tattered rags of American culture."[5] He is an aggressive, troubled, and disappointed man in the city of Chicago, whose impulses and fears can find no cultural or religious ground. In remarks on *Native Son*, Wright recognized a disconnection between America's finest virtues and values and the life of his character; he wrote, "We live by an ideal that makes us believe that the Constitution and the Bill of Rights safeguard civil liberties and all should have opportunity to realize their potential: his own peculiar and untranslatable destiny."[6]

Bigger Thomas is portrayed as isolated, as "sullen, angry, ignorant, emotionally unstable, depressed and unaccountably elated at times," and in his reflections on *Native Son*, Wright points out that Bigger is "the product of a dislocated society; he is a dispossessed and disinherited man."[7] Wright realized that he had to create this character to show this "symbol of all the larger things" that he saw in him. Bigger Thomas would confront readers with his anguish and "they would not relish being publicly reminded of the lowly, shameful depths."[8] Have some pride, Mr. Wright, he expected his readers would say. Think of all that we have accomplished in spite of oppression. Yet, Bigger had to take on life as a troubled individual in the pages of his novel. Wright realized that what Bigger meant had claimed him.[9]

Richard Wright's observation of African American life in America remains an important point of reference today. He referred to his character as a meaningful and "prophetic" symbol.[10] Bigger was "estranged from the religion and folk culture of his race."[11] He was a modern person "whose glitter came to him through the newspapers, magazines, radios, movies, and the mere imposing sight and sound of daily American life."[12] We might add television, the Internet, Facebook, iPhones, and advertising to this list of media that offers enticements and shapes our perception today. In an essay in which he recalls his character, Wright addresses a feeling among black youth: "a wild and intense longing . . . to belong, to be identified, to feel that they were alive as other people were." He speaks of a desire to be involved in events, to "do a job in common with others."[13]

Wright recognized that this drive to participate may be dampened by some features of the environment in which one lives. He wrote that "Chicago's physical aspect—noisy, crowded, filled with the sense of power and fulfillment—did so much more to dazzle the mind with a taunting sense of possible achievement."[14] Wright brought his experience and imagination, the techniques of social science, and an approach that reflected the naturalism of Theodore Dreiser and James Farrell to his novel. While Wright was influenced by literary naturalism, he approached the situation of Bigger Thomas, a black man in Chicago, in a unique manner informed by Marxism and socialist theory. Wright became a committed critic: "I faced ways and techniques of gauging meaningfully the effects of American civilization upon the personalities of people."[15] He consciously practiced and developed ways of seeing American life and saw what he called "a complex struggle for life in my country, a struggle in which I was involved."[16]

Native Son was a novel that Wright found necessary. He had to write it, he said, "for my race possessed no fictional works dealing with such problems." Wright dealt with issues of prejudice, economic deprivation, alienation, and anger head-on, and sought to work "with a deep and fearless will down to the dark roots of life."[17] He began with the character of Bigger Thomas, and without any plot. He had thought about this character for a long time. Wright began his novel while living in Chicago. To develop Bigger Thomas, he took a job at the South Side Boys Club. This was a place that sought to improve boys' lives or, as Wright put it, reclaim them from "the dives and the alleys of the Black Belt."[18]

Wright became cynical about the work of the Boys Club. It seemed to him that the organization's goal was to distract boys like Bigger Thomas with sports to keep them off the streets, so that they would not "harm the valuable white property" on the outskirts of Chicago's South Side. He wanted to prove that "full-blooded" life is "stronger than ping-pong."[19] There was more to building up these young boys' minds and lives than pacifying them with Ping-Pong, checkers, swimming, and basketball.

Wright says that he wrote his first draft of the novel in four months, producing 576 pages by working daily. He worked "scene after scene" and says that he always "tried to render, depict, not merely tell the story."[20] He experimented with stream-of-consciousness, interior monologue, and focused on the unfolding of action in the present. He centered his story on what Bigger Thomas "saw and felt" while keeping himself "out of the story as much as possible."[21]

Wright picked up the work again after he moved to Brooklyn in 1938. By October 1938, most of *Native Son* had been written, and he revised his novel in 1939. It would be a best seller in 1940. Wright spoke about *Native Son* in 1940 at Columbia University and at the Negro Playwrights Company in Harlem. In his essay, "How Bigger Was Born," he traces the process of his composition. He showed the work to his agent, Paul Reynolds, and to his editor, Ed Aswell. Dorothy Canfield also responded to the book; she would later write the introduction.

Wright suggests that most of Bigger Thomas's limitations are socially conditioned. The forces that created this character drive him toward disaster. The mistakes that he makes land him in trouble. He carries a drunken girl upstairs. Covering her mouth to keep her quiet, he inadvertently smothers her. The father of the girl is a real-estate businessman. If he had truly responded to the inner city he profited from and had created playgrounds, basketball courts, recreational grounds, and employment opportunities for, there might not be someone like Bigger Thomas to take his daughter's life. Even so, in Wright's view the issue is larger than civic responses such as providing recreational opportunities and jobs for people like Bigger Thomas. Bigger's dilemma is situated in his limitations as a black man in a socioeconomically deprived context. He is an alienated individual in a dehumanizing industrial modern city. Bigger's case parallels Theodore Dreiser's story of Clyde Griffiths in *An American Tragedy*, which moves from an accidental murder to a court trial. Bigger's defense lawyer, Boris Max, is a radical who is disposed toward communist positions and argumentation. He is inclined to attempt to hold capitalism responsible for Bigger Thomas's situation. However, Max does not challenge the false rape charge, nor does he launch out against racial prejudice.

The philosophy of Karl Marx lay behind Wright's critique, but Wright was already anticipating existentialism as well. This presents an interesting tension between determinism and free will. Marx emphasizes humanity's social being, or species-being, and existentialism focused on individualism, or self-making. There is a tension between those perspectives. Wright's novel may be set alongside Albert Camus's *The Stranger* (1942), which appeared two years after *Native Son*. Camus gives us Merseult's story of alienation. There is a shooting in the blinding light on an Algerian beach, and a trail that Merseult approaches dispassionately. Merseult is put on trial. In Wright's novel, a murder is followed by the arrest and trial of Bigger Thomas. To the court scenes Wright brings communist musings.

The dilemma of Bigger Thomas also reminds us of William Faulkner's *Light in August*, which suggests the absurdity of the situation of Joe Christmas. He is a tragic figure—a black man, racially mixed, who is caught in a perplexing mess. He has been charged with the rape and murder of a white girl, Joanna Burden, and he is pursued as a fugitive. One critic, Esther Merle Jackson, distinguishes Bigger Thomas from Joe Christmas and suggests that Wright realizes Bigger's psychology more completely than Faulkner renders the psychology of Joe Christmas. However, Faulkner's text shifts in time and calls for a different approach to his character's consciousness. Bigger Thomas is indeed lost within "a shadowy region, a no man's land, the ground that separated the white world from the black world that he stood upon," but so too is Joe Christmas cut off from these worlds, both white and black. Jackson claims that Bigger is "more complex . . . for he sees his situation as the face of a profound universal disorder."[22] However, Faulkner's creation of his character's limitations appears to be intentional, and his character's personal crisis is equally a cosmic matter.

12 Million Black Voices and Civil Rights

In 1940, Wright raised an argument about the police response to a black youth in Chicago, a response that was sharply criticized by Supreme Court Justice Hugo Black. A crime wave was occurring in the city, and the police cruised through neighborhoods in patrol cars. Wright claimed that there was racial profiling occurring—that the Chicago police would "grab the first Negro boy who seems to be unattached and homeless."[23] Wright asserted that this suspect would be held for about a week without charge or bail, and would be unable to communicate with anyone while he was pressured to confess.[24] Incensed by this apparent intimidation, Wright argued against the injustice in this situation. He added: "So far removed are these practices from what the average American encounters in his daily life that it takes a huge act of his imagination to believe that it is true."[25]

In the 1940s, Wright broke through the color barrier of the bestseller lists much like Jackie Robinson broke through the color barrier in baseball. In 1941–1942, Richard Wright's *Native Son* was adapted for a stage play directed by Orson Welles, with Canada Lee in the lead role. Wright's story, "The Man Who Lived Underground," was published in *Accent*. A work of nonfiction also appeared: *12 Million Black Voices: A Folk History of the Negro in the United States* (1941), illustrated with photographs taken by Edwin Rosskam. It begins with "Our Strange Birth," an essay on black history. Wright immediately asserts that the men in Europe subjugated the Negro race: they "denied our human personalities, tore us from our native soil, weighted our legs and stacked us like cord-wood in the foul holes of clipper ships, dragged us across thousands of miles of ocean, and hurled us into another land, strange and hostile." Yet, this sentence goes on to recognize that in this strange and difficult journey of bondage lay "the slow, painful process of a new birth amid conditions harsh and raw."[26]

The decade of the 1940s was a time of increased movement of African Americans from the South to northern cities and, sometimes, to West Coast cities.[27] Wright himself was part of this movement, emerging from Mississippi roots and living and working in Chicago. The "folk" place that Wright discusses includes a family and kinship system that Houston A. Baker Jr. recognizes as "fragile."[28] There is a tradition, he reminds us, one that includes "standards of love, hope, and value."

There is a religious tradition that includes people getting ready for church—the center of community life—singing hymns and avidly echoing the pronouncements of the preacher. There are the secular sermons of jazz and the blues, a declaration of life that Wright says is present "in our wild, raw music, in our invention of slang that winds its way all across America."[29] Wright observes how the black culture encounters industry and women become domestics. Men are the laborers, and "it is in industry that we [black men] encounter experiences that tend to break down the structure of our folk characters and project us toward the vortex of modern life."[30] This is a dilemma of modernization, not exclusive to African Americans, that has been critiqued by sociologists who have examined the shifts of community life in America. In Wright's view, modernity and industrialization have eroded the basis of black folk life that long supported family and community.

Reflecting on Wright's *12 Million Black Voices*, critic Houston Baker observes the condition of confinement experienced by African Americans, crammed into small spaces on slave ships and bound in slavery. His point is that boundaries set for African Americans persisted in America; Baker writes: "This hole thus stands as an ironic indictment of the commercial birth of modern man."[31] The "hole" he speaks of may be the plantation system of the eighteenth and nineteenth centuries, or the urban ghetto of the twentieth and twenty-first centuries. Baker recognizes that turning human beings into commodities was a displacement of bodies for commercial purposes.[32] Wright's picture of Bigger Thomas in Chicago is consistent with this view.

The world that Wright wrote was within established narrow geographies for African Americans. At best, most made what Martin Luther King Jr., in his "I Have a Dream" speech, later referred to as transitions from one ghetto to another. Women became representatives of folk wisdom and spiritual centers of the home. Wright asserts that at work, black men are "gripped and influenced by the world-wide forces that shape and mold the life of Western civilization."[33] Black women learn that the "orbit of life is narrow . . . from their kitchenette to the white folk's kitchen and back home again"; while the men may find expression for their lives in their work in the mills and factories, the women find it in the churches and "they love the church more than do our men."[34] Baker points out that this does not account for women who ventured out beyond domesticity. There were black professional women who attended college, women who joined the labor movement became involved with industry during the war. Baker observes that Wright appears intent on constructing for us a history that emerges from his own perspective as an African American man in the 1940s, a socialist with a grasp of social science. Wright is quite aware that he is offering a perspective. Baker points out that four years before Wright created this book, he penned an essay, "Blueprint for Negro Writing," in which he says that a perspective is a "fixed point in intellectual space where a writer stands to view the struggle, hopes, and sufferings of his people."[35]

Black Boy

Wright's "space," when he writes *Black Boy*, is that of a writer situated in 1940s America. His space is that of a working writer concerned with the working class, a man with a Marxist socialist ideology concerned with the proletariat. Baker concludes that both Wright and Ralph Ellison placed too much faith in the machine of industrialism as "a potentially productive womb" from which a modern, "redemptive Afro-American consciousness will be born."[36] Wright's fiction draws on the insights of the Chicago School of social science and urban sociology. With *Native Son*, he creates a case study narrative; he seeks social explanations. But he engages in a personal quest for understanding with his life story in *Black Boy*, his autobiography.

Black Boy is three times the length of his story *American Hunger*, which appeared as a sequel to the autobiography. It opens in Chicago: "an unreal city whose mythical houses were built of slabs of black coal wreathed in palls of gray smoke, houses whose foundations were sinking slowly into the dank prairie."[37] Wright's editor submitted *Black Boy* to the Book of the Month Club under its original title, "American Hunger." The BOMC wanted revisions, including the deletion of part 2, "The Horror and the Glory," about Chicago and the activity of the Communist Party there. Wright made the revisions, and this expurgated version of *Black Boy* is the one that appeared in print.

Bigger Thomas in book 1 of *Native Son* is inarticulate and illiterate. In contrast, the narrative voice in *Black Boy* is quite articulate and literate. Wright's intelligence and curiosity about language prompted the emergence of his career. Wright's urban enslavement was not that of Frederick Douglass, as Robert Stepto points out; Douglass reached for the possibilities offered by literacy, but Wright applied different rhetorical strategies.[38] James Baldwin, Toni Morrison, Ralph Ellison, Ernest Gaines, Alice Walker, and other African American authors have created work that "dispels the deathlike chill of Wright's (albeit rhetorical) vision of Negro America," Stepto concludes.[39]

The Outsider

Richard Wright's existentialist thinking preceded his acquaintance with Jean-Paul Sartre and Albert Camus and his work on his 1953 novel, *The Outsider*. The existential condition is something he realized in his own experiences. These existentialist concerns appear in his autobiography, *Black Boy*, and in his story "The Underground Man" (1942). Wright's time in Paris contributed to *The Outsider*.

In *The Outsider*, Cross Damon tries to escape his identity. He is a Chicago African American who is in debt and is in a troubled marriage. He has a mistress who is pregnant. Caught in a subway accident, he fakes his death and takes the identity of another man who has been killed. Then he conceals who he is, and goes to New York, where he joins the Communist Party and he gets caught in a murder. Cross Damon cannot run away from consciousness, nor can the reader flee from the obvious existentialism of Sartre and Camus that runs through this novel.

Cross Damon is a modern man who breaks from his roots. He must reinvent his life: "Cross had to discover what was good or evil through his own actions."[40] He had become no one—an individual in the modern dilemma. He was not an individual murderer, like the Dallas sniper who shot police officers after a peaceful demonstration in July 2016. Neither is he Ralph Ellison's invisible man. Wright's outsider is no man, an individual of no race and no tradition, of no faith and no culture. Bereft of any depth of spirit, any sustaining myth or sense of purpose, he tries to make a getaway from responsibility and from identity. Yet, to Damon Cross (perhaps a demon who is cross) we must say, with the existentialists, that an individual who is thrown here into life on earth must choose and act. Running away is not really an option.

CHESTER HIMES

Chester Himes's novel, *If He Hollers Let Him Go* (1945), documents worker experiences in the shipyards. Ship assembly was a major industry during World War II, and Himes was involved in this work. He writes a story about Bob, Jones, and Madge, who work at the Atlas Shipyards. In chapter 12, we read about Bob waking up from a dream: "I started drawing in my emotions, trying them, whittling them off, nailing them down."[41] Bob's sleep is haunted by dreams. He experiences internal pressures, and his life is dictated by the ship assembly pace.

Himes moved to Los Angeles in 1942, and was one of 340,000 African Americans who moved to L.A. between 1942 and 1945.[42] Shipbuilding was an industry in which they could find work; aircraft building was segregated. Himes worked at Kaiser Shipyard in the San Francisco Bay Area, and in San Pedro as an assistant to a shipwright. Throughout this time, he hoped to do some screenwriting in Los Angeles, but there was little opportunity to be found. Himes and other blacks could work in the shipyards because President Roosevelt signed Executive Order 8802, making this possible. A. Philip Randolph, the leader of the Brotherhood of Sleeping Car Porters, threatened to have one hundred thousand blacks march on Washington, D.C. to protest segregation in the defense industry. He and Roosevelt met in June 1941 to work out defense policies and issues of segregation in the military. North American Aviation would not employ blacks until Roosevelt signed a law opposing discrimination in defense industries.

Of course, the work environment was not always hospitable. Himes wrote: "The air was so thick with welding fumes, acid smell, body odor, and cigarette smoke, even the steam from the blower couldn't get it out." He saw around him "the immensity of production" and wrote: "It was stifling hot, and the din was terrific." Himes writes of a bustling industrial place where a person feels rather alienated and fragmented. He lives his job, however disrupted he feels in his life. He feels connected with the war and "included in it all."[43]

ANN PETRY

What is the look, the sound, the feel of the street in 1940s Harlem? If brick and concrete could speak, what story would echo there? In *The Street* (1946) by Ann Petry (1908–1997), Lutie Johnson must find a place to live. She locates a Harlem apartment, a three-story walk-up where she lives with Bub, her eight-year-old son. It is a place that is urban and black, a space that is "ever closing in." The street seems to own these people. Lutie's blackness limits her possibilities for work: "The women work because the white folks give them work: washing dishes and clothes and floors and windows." Lutie does not have any opportunity for upward mobility. She recognizes that the races are separate and that women are hardworking: "Here on this street women trudged along overburdened, overworked, their own homes neglected while they looked after someone else's while the men of the street swung empty-handed, well-dressed, and carefree."[44]

Lutie Johnson is dealing with the collapse of her marriage, and she is on her own. Bub, her son, is persuaded into a scheme to steal mail. He is caught and ends up in a children's shelter. Lutie seeks money to pay for a lawyer and goes to a man named Boots, who is a nightclub owner. Boots tells her that he will provide money in exchange for sex. She protests vehemently and resists his advances with an iron candlestick and strikes him with it. Realizing that she has killed Boots, she knows that she must get out of town and buys a train ticket for Chicago: one way, never to return.

The Street sold swiftly, selling more than a million copies: the first novel by an African American woman to do so. The lurid incident with Boots, with its sex and violence, probably accounted for some of the popular interest in the story. Petry provided a keen portrayal of the urban world of the 1940s, and how Lutie's race limited her prospects for jobs, income, and upward mobility. Her narration is written with a third-person point of view that shifts perspective and shows the connections between people. She creates a character who protests the abuse that she personally experiences, as well as the abuse she believes that blacks experience.

Petry knew the sights and sounds around P.S. 10 in Harlem, where she worked. She wrote about black lives that indeed mattered to her. Petry's short stories first appeared in W. E. B. Du Bois's magazine, *The*

Crisis. Her character Lutie Johnson has been called the most politically aware female character in the novels of the day. As David Wyatt points out, there are social barriers for African American females, which are as equally present as economic ones.[45]

JAMES BALDWIN

> *If history were the past, history wouldn't matter. History is the present. You and I are history.*
>
> —James Baldwin

James Baldwin asserted that a culture and its literature are connected. He became one of the most powerful literary voices of the 1950s and the 1960s by taking that idea seriously. A writer, Baldwin believed, presents an image of the lives of people in a culture. The novel that he writes can engage in a social and cultural focus, although it is not sociology. A novel is an aesthetic work and can also be an art of revelation. Baldwin wrote: "It is this power of revelation which is the business of the novelist, the journey toward a more vast reality which must take precedence over all other claims."[46] In the 1950s, Langston Hughes wrote that Baldwin "uses words as the sea uses waves, to flow and beat, advance and retreat, rise and take a bow in disappearing."[47]

Baldwin began to move toward his role as a social critic while writing book reviews in the 1940s. Between 1947 and 1949, he wrote twenty-nine reviews. "Eight Men" and "The Male Prison" reappeared in *Nobody Knows My Name.* In "History as Nightmare," Baldwin responds to Chester Himes's *Lonely Crusade,* concerning black efforts to survive in a white society. Baldwin writes that Himes expresses a "desperate, implacable determination to find out the truth . . . to understand the psychology of the oppressed and oppressor in their relation to each other."[48] This becomes a repeated theme in Baldwin's writing.

In 1949, Baldwin reviewed five books in a review essay, "Too Late, Too Late," that appeared in *Commentary.* In this essay he wrote that "the full story of white and black in this country is more vast and shattering than we would like to believe." Baldwin's comments in January 1949 continue to have relevance for our own time: "We are sick now and relations between the races is only one of the symptoms," he asserted. These happenings, he said, are becoming more a part of America every day.[49] Despite these problems, Baldwin held out a hopeful role for literature: that it could contribute to uniting diverse people. Writing had to be objective to represent social reality, Baldwin said. "I want to be an honest man and a good writer," he wrote.[50] Baldwin held that literature must explore the past, examining U.S. history and its meaning and relevance. Literature would then be a means to reflect social reality and seek truth.

In "The Image of the Negro," another review of five novels, Baldwin examined the values he saw embodied in literary texts. He asked: "With what reality are they concerned, how is it probed, exactly what message is being brought to this amorphous public mind?"[51] He reviewed *There Was Once a Slave*, a biography of Frederick Douglass by Shirley Graham, in which he probed the heroic black "superman" figure: "She has reduced a significant, passionate human being to the obscene level of a Hollywood caricature," he wrote.[52] In the "Dead Hand of Caldwell," Baldwin reviewed Erskine Caldwell's *The Sure Hand of God*. It was a story of Southern life and concern for individuals facing predicaments, experiencing the difficult odds against them.[53] Baldwin also reviewed Jacques Maritain's *The Person and the Good*. Maritain, a Scholastic philosopher, presented ethical issues that must be confronted within a framework of faith. Baldwin insisted, "It is unhelpful to be assured of future angels when the mysteries of the present flesh are so far from being solved."[54]

Baldwin's comments on two of Richard Wright's stories, "The Man Who Was Almost a Man" and "The Man Who Saw the Flood," are of interest partly because he would later launch out critically with his perspectives on Wright's *Native Son* and *Black Boy*. Baldwin wrote: "Perhaps it is odd, but they did not make me think of the 1930s, or even particularly of Negroes. They made me think of human loss and helplessness." Here, Baldwin considers Wright as a voice tuned in to universal human concerns. Indeed, black lives matter, but this recognition points to the universal: the dignity of the human person.[55] Wright responded sensitively to Baldwin's criticism. Maurice Charney called this Wright's feeling of having been "betrayed by this writer that he much admired."[56]

James Baldwin's attitudes toward Richard Wright's *Native Son* are expressed in his essays, "Everybody's Protest Novel" (1949), "Many

Thousands Gone" (1955), and "Alas, Poor Richard" (1962). Baldwin recognizes Wright's significance and sees him as a "spiritual father," and acknowledges Wright's efforts as valuable ones "during a bewildering and demoralizing era in Western history."[57] *Black Boy* was especially important to him. Recognizing his debt to Richard Wright, he stated: "His work was an immense liberation and revelation for me."[58]

However, Baldwin and Wright were different writers with different aesthetic concerns and social visions. In the personal essay and autobiographical writing, James Baldwin was concerned with the theme of identity. "One writes out of one thing only—one's own experiences," he acknowledged; "Everything depends upon how relentlessly one forces out from this experience the last drop, sweet or bitter, it can possibly give." Baldwin asserted: "This is the only real concern of the artist, to recreate out of the disorder of life that order which is art."[59]

When James Baldwin wrote "Many Thousands Gone," he critiqued what he saw as Wright's omission of a "necessary dimension" of African American life: "this dimension being the relationship that Negroes bear to one another, the depth of involvement and unspoken recognition of shared experience which creates a way of life."[60] Of course, Wright was arguing that modernity and industrialism broke down these community relations and left individuals like Bigger Thomas cut off and alienated from these sources of life.

In the 1940s, James Baldwin began to arrive at his perspective that the oppressor and the oppressed are "bound inextricably in American culture," a view that he held throughout the 1960s. In "Everybody's Protest Novel" he says that Richard Wright's novel is mostly concerned with "something resolutely indefinable, unpredictable." The novel is about "the complexity of ourselves." Baldwin claims that Bigger Thomas is only part of a more complex reality. He concludes: "What is missing in Bigger's situation is the representation of his psychology—which makes his situation false and his psychology incapable of development."[61] Wright had not sufficiently conveyed a sense of African American life as a complex group reality.[62] "[S]ince literature and sociology are not one and the same, it is impossible to discuss them as if they were," Baldwin wrote.[63] The protest novel responds to a human need for "categorization, life fitted into pegs." It helps us to feel good by distancing real problems from ourselves. So, it becomes "a mirror of confusion," Baldwin wrote. It ultimately is more fantasy than reality.[64]

In *Notes of a Native Son* (1955), Baldwin reflects on alienation and discrimination, asserting that America is "deeply involved in the lives of black men." The American experience, in this sense, is repressive. He writes that "his past was taken from him, almost literally, at one blow."[65]

Richard Wright's *Native Son* made a lasting impression on Baldwin. However, Baldwin asserted that Bigger Thomas was Uncle Tom's descendant: "flesh of his flesh."[66] Whereas Wright reported on social and economic inequality and prejudice and how this had affected Bigger Thomas, Baldwin argued for a change of image. Wright had placed before his readers a negative monster, deterministically shaped by forces in America. Baldwin sought a refashioning of the heart and a vision that was different from the one Wright had presented. Baldwin opposed Wright's determinism. He wanted to see a hopeful move beyond Chicago's troubled streets to broader concerns: "that of the world, of the human heart."[67] In "Many Thousands Gone," Baldwin wrote: "We cannot escape our origins, however hard we try, those origins which contain the key—could we but find it—to all that we later become."[68] Baldwin's search for identity in his work was coupled with a belief in will and self-creation. He held that approaching protest as venting would not in itself change anything. Rather, what is necessary is decision, action, and personal transformation. One can shape things and create art, and thereby create a new work within society.

Baldwin rejected the self-destructive rage in Bigger Thomas. He likely recognized it in himself. In *Notes of a Native Son*, Baldwin tells the story of his encounter with a waitress in a New Jersey diner who would not take his food order and serve him his meal. He hurled a glass of water at her and left the diner. His anger was justified, but he recognized that hate can warp the mind, affect a person's life and history. To characterize a symbolic, representative figure like Bigger Thomas was a starting point. However, it would be necessary to go further, and face the pain of alienation and the complexity of African American experience in America.

Baldwin and Ralph Ellison rejected the notion that either of them had in any respect betrayed Richard Wright. They both acknowledged his influence, while asserting their freedom from it as artists. Baldwin, in "Everybody's Protest Novel," asserted that *Native Son* did not "deal with man in his wholeness and complexity," instead forcefully pointing out that a novel is not sociology, and indicating his belief that protest novels fell short of their aims. Ellison argued that Bigger Thomas was not by any means the "final image of Negro personality."[69]

James Baldwin's novel, *Go Tell It on the Mountain* (1954), provides another image. It is an affirmation of tenacity and endurance despite adversity, of faith that there will be victory after struggle. It is what theologians call *kerygma*: a proclamation of the good news that Jesus Christ is born. It is also a cry in the wilderness that recalls Moses on the mountain looking out toward the Promised Land. It is a song that evokes history, an exodus from bondage: "Let my people go!" The novel's title recalls the Negro spiritual, and is an allusion to Mount Sinai and to Mount Zion in Second Isaiah: "O Zion . . . that bringest good tidings, get thee up into the high mountain. O Jerusalem. Lift up thy voice with strength." Thus, it is symbolic of the past, a song that echoes a history, and it is also an affirmation of God's protection and a hope in possibility for the future. It is much like Martin Luther King's "I Have a Dream" speech affirmation, calling on all to ring out and shout freedom from the mountain tops across the country.

In his review of Bruce Watson's book *Freedom Summer* (2010), Dwight Garner of the *New York Times* (July 18, 2010) pointed out that when Baldwin was on the *Today* show, NBC stations in Mississippi cut to an old movie. Baldwin wrote a two-page fundraising letter to friends, which is kept in the Kathleen Dahl Collection at the Civil Rights Museum, urging continuing support for those who have traveled to Mississippi, and mentions three workers who have disappeared. At that time, Baldwin wrote, "For these are all our children. We will profit by or pay for what they become."[70]

Baldwin asserted the importance of maintaining the nation while critiquing its flaws. He contended that mostly we hold to myths, democratic ideals, while in practice denying minority groups rights and privileges. Baldwin addressed the need to "disrupt the comforting beat, in order to be heard."[71] Like a jazz artist, he would break rhythm. In a letter to Archbishop Desmond Tutu, he insisted that "black freedom will make white freedom possible."[72] In 1963, Baldwin emphasized the objective: "One is attempting to save an entire country. . . . The price for that is to understand oneself."[73]

RALPH ELLISON

Ralph Ellison's trumpet playing brought him to the Tuskegee Institute with dreams of someday composing a symphony. Ellison was deeply moved by jazz and classical music, and he had an interest in sculpture. He moved to New York with the thought of working and then returning to the institute to complete his degree. However, he never did return. He roomed at the Harlem YMCA, and there he met Langston Hughes. Hughes introduced him to Richard Wright. Wright had grown up in poverty, and he was concerned with racial and socioeconomic struggles. Ellison grew up in Oklahoma, a state which had no history of slavery. He had friends from many different backgrounds.

Ralph Ellison's star rose most powerfully with *Invisible Man* (1952), a novel of eloquence about the position of blacks in the contemporary world. His novel was a call for inclusion and human dignity. Among his first appearances in print was his review of Arthur Huff Faucett's *So-journer Truth: God's Faithful Pilgrim* in the radical journal *New Masses*, in 1938. He studied dialectical materialism and radicalism. He read Andre Malraux, Fyodor Dostoevsky, and Ernest Hemingway, and he especially felt stirred by Richard Wright's *Native Son*. By 1940, he was writing reviews for *Tomorrow: The Magazine of the Future*. He was becoming a man concerned about social decay and moral values in America, a witness to black life and the need to construct a dignified future. Ellison's biographer, Arnold Rampersad, points out that the young Ralph Ellison sought to create a bridge of friendship between black and white while holding onto "black racial feeling."[74]

In the summer of 1941, Ralph Ellison was living at 453 West 140th Street in Harlem. He drew from his childhood and from his present experiences for stories like "Mister Toussan," which appeared in *New Masses* (November 1941). In April 1942, he discontinued his affiliation with the Federal Writer's Project. He joined the U.S. Merchant Marine in 1943 and in December was assigned to the SS *Sun Yat Sen*, which sailed from New York to Swansea, South Wales. He wrote that he regarded the Welsh people as "a mature people while we Americans are yet in painful adolescence."[75] He was stationed for a time in London. He returned to New York and lived at West 141st Street. During this period, Ellison wrote "In a Strange Country," in which a black soldier faces a rough crowd outside a Welsh pub. He then wrote "A Storm of

Blizzard Proportions," about an interracial relationship, in which a black man visiting Wales meets a white woman and feels that he must leave her rather than bring her back to the United States, where they would face prejudice and be despised for miscegenation. Jack Johnson, a black boxer whose marriage crossed racial lines, might be able to stand strong against such racism, but he feels that he cannot. In 1944, Ellison's story "Flying Home" earned attention when it appeared in a collection with novelettes from Richard Wright and Jane Bowles. The collection also included an excerpt from Norman Mailer's forthcoming *The Naked and the Dead*, poems by Langston Hughes and fourteen other poets, a play by Arthur Miller, and seventeen stories, including one by Shirley Jackson.[76]

The young black writer responded with a sense of wonder and urgency to Richard Wright's *12 Million Black Voices*, with its black-and-white photographs by Edwin Rosskam. Wright described black lives within "the dusty land" and "the hard pavement." His writing caused Ellison to look hard at his own life and to reflect on black America. He wrote: "You usually take us for granted and think you know us, but our history is far stranger than you suspect, and we are not what we seem."[77] Ellison affirmed the connection that he felt with Wright: "I am now more sure than ever: that you and I are brothers," and declared that he would not forget the struggle, the suffering of "passing from the country to the city of destruction" as Wright had done. "We are immersed in the same flow of reality," he added.[78]

Ellison was moved by Wright's autobiography, *Black Boy*, and wrote a review for *Tomorrow*. He focused on the final third of the book, in which Wright discussed his involvement with communism. That part was cut, at the request of the Book of the Month Club. Ellison's review was not published. Ellison's essay emphasized the "innate dignity" and humanity of blacks, regretting their exclusion from America's intellectual life. *The Antioch Review* published the essay in 1945. That same publication had asked him to respond to Swedish sociologist Gunnar Myrdal's *An American Dilemma: The Negro Problem and Modern Democracy*. Ellison took Myrdal's study to task for analyzing black culture as replete with problems. He asserted that black culture had many valuable aspects. This review also was not published until many years later, in *Shadow and Act*. Ellison was interviewed on WHN radio, and

Langston Hughes, in *Chicago Sun Book Week*, called him "among the most promising of the younger Negro writers."[79]

Langston Hughes was very supportive of Ralph Ellison's work and development as a writer. For Ellison, meeting Hughes was life-changing. Hughes introduced him to Claude McKay, whose poetry and novel *Home to Harlem* (1928) was at the center of the Harlem Renaissance, and welcomed him to the American Academy and the National Institute of Letters, where Hughes received honors.[80] The talented young writer gained some other influential literary friends; among them was Kenneth Burke, whose *A Grammar of Motives* (1945) contributed to Ellison's writing of *Invisible Man*. Burke's *Counterstatement* (1931) and *Philosophy of Literary Form* (1941) lay behind Ellison's development of his ideas about his fiction. In Burke, Ellison found a formalist literary approach, an attention to linguistic structures, symbolic forms, and social psychology. Ellison began to move away from his socialist approach to literature. He felt free to stretch out across a variety of disciplines. (Psychology was one of these areas of his interest; he had worked as a receptionist and clerk for psychologist Henry Stack Sullivan.) Stanley Edgar Hyman, a staff writer for the *New Yorker* and a teacher, became a good friend. Hyman introduced him to the stories of the woman who would become his wife: Shirley Jackson.

Ralph Ellison's deep interest in music and in art led him to many hours of listening to bebop jazz, the blues, and symphonic music. He also liked visual art, but there were unspoken cultural barriers for African Americans like Ralph Ellison. Arnold Rampersad points out that the art galleries, symphonies, and museums did not immediately welcome and embrace black visitors, and mentions that the New York Public Library lions "were too fierce to be crossed."[81]

As a young man, Ellison was concerned about the war in Europe. He considered writing a novel set in a Nazi prison camp, but that never quite materialized. He tried starting a novel set at a Southern college, with a black man named Bard as his protagonist. Nothing much came of that either. Richard Wright wondered if Ralph Ellison's skill might be best suited for nonfiction prose. Arnold Rampersad observes that Ellison wondered if perhaps he was not a natural novelist. He was already a vital short-story writer in the 1940s; "King of the Bingo Game" first appeared in *Tomorrow* in 1944. Ellison applies in the story a surrealist touch and a subtle critique of society. A man goes to the movies and awaits the Bingo game afterward. He wants to get money to help his sick wife. He wins, and can press a cord that spins a wheel. He will win the jackpot if the wheel stops on the right number. He keeps holding the button down, until men in uniforms come for him. They disrupt his holding of the wheel, but then the wheel sails around to double zero. He thinks that he has won but then he is hit by a man and realizes he is out of luck.

The war brought Ellison into the ranks of the military. In February 1945, Ellison was aboard the SS *Sea Nymph*, which plodded across the Atlantic on high alert. The ship carried supplies and ammunition for the Allied push toward Germany. In the first days of March, Ellison was in France, first sailing up the Seine and then exploring things onshore in Rouen. He felt a "lost vitality" in France, a shadow of war, but recalled Van Gogh as he viewed the fields of Normandy.[82] Rampersad suggests that Ellison began work on *Invisible Man* in July 1945. Ellison wrote to Ida Ellison on his attempt to get "down on paper the most ambitious and conceptually mature fiction idea that I have ever attempted."[83] He began: "I am an invisible man."

Ellison became a managing editor for the *Negro Quarterly*, a publication primarily directed toward black intellectuals more than toward the wider public. Joseph North and Sam Silla attempted to keep Ellison connected with *New Masses* as a contributing editor. He wrote "The Negro and Victory" and "The Way It Is"—his last essay in that publication. There would be no more writing for radical left journals.[84]

CIVIL RIGHTS

In 1940, 77 percent of black Americans lived in the South; 5 million migrated north. Chicago rapidly expanded, with more than two thousand African Americans moving to Chicago weekly. In the South, blacks were frequently prevented or discouraged from voting. Only about 2 percent were regarded as "qualified" to vote. Yet, African Americans were soon to fight in the Second World War. The principles of American democracy must be upheld, wrote one twenty-two-year-old American soldier: "If I fight, suffer or die it will be for the freedom of every black, any black man, to live equally with other races," and the fight must be for "a cause he can understand" rather than "against any enemy whose principles are the same as our so-called democracy."[85] In *Smith v. Albright* (1944), the Supreme Court rejected the "white primary device of some Southern states to exclude black voters." On September 8, 1948, a black man named Isaac Nixon was killed as he attempted to vote in Wrightsville, Georgia. His alleged murderers were set free by an all-white jury.

In 1946, Isaac Woodward, an African American passenger on a bus, insisted that the driver treat him like a man. This case went to the U.S. Federal Court in Columbia, South Carolina. Woodward's assertion that he be treated like a man caused the driver to single Woodward out for arrest at Batesburg.[86] This incident came to blows and a claim that Woodward resisted arrest. Police Chief Lynwood Shull blinded this black war veteran by blows with a blackjack. He was acquitted at the trial.[87]

In November 1946, Alabama passed the Boswell Amendment requiring voting applicants to "understand and explain" sections of the United States Constitution "to the satisfaction of the Board of Registrars."[88] The Alabama governor, Big Jim Folsom, opposed this. He said, "As long as the Negroes are held down by deprivation and lack of opportunity, the other poor people will be held down beside them."[89]

Jack H. Pollack in the *American Mercury* (May 1947) examined devices like literacy tests that were used to keep the ballot from black voters. He noted numerous instances in which a "Southern Negro must be approved by" a white Board of Regents and "literacy tests" were used to disenfranchise that person.[90]

Justice Hugo Black, from Alabama, was appointed to the Supreme Court by President Roosevelt in 1937. He was a Southern populist and New Dealer who loved the South, and provided the basis for several Warren Court decisions. Despite a brief Klan membership as a young man, he became a progressive in race relations. For Hugo Black, desegregation was among the Supreme Court's most important issues.

In the 1940s Thurgood Marshall traveled throughout the south, witnessing segregation and discrimination firsthand. In 1950, Marshall pushed the Supreme Court on "separate but equal," arguing *McLaurin v. Board of Regents*. George McLaurin was accepted as a law student in Oklahoma "on a segregated basis." Marshall argued that such a "badge of inferiority" would affect McLaurin's relationship with other students. McLaurin ought not to be restricted to a designated area in the library, but should be allowed to use the facilities freely. Marshall pointed to the findings of psychologist Kenneth Clark, whose empirical studies indicated that black students who were educated at segregated schools developed a negative self-image. His legal opponents rejected this.

In 1950, Marshall pushed the court on separate but equal, also arguing *Sweatt v. Painter* (1950), in which the Supreme Court found that the Texas School for Negroes was not sufficient in comparison with the University of Texas. *Brown v. Board of Education* (May 17, 1954) was a landmark decision that called for eliminating racial segregation in U.S. schools. Justice Warren asserted: "in the field of public education, the doctrine of separate but equal has no place; separate educational facilities are inherently unequal."[91]

In 1955, Rosa Parks had the courage to refuse to give up her seat on a bus. She had been in the workshops run by Septima Clark (1898–1987), who is mentioned by Martin Luther King Jr. in his "Letter from the Birmingham Jail." Septima Clark's workshops were based on nonviolence, and became an inspiration for the Civil Rights movement. She begins her story: "I wanted to start my story with the end of World War II, because that is when the Civil Rights movement really got going."[92]

4

WAR STORIES

James Gould Cozzens, Irwin Shaw, Norman Mailer,
James Michener, Pearl S. Buck, and John Hersey

The 1940s emerged as one of the most momentous decades in modern history. A world war broke around the globe, absorbed the energies of millions of people, and had lasting repercussions. On September 1, 1939, the German army struck across the border of Poland. In Asia, Japan expanded its military activity and designs of conquest across the region. As Europe and Asia were plunged into war, America remained neutral, but this position of neutrality could not be held for long in a world on fire with the political tension and wide destruction of war.

The American novel during this period dwelled on both domestic and international concerns. Fiction addressed issues of family and region, race, work, and society. Novels probed personal issues, as well as those concerns about the war that came to bear on people's lives. Ernest Hemingway directed his attention to the Spanish Civil War in *For Whom the Bell Tolls*. Steinbeck began writing *The Moon Is Down* before the United States committed troops and resources to the war effort. Following Pearl Harbor and entry into the war, American writers got busy. William Bradford Huie's *Mud on the Stars* appeared in May 1942. John Hersey's *A Bell for Adano* (1944) and Harry Bowman's *A Walk in the Sun* (1944) brought readers to the conflict in Italy. *Beach Red* (1945) was a Book of the Month Club selection that looked at the American military effort to gain a Japanese atoll in the Pacific.

The American war novel is a form of memory, one of those time capsules that help us to remember this time. The lives and memories of a generation of Americans were entirely bound up with the war, and their stories have become a matter of retrospective analysis. Indeed, the Second World War became an industry of recollection across the next several decades. In the immediate aftermath of battle, Norman Mailer's *The Naked and the Dead* (1948) carried a powerful account that was widely popular. His story concerned the war in the Philippines rather than the massive war effort in Europe. James Michener wrote about sailors in *Tales of the South Pacific* (1947), which was adapted by Rodgers and Hammerstein into the popular musical, *South Pacific*. John Horne Burns's *The Gallery* (1947) emerged from his involvement with the war in North Africa and the Allied invasion and occupation of Naples. His novel includes the recollections of a corporal named John about what he encountered in Casablanca, in Oran, and in Naples. The corporal's "promenades" are accompanied by longer "portraits," which read like a series of short stories. The American soldier must come to terms with being moved outside of the familiarity of home into a combat zone: "In the nineteen days of crossing the Atlantic I remember that something happened to me inside," he says. Burns is critical of isolationism and American self-focus, and calls for stepping out of one's comfort zone to face the struggles that others are experiencing in a life battered by war. The narrator says that "perhaps we must all soon come to the point where we're proud only to say: 'I am a human being, a citizen of the world.'"[1]

These novels provide us with imaginative forms of cultural memory. They were written by people who experienced the war firsthand, like Irwin Shaw, who served in Europe, and Norman Mailer and James Michener, who served in the Pacific. However, when Studs Terkel commented that World War II was the "good war," James Jones, the author of *From Here to Eternity*, replied that it was not so good: "The truth is, thirty-five years has glossed it all over and given World War II a polish that it didn't have at the time." He reflected on what the passing of time does with historical perspective, and especially with the recollection of wars: "In countless Hollywood features, government sanctioned newsreels, and animated shorts, the war was transformed into a global morality play, a clash of civilizations on a near apocalyptic scale."[2]

The years immediately after the war were enriched by fiction that has waned in popularity with the years. Some of these books deserve to be recovered and introduced to new readers. For example, James Gould Cozzens wrote *Guard of Honor* (1948), a Pulitzer Prize–winning novel that takes place mostly on an Air Force base in Florida. The action is confined to a period of forty-eight hours. Cozzens had written ten novels before he entered the military and began writing speeches for Henry "Hap" Arnold, working in the Office of Information Services. Irwin Shaw's *The Young Lions* (1948) was also a popular best seller. It offers a long and enjoyable read. Shaw served overseas in Europe, and spent part of the war writing training scripts in Queens. Thomas Heggen's *Mister Roberts* became a stage play and a film. Gore Vidal's *Williwaw* (1946) concerned an American ship attempting to transport cargo in a storm. His novel, written when Vidal was nineteen, brought attention to a gay relationship. When Warren French discussed these war novels, he asserted that *The Gallery* and *Mister Roberts* "stand out above the other American novels about World War II because they are accounts of an individual's discovery of his capacity for feeling" that are rendered well and enable readers to share in those feelings.[3]

In the 1950s and 1960s the war recollections of this generation of writers would continue to appear. Joseph Heller recalled the trials of airmen in *Catch-22*; Kurt Vonnegut, who was a prisoner of war in Dresden during the bombing of that city, told a story of devastation in *Slaughterhouse Five*. Herman Wouk, who wrote *The Caine Mutiny* during the war, reached a wide popular audience with *War and Remembrance* and *The Winds of War*.

JAMES GOULD COZZENS, *GUARD OF HONOR*

Some of the important writers of the 1940s are seldom read today. Among them is James Cozzens, whose novel *Guard of Honor* won the Pulitzer Prize in 1948. Cozzens was a writer of social novels of moral concern that engaged in social critique and in a search for order during difficult times. His novels of the 1940s, all published by Harcourt Brace, provide studies of professions—lawyers and military men. They are unlike the social novels of the 1930s, since they do not include factory workers or farmworkers, like the novels of James T. Farrell or

John Steinbeck. Cozzens's novels assert that dispassionate reason will overcome irrationality. He writes with considerable respect for military rank, rational legal thought, and conservative social values. Clearly, he tapped into a cultural milieu of readers for whom his themes of reason and honor resonated.

Cozzens may at first appear to be an admirer of the expatriate Henry James. He began the 1940s with *Ask Me Tomorrow* (1940), a novel set in Europe in 1926–1927, rather than in the United States. Some critics have suggested that the novel may be autobiographical. Frank Ellery is leaving Florence to become a tutor in Montreaux. His mother asks him to look out for Faith Robertson on the train journey. Frank and Faith agree that Milan is boring, and their encounter suggests that they might find something more exciting with each other. Ellery must tutor the asthmatic, physically challenged Walter Cunningham, and must deal with the wealthy and bossy Mrs. Cunningham. Literary critic Granville Hicks asserted that Ellery is not at all likeable.[4] Ellery argues with a hotel manager, and makes derisive remarks about the French, the Germans, and the Russians.

With his next novel, *The Just and the Unjust* (1942), Cozzens set his story in a small town in eastern Pennsylvania. Abner Coates has been the district attorney for the past four years. He is now involved in a murder case. Four men have kidnapped a drug dealer and killed him. The leader of the kidnapping plan was also killed as he tried to escape from the police. Another member of the group of kidnappers has agreed to confess and turn state's evidence. However, now the other two members of the gang are on trial.

Cozzens carefully researched trial procedure and legal cases as he prepared his novel. His story is rich with details about law and reflections on society. There is a party on a barge given by the Calumet Club on the eve of the trial. Abner is accompanied by Bonnie Drummond. Abner's father, Judge Coates, tells him that if he wants to get away from politicians he will have to get away from society. The hard fact about politicians is that "[e]ither they learn how to be politicians pretty quick, or they don't last." Martin Bunting, Abner's boss, also has worldly advice for him: "You can't just stand off and say you don't like how things are run."[5]

The action of the novel takes place across three days. Judge Coates is the "man of reason," a realistic individual who distrusts emotion, observes Granville Hicks.[6] A few peculiarities are thrown into the mix. There appears to be a pedophile schoolteacher who has persuaded students to pose naked. The newspaper editor tries to get the school's principal fired. This may seem more sensational than the murder trial. Thematically, the story focuses upon conscience and wisdom. Judge Coates, the man of reason, advises Abner: "It's a good thing to be steady and level headed, but the defect of the virtue can make you seem a little remote or apathetic."[7] The phrase "man of reason" also appears in Cozzens's novel *By Love Possessed* (1957).

Published in 1947, *Guard of Honor* sold less than fifteen thousand copies by the end of the year.[8] However, the novel received critical acclaim; it was called "the best novel of the year" by the *Yale Review* and was cited as a novel of "Olympian objectivity."[9] Noel Perrin, a Dartmouth professor and essayist, who was about twenty years old when the novel appeared, recalled it as "probably the best novel of the twentieth century."[10] Cozzens was touted as a legitimate heir to George Eliot and Joseph Conrad by Louis O. Coxe, who adapted Melville's *Billy Budd* to the stage. Coxe wrote: "Cozzens creates a world of particulars, a world of men and women at their tasks and duties, and then tries to show the intricacy of the web of will and desire, the stuff of action, as these work out men's involvement with one another, with themselves, and with their tasks—all these relationships described with irony, shown in action, brought to a climax best characterized as heroic."[11] Cozzens underscored a faith in authority that contrasted with Norman Mailer's sharp critiques of it in his popular war novel, *The Naked and the Dead*.

In *Guard of Honor*, Cozzens explores the conscience of Colonel Ross and the conditions of the war through shifting points of view. He writes a novel of ideas, a social novel that examines the complexity of human interactions. Cozzens was not a popular culture writer. In 1957, a *Time* magazine writer pointed out that Cozzens and his wife had not seen a movie in seventeen years—it was "more than twenty since they went to a theater, to a concert, or an art gallery."[12] Instead, we encounter a density of content written by a stoic, rationalistic, secular writer who was concerned with "the psychological impact of wartime tensions."[13] Cozzens served his country as a major in the Air Force, but the action of the war itself does not play a large part in his novel. *Guard of*

Honor is not set in a combat zone, but at the fictional Occanara Air Force Base in Florida.

The camp that we see in *Guard of Honor* is in the South: in Florida, rather than in what is sometimes called the Deep South. Even so, a Florida base was a place where in 1944, as Lucille Milner notes, "North and South as well as white and colored are thrown together."[14] This led to some inevitable concerns, she said: "The segregation question will be a burning postwar issue."[15] Of course, it was just that. These concerns led toward the *Brown v. Board of Education* ruling of 1954 and subsequent civil rights struggles.

Chapter 1 begins on a plane bound for Occanara, and introduces some of the novel's principal characters: General Beal, Colonel Ross, Lieutenant Colonel Carricker, Captain Hicks, Lieutenant Turck, and Master Sergeant Pellegrino. There is also Mortimer McIntyre, a black serviceman who appears in the first pages of *Guard of Honor*. McIntyre is seated on the plane returning to the Florida airbase. He is seated on the closed cover of a chemical toilet, segregated to that lowly station: "the only place left to sit."[16] In the first pages of the novel, his wonder at the flight suggests that he might become an interesting character in the story. Yet, Cozzens does not develop this character, and McIntyre disappears in the pages that follow.

Upon landing, Benny Carricker punches Lieutenant Willis, an African American officer who landed by mistake in Carricker's flight path. The racial problem immediately arises as an urgent concern. Benny Carricker is a war hero, but he is "impulsive and reckless."[17] Colonel Ross, who was a judge in civilian life, is a man of reason who tries to save General Beal from his missteps. A celebration of General Beal's birthday results in disaster as paratroopers are drowned. Cozzens brings us into Colonel Ross's thoughts; the man of reason calls people to face reality: "Credulity has been renamed faith," he says. People are fallible. A person ought not to bet his or her future on Christianity, or on an ideology like Marxism, Colonel Ross believes. This appears to echo Cozzens's own view of religion as a context for "superstition and sentimentality."[18] Colonel Ross thinks about the war. He asserts that the best approach to the war (and indeed to all of life) is one of dispassionate reason. Lieutenant Edsell, a liberal, is cast as a hypocrite. Captain Hicks tries to be a man of reason, but he ends up in bed with Amanda Turck. Captain Duchemek has no qualms about his repeated affairs.

Captain Andrews, who is a math whiz, is deeply devoted to his wife, and is always upset to think of ever losing her.

A concern with racial justice is central to *Guard of Honor*. The story is set in a Southern town. African American flyers are trained at Occanara. The language of white officers indicates racial prejudice. Cozzens himself did not agree with segregation, but recognized the facts of the situation in the American South. In *Guard of Honor*, Lieutenant Edsell supports the black servicemen. Colonel Ross also sees the unfair treatment that they are subjected to. Ross remarks to his wife: "We are having a little trouble with some Negro officers. They feel they are unjustly treated." He adds that he agrees with them, but sees "insurmountable difficulties to doing them justice." Ross affirms: "There are no Army Regulations that make any distinction on the basis of race, creed, or color. A soldier is a soldier."[19] Racist attitudes work against the unity of the nation and of this military unit. Principles of democracy and freedom are crucial. However, through the work of good men like Colonel Ross, perhaps things can be changed, and such men can lead the nation through difficult times.

Cozzens's worldview has been characterized as pessimistic. He suggests that the fates of do not play fairly with us. There are not many strong emotions in his characters. There is some sex, but not a great deal of passion. Rather, in Cozzens's fiction there is, as Hicks points out, an "anti-romantic approach."[20] Hicks adds that Cozzens may be guilty of snobbishness, but not of racial prejudice. *Guard of Honor*, for example, repeatedly suggests the author's concern for African American servicemen and military officers. Cozzens also appears to be concerned with the impact of systems on people. Frederick Bracher quotes a letter that Cozzens wrote to his publisher in England, in which he says that he "wanted to show . . . the peculiar effects of the interaction of innumerable individuals functioning in ways at once determined by and determining the functioning of others."[21] In other words, Cozzens was a social novelist who concerned himself with how individuals influenced each other within group contexts. He was also interested in exploring perspective through techniques that engaged with point of view. Hicks points out that while Colonel Ross serves as a viewpoint character, in the novel "the point of view moves about so that various themes can be developed simultaneously."[22]

Cozzens is a writer of the traditional social novel, observes Bracher: "The best of Cozzens's works are evidence that the traditional social novel with its high seriousness and moral urgency is still viable in a period of experiment and disorder."[23] John M. Kinder notes that in Cozzens's novel, "conflicts over free speech, the intrusive presence of the press, and changing social mores frequently undermine the war effort and disrupt the military's balance of power."[24] The novel, he asserts, suggests that career soldiers are "more threatened by the presence of women, college educated liberals, civilian officials, and African American officers than by the forces of Fascism abroad."[25] The novel faces the reality of institutional racism during the war, rather than concealing it. To his credit, Cozzens contrasts a vital democracy with the poor treatment of African American soldiers. He rejects the practice of placing them in menial positions or under surveillance, or casting verbal insults at them.[26]

Cozzens's worldview of rationalist logic, honor, and stoicism seems to reflect the attitude and stance of many American men of the wartime generation. In contrast with the rationalism and secular conservatism of Cozzens, the novel or nonfiction text of religious disposition was also quite popular during the war period. *The Nazarene, The Keys of the Kingdom, The Song of Bernadette, The Robe,* and *The Seven Storey Mountain,* Thomas Merton's autobiography, were all best sellers during the first years of the war. Postwar America also saw the epics *Ben Hur* and *The Ten Commandments.* "Cozzens's novel debunks the myth that World War II transformed all patriotic Americans into an inseparable band of brothers," Kinder observes.[27] The notion of World War II as "the good war" found expression in film, memorialization, images, and narratives. This simplifies the magnitude and difficulty of the war and this era.

Cozzens's *Guard of Honor* and Mailer's *The Naked and the Dead* offer different perspectives on the Second World War and its impact on postwar America. Mailer argues that the United States emerges from its engagement as a quasi-totalitarian state with a "military style hierarchy and rigid social controls," observes Kinder, while Cozzens offers "a glimmer of hope" in the guidance of good men who are responsible, though flawed.[28] Cozzens's novel asserts that reason will prevail.

Before December 7, 1941, the United States had started to create what Army Air Force Commander H. H. (Hap) Arnold called for "overwhelming air superiority over our enemies in the shortest possible time."[29] In January 1941, the Army Air Force had 6,180 officers, 7,000 cadet flyers, and 88,000 enlisted men.[30] In April 1941, the United States established bases in Greenland, including airfields and weather stations. Arnold wrote: "The entire year 1941 was one of acceleration in building bases and training facilities, teaching air crews and ground crews, establishing supply depots and supply lines, strengthening our continental defenses."[31]

The setting of *Guard of Honor* on an air base in Florida reflects reality. "In Florida the Army Air Force has a Tactical Center," Arnold pointed out. This base was established for training for fighter bomber and patrol missions. It was conceived of as "the last dress rehearsal for our war," Arnold said. "The men live, work, and fight as they will abroad, in organizational units as large as a complete task force."[32] Cozzens's novel does not show operations on a grand scale, but it does describe training flights. The goal, Arnold wrote, was "to reduce the hazards of combat."[33]

Once America entered the war, the Army Air Force went heavily into action. The hazards of combat were inevitable. In 1943, the Army Air Force flew 3,352,000 miles, or some 134,000 trips around the world.[34] The flights were now often into harm's way. Meanwhile, the United States increased airplane production. In January 1942, there were 2,972 new planes built. A year later, in January 1943, there were 5,013 more, with an additional 7,598 planes by September. Women contributed their work to airplane manufacture. About 22,000 women at airfields were in the Women's Army Corps (WACS), with most of these women involved with clerical work, communications, or motor transport.[35] "In no other industry has women power been more effective," Arnold wrote.[36]

In the Pacific, the fleet and airfields at Pearl Harbor were damaged by the Japanese attack. Hickham and Wheeler fields in Oahu were "smashed."[37] The airfield at Luzon in the Philippines was also destroyed. However, despite the losses, some of this damaged military material was reparable. The early losses engendered a fighting spirit. At Coral Sea, U.S. forces sank nineteen Japanese ships. At Midway, they sank ten, including four carriers and two heavy cruisers.[38] On April 18, 1942, General James Doolittle took off from the carrier USS *Hornet* to lead a devastating raid of the Japanese mainland.

In North Africa, the British Royal Air Force (RAF) faced a well-equipped German Luftwaffe. H. H. Arnold recognized that the RAF "kept Erwin Rommel's forces from annihilating the British Army and helped, finally, to halt him at El Alamein."[39] The ground force campaign in Tunisia, culminating in an attack on April 22, was preceded by four nights of bombing.[40] The U.S. Army Air Force sent an advance force ahead of the Salerno landing in Italy. Its goal was to disrupt the enemy flow of supplies and reinforcements, Arnold stated.[41] Once the war was over, General Arnold called for postwar attention to technological research. He wrote that these times would "demand continuous scientific research to insure the maintenance of our national security and world peace."[42]

James Gould Cozzens was nominated for a second Pulitzer Prize in 1957 for *By Love Possessed*. His reputation subsequently declined in the 1960s. He was criticized by Dwight MacDonald and Irving Howe, and was sharply critiqued by John Updike. Some critics associated his apolitical conservatism with the establishment, and he was viewed as out of step with emerging trends. However, in *Guard of Honor*, James Cozzens takes on the problem of segregation in an officer's club, and the issue of morale among the black officers. These were not typical conservative positions. He held a position similar to that outlined by Lucille B. Milner in *The New Republic* (March 13, 1944), who utilized letters from African American servicemen to demonstrate that segregation in the military was "demoralizing." Milner addressed the issue by referring to the Selective Training and Service Act of 1940, which asserted that there would be "no discrimination against any person because of race or color."[43] Milner then pointed out how this was discredited by Jim Crow laws. She wrote that "today's confusion" stemmed from "the inherited tradition" that had come from prewar days. "The racial attitude of the military is a curious anachronism," she said. In the camps of the South in particular, there was "a reversion to dark and ignorant prejudice."[44]

It is to Cozzens's credit that he raises the issue of segregation and Jim Crow regulations. Lieutenant Edsell is particularly irritated by what he calls "a lot of sadistic sub-morons down in dear old Dixie [who] can do whatever they want to any Negro, any time."[45] Cozzens might have given more emphasis to his point with further development of characters, black enlisted men as well as officers, with strong voices and honorable claims.

IRWIN SHAW, *THE YOUNG LIONS*

Irwin Shaw served in the war as a soldier. He was successful as a playwright before the war, and he became a commercial storyteller after it. He wrote *Bury the Dead* (1936) for the stage, and had written radio show scripts for Dick Tracy episodes. He was popularly successful as a novelist with *The Young Lions* (1948). Shaw was in Signal Corps as a writer, and spent time overseas as a warrant officer and as a war correspondent. He welcomed his role as a middlebrow writer. Shaw's best-selling novels included *Rich Man, Poor Man* (1969), which was later made into a television miniseries.

The story begins in Austria before the Anschluss, in which Austria allowed itself to become part of Nazi-controlled Germany. Shaw introduces us to a fine young woman named Margaret Freemantle, an American art student who is twenty-one years old. Within the first few pages she is sexually assaulted by a brutal proto-Nazi named Frederick. She then meets a sympathetic ski instructor, Christian Diestl, who is also a Nazi but appears to be a gentleman. "Frederick did not climb into your room because he is a Nazi," he says. Rather, he climbed into her room "because he is a pig. He's a bad human being."[46] Yet, while Diestl is a sign that the National Socialist Party has carried along the good as well as the bad, it is clear that something troubling is occurring in Austria. Margaret waits for her boyfriend Joseph to arrive on the train from Vienna. Joseph does not survive the war.

The first scene of Shaw's novel makes clear that there was considerable local support in Austria for German occupation. The emergence of Nazi power in Austria was part of a long process. Engelbert Dollfuss became the chancellor of Austria on April 24, 1932. He survived a call of no confidence by pan-Germans in August, and sought to dissolve parliament. Austria's parliamentary democracy was suspended in 1933. Dollfuss outlawed the Schutzbund, the Social Democratic militia, and ruled by decree. He then attempted to outlaw the Nazi Party, which had been terrorizing Vienna and bombing stores with Jewish owners. In February 1934 Dollfuss ended the Social Democratic Party in a four-day civil conflict. In July, the Nazis responded with a putsch to take over the government and silence Dollfuss, which they did by killing him. A crowd in Vienna posted the Dollfuss death mask on a pedestal to be witnessed by the German visitor Franz von Papen, who arrived on August 15, 1934. The new chancellor, Kurt von Schuschnigg, ordered a plebiscite, a vote of the people, to try to hold back German influence and regain some consensus. In February 1938, he was summoned to meet with Hitler at Berchtesgaden, where he was berated and forced to comply with Nazi ultimatums.[47]

Church bells rang on Monday, March 14, and people cheered from sidewalks and watched from rooftops as Hitler arrived and his Mercedes rolled up to Hotel Imperial. The next morning, Adolph Hitler strode up to speak on the Heldenplatz. There were "streets dipped in a frenzy of color," shouts across the square, thousands of arms raised in the Nazi salute. Hitler proclaimed: "I can announce before history the entry of my homeland into the German Reich."[48]

The Young Lions immediately brings us back to the United States, to Times Square in New York City on New Year's Eve. We are introduced to Michael Whitacre, a stage manager for a theater who is on his way to a New Year's party. The city is alive with animated merrymaking and the energy of revelers from a variety of cultures. Yet, amid the horns and confetti and laughter, Shaw casually drops the information that a girl's throat was cut on 50th Street. This is a night of vitality in a city of "[p]ickpockets, whores, gamblers, pimps, confidence men, taxi-drivers, bartenders, and hotel owners."[49] It is a strange backdrop for the appearance of this character, who has arrived to see Laura. He drinks scotch that tastes as if someone has poured lemon soda into it. Something is sour here.

In the curious crowd at the party are some entertaining personalities. The wife of an alcoholic playwright insists that he not drink, although the dramatist has a teacup available for some clandestine imbibing. His wife has imagined that getting him out to the party would be good for him. But it turns out that they must keep him from jumping out a window. Meanwhile, the marriage between Michael and Laura is not doing much better than the playwright is. The marriage dissolves, and Michael goes to California, hoping that a play production there will be successful. Its writer pulls out of the project, saying that movies are more profitable. The war is on, and if he writes for film he can avoid military service. Michael thinks otherwise: maybe he should enlist in the Army. At a home in Pennsylvania, Michael meets Margaret, the character we were introduced to in the first chapters of Shaw's story. It seems that Margaret, now called Peggy, might have been developed further to this point. However, the focus is on Michael, who enters the Army.

Christian Diestl will prove to be not as pleasant as he seemed at first. However, he is not so despicable as Lieutenant Hardenberg, his immediate supervisor in the Nazi ranks. Hardenberg is a callous man of calculation, who intentionally sends those under his command into harm's way and cheats on his profligate wife, who is having multiple affairs in Germany. He asks Christian, who is on leave to Berlin, to deliver a package of black lace to her. Christian gets caught up in her seductions, like Odysseus by Circe. When he returns to active duty, he watches Hardenberg sentence thirty-seven men, who were on a mission, to their deaths. He watches as Hardenberg kills a man who is slow to obey his orders. Then he and the lieutenant are swept up in a fierce battle. Trying to flee, they are hit by mortar fire. Hardenberg, shredded by the explosion, becomes a faceless man. Diestl, the ski instructor, is told that he will never ski again.

We also follow the story of Noah Ackerman, who travels from Chicago to Santa Monica to bid farewell to his dying father. He uses a pay phone at a seedy bar to make funeral arrangements. A woman with blond hair, smelling of perfume and onion breath, comes on to him at the bar. Sailors from the San Diego naval base wonder what she sees in him. They tell him that she would probably rob him. The next time we see Noah, he is in New York City, where he has started living near Riverside Drive with a friend, Roger, whom he has met in the Columbia University Library. Roger arranges for a party so that Noah can meet one of the women he knows. Noah is stunned by Hope, whom he thinks is Roger's girl. Terribly shy, he can barely talk with her. However, when he says that he will go to the store for some soda, she joins him. He admits that he has no idea where the store is. When they return from their long walk together, with the lights of the George Washington Bridge shining in the distance, the apartment is dark and the party is over. Hope asks Noah to get her home—to Brooklyn. A subway ride and a trolley ride later, Noah finds himself on the doorstep of Hope's home. He summons up the courage to kiss her good night and she smacks him.

With Noah's first encounter with Hope begins the story of their romance and marriage, and Noah's decision to enlist in the military. Hope is his strength in marriage, but he is not well equipped for military life. Despite a medical exam that suggests traces of tuberculosis, he persists and is soon in the Army. Noah is in the same barracks as Michael Whitacre. Noah is a sensitive individual, and he is picked on by some of the other men and by a sergeant who pesters him abusively. He is charged with desertion for trying to get away from this abuse. He later surprises many of the men in his company with his heroism.

Meanwhile, Shaw shows a strong tendency to associate his more insensitive characters with their disregard for literature. Hardenberg, for example, would "have all the novels burned, too . . . and the poems of Heine."[50] Hardenberg's worldview is characterized by his statement that war most completely fits with the nature of man, who is predatory and egoistic.[51] Colclough, the sergeant who repeatedly shames and beats up on Noah, pushes aside Noah's books. The satire is clear when he asserts that T. S. Eliot and James Joyce's *Ulysses* are not "government issue." *Ulysses* is a "dirty filthy book," asserts Colclough, who clearly has never read any of it. He declares: "Get rid of it. Get rid of them. This is not a library, soldier."[52] Shaw, meanwhile, urges optimism and criticizes a nation of sour critics whose criticism has resulted in a "barren country because of it."[53] Even with such cultural criticism, Shaw's novel remains patriotic, entertaining, and full of verve and life.

NORMAN MAILER, *THE NAKED AND THE DEAD*

Norman Mailer's *The Naked and the Dead* (1948) begins in stark realism. He sharply presents the landscape of his wartime setting in the Philippines, the experience of soldiers sleepless in their bunks anticipating the bombardment of Anopopei. We meet Sergeant Croft, Wilson, and Gallagher, who is from Boston—men initially introduced only by their last names. We meet Red, who is aboard a ship and is looking out to sea. The moon is high in the sky and the water hardly rocks the ship. Tomorrow will be different when they make their landing on the shore. It is the calm before the storm.

The cast of characters continues to emerge. Lieutenant Hearn, a central character who has Marxist sympathies, must contend with General Cummings, a difficult man, who is the commander. In their perspectives and temperaments, they are at odds with each other. There are the Jews, Roth and Goldstein, and there is Mineta, who is injured and is sent to the Division Clearing Hospital. Croft predicts that Hennesey, a recent recruit, will die in combat, and he feels a sense of omnipotence or "portents of power" about his foresight when this occurs. We have begun the story with Croft, and we follow him through the novel to the end. Mailer's naturalistic method is accented with moments of descriptive lyricism. There is sex as well as violence: "Still there are moments. Different women, different nights when he lies in embrace, steeped in a woman's flesh until the brew is intolerably joyous."[54] Mailer manages his crowded cast of characters with techniques that critic Diana Trilling recognized as drawing on the influence of John Dos Passos's U.S.A. trilogy.[55]

In *The Naked and the Dead*, the narrative voice of Norman Mailer's novel tells us that most of the men "fight out of fear or a sense of personal shame."[56] The story highlights the pressures of army life, authority and bureaucracy, the call to duty, and the problem of anti-Semitism. The four sections of the novel (Wave, Argil and Mold, Plant and Phantom, Wake) provide flashbacks to the lives of the characters. The story presents a deep concern with dehumanization of the soldiers, who are caught up in the machine of war. There is an examination of power and an exposition of the loneliness of the soldiers, offset by the community that they experience in company with each other.

Norman Mailer was a rifleman. He observed the war in the Pacific with the intention of writing about it, and the novel he wrote launched his career. For a time, Mailer was America's most famous postwar writer of literary fiction after J. D. Salinger, observed Terry Teachout in an article in *Commentary*: "Today Mailer's name no longer figures other than sporadically on lists of important postwar writers."[57] This may be true despite Mailer's "brazen demeanor," politics, exuberant journalism, and creative nonfiction. Teachout says that *The Naked and the Dead* shows Mailer as "a natural born describer."[58] J. Michael Lennon offers a harsher view of Mailer in his lengthy authorized biography, to which Teachout responds: "Lennon views Mailer as something not far removed from a lifelong drunken adolescent, albeit one of genius and, even more important, of near Dickensian industry."[59] Indeed, Mailer wrote prodigiously, and maintained a public profile amplified by his vigorous and feisty personality. From 1968 to 1983 Mailer wrote twenty books, none of which were novels. He explored the world of a death row inmate in *Executioner's Song*. He called that "a true life novel," but that was more a matter of blending genres. This cross between the novel and factual narrative can also be seen in John Hersey's *Bells for Adano*, *The Wall*, and *Hiroshima*.

Mailer biographer J. Michael Lennon claims that the author may have risen to prominence too quickly for his own good as an artist. *The Naked and the Dead* reached the best-seller list as a postwar novel, and Mailer "found himself at a loss creatively," says Lennon.[60] As the 1950s began, Mailer produced *Barbary Shore* (1951) and *The Deer Park* (1955). He would remain a novelist, producing mammoth works like *Ancient Evenings*, but it was as a writer of nonfiction that he became particularly notable. Mailer wrote of himself in *Advertisements for Myself* (1959) and as a participant in *Armies of the Night* (1968), which is subtitled "History as a Novel, The Novel as History." In *Pieces and Pontifications* (1980), we hear Mailer calling history "a series of immensely sober novels written by men who don't have large literary talents."[61] Novels say more, he insists. Historians are dealing with hypotheses formulated in relation to accumulated data.

"One cannot read a page or two of Mailer without a visceral reaction," wrote David Cowart in an article with the provocative title "Norman Mailer: Like a Wrecking Ball from Outer Space."[62] Mailer wrote as a social critic, a sometimes bombastic commentator. He was a magazine feature writer and an artist, not a newspaper journalist. In *Advertisements for Myself*, Mailer said that he believed that art has to "intensify, even, if necessary, to exacerbate the moral consciousness of people" and added that the novel is best suited to do this because it is "immediate . . . overbearing . . . inescapable."[63] Mailer's first novel, in 1948, was a testosterone-driven study of war and society with an all-male cast. By the 1970s, Mailer was getting into trouble with feminists. Responding to Kate Millet's *Sexual Politics* (1970), Mailer wrote "The Prisoner of Sex." In a live discussion with Betty Friedan, Susan Sontag, and Germaine Greer, Mailer asserted: "I'm not going to sit here and let you harridans harangue me." Novelist and playwright Gore Vidal took the opportunity of a review on Eva Figes's *Patriarchal Attitudes* (1971) to launch out at Mailer. Vidal had emerged in the forties as a young writer who crafted the story of a gay romance in *The City and the Pillar* (1948). With *Myra Breckinridge* (1968), a satirical novel in diary form, he explored gender, transsexuality, feminism, Hollywood, and sexual expression beyond conventional norms. Vidal remained sensitive to gender concerns, and was fully in support of the women's liberation movement. He was sharply critical of Mailer's apparent male chauvinism. *New York Review of Books* published Vidal's remarks on Figes's book as an essay, "In Another Country," where he observed that the public reaction to Millet's *Sexual Politics* and to Friedan's *The Feminine Mystique* was one of the most interesting responses in American culture next to Richard Nixon's politics. He asserted that there had been a clear patriarchal progression from Henry Miller to Norman Mailer to Charles Manson.[64] Mailer was not pleased.

On the *Dick Cavett Show* on December 15, 1971, Mailer and Gore Vidal mixed it up over this *New York Review of Books* essay. HBO repeated this telecast as *The Fifty Year Argument*, a Martin Scorsese documentary codirected by David Tedeschi. Dick Cavett wrote about it in his autobiography; he said that he had to wait for a week to see the show because the producers were reviewing it. Mailer was so irritated at Vidal that he butted him with his head backstage before the show was taped. Cavett says that he knew that there was trouble when Mailer entered: "He had his pugilistic walk and looked a little pissed, in the British sense."[65]

JAMES MICHENER, *TALES OF THE SOUTH PACIFIC*

James Michener, Norman Mailer, and Irwin Shaw all had military experiences. Michener served in the U.S. Navy on forty-nine islands, including Iwo Jima, Pitcairn, and the Polynesian islands of the South Pacific. His experiences became the raw material for his *Tales of the South Pacific* (1947), the basis for the Rodgers and Hammerstein musical *South Pacific*. Michener later made further use of this experience when he wrote his best seller *Hawaii* (1960). His South Pacific stories evoke the same imaginative awakening that some sailors likely had to a part of the world they had never seen before.

Michener's book must be distinguished from the musical, which used only two sections of his manuscript. These sections focused on romantic, exotic locales, not on the war itself. Overall, Michener wrote nineteen related episodes about men in service in the South Pacific whose lives are in the balance. The stories are patriotic, but they do not add up to a war novel. His characters encounter island culture, but some passages indicate that all was not as romantic as a torch song like "Some Enchanted Evening" would make it seem. We read: "You rotted on New Caledonia waiting for Guadalcanal." Battles were "flaming things of the bitter moment." Michener witnessed the major naval action of Korelei and the Battle of Coral Sea, as well as the 1942 mission, "Alligator," which he says "changed lives in every country in the world."[66]

PEARL S. BUCK, *THE PROMISE*

Pearl S. Buck is perhaps best known as the Nobel Prize–winning novelist who wrote *The Good Earth* (1931). Yet she was also a committed advocate for racial justice and international peace. Her novelette, *The Promise*, is a testimony to her support for Chinese resistance against imperial Japan. Buck was a member of the Chinese Emergency Relief Committee that was created in 1938. She and Richard J. Walsh started the East-West Association in 1941. Buck saw the war as a test of American ideals of democracy and equality. Citing racial issues, she called the 1940s "a new era of nationalism," in which minorities would not accept being dominated. In Herbert Agar's 1942 review of her collection *American Unity and Asia*, he suggested that she might turn out to be "the Tom Paine of our world-wide civil war." Chester Kerr, the chief of the Office of War Information, recommended Pearl Buck's *American Unity and Asia* and said that it should be read by "every member of this Government who has a hand in shaping American opinion."[67]

Pearl Buck's views were formulated by her experiences in China. She was born into a missionary family, and knew China better than most Americans. This made her, within the perceptions of the American public, an authority on Chinese life, which enabled her "to address American race issues in an international context," observes Karen J. Leong.[68] Pearl Buck was born in the United States, but her family returned to China to Christianize the Chinese. As a young adult, she left China to attend Randolph-Macon Woman's College in Lynchburg, Virginia. At the age of eighteen she was a stranger to American culture. She then married J. Lossing Buck, a missionary and agriculturalist, in 1916. They went to rural north China. In the 1930s, Pearl Buck wrote *The Fighting Angels* (1936) and *The Exile* (1936). She witnessed what she regarded as oppression of women in China, and commented that "all subjected women suffer." In 1931 she visited Harlem, and spoke with an audience about her sense of being different and treated as an alien in China. She made a vow to write on behalf of people of minorities: "I made up my mind that if I ever returned to America to live, I would make these people my first concern."[69]

Pearl Buck wrote with realism. That she was American, a white woman raised in China, influenced her perspective. In 1940, she was one of the few American public intellectuals familiar with China. For some of her readers she was a novelty; for most Americans, China was mysterious, distant, and exotic. For Buck, it was a place that had been her home. Her experiences in China enabled her to think internationally and reflect on America from a distance. The U.S. media, meanwhile, looked to Pearl Buck for insight into China.

The Good Earth was chosen as a Book of the Month Club selection for March 1931, soon after it was published. Chinese papers reviewed the novel positively. Buck wrote to her publisher Richard J. Walsh that "doubtless many Americans are asking and wondering how true the books are to life here and what the Chinese themselves think of them."[70] This was not merely a travel book or a curiosity, said Dorothy Canfield Fisher; the novel "makes us belong to the Chinese characters."[71]

Buck's childhood experiences in China gave her a markedly international worldview. She urged the United States to respond to the world. India and China were waiting for the United States to "take the lead for democracy and are growing disheartened and discouraged because of our delay."[72] She urged strengthening democracy, fervently approved of immigration, and believed that America had a political unity that supported stability. She remained concerned about racial discrimination. In a November 15, 1941, letter to the *New York Times*, "The Other Side of Harlem," she responded to an editorial of November 12 with a concern about racial injustice. In her commencement address at Harvard University in June 1942, she said: "I confess . . . I have been completely perplexed by this race prejudice in my own country."[73] She was a white woman who could identify with Chinese and with being an outsider. She concluded that the war had given American soldiers a more international perspective. Soldiers will return, she said, "with a certain partial knowledge of these peoples . . . and yet the experience will change them into different men."[74]

In *The Promise* (1942), Pearl Buck sets up a romance in the midst of war. Her story presents an extraordinary young woman and a virile young soldier. We follow the young warrior, Sheng, to the house of Wei Mayli, where he announces that he must leave for the war. "Beauty will not win a war," he insists.[75] The drone of planes sounds above them, and an aerial attack assaults the town. The bombing raid casts thunder down upon the town. A child is pulled from the rubble. Beset by the war and a call to service, the characters will both leave their town and join the military march on the Burma Road in southwest China.

The story is set in 1942, after the Japanese overtook Burma. The British attempted to wrest Burma back again, and China was engaged in this effort. British, Chinese, and American forces, under General Joseph Stilwell, recaptured the northern territory of Burma. Pearl Buck's novelette brings us into this time of struggle and offers readers a deeply humanitarian story. We learn that Wei Mayli is strong and resourceful, yet the limitations of a female in China are made strikingly clear. When Mayli reaches the house of the One Above, she meets his lady, who is not named. Mayli wonders at this lady in the dark blue silk robe and blue velvet jacket. "Oh, what a disadvantage it is today to be a woman!" she says. Surely you are not at any disadvantage, Mayli replies. Oh, yes, says the lady in blue. "I long to do this and that—anything and everything. I see so much to do. Then my husband says to me, 'Remember that you are a woman, please.'"[76]

The man called the One Above is sending his best troops on the road to Burma. There they will join with the Americans to fight "to keep the Big Road open."[77] The lady in blue is apprehensive about the military campaign. She wishes that she was a man so that she can go with the soldiers and see things unfold. Mayli tells her that she will go and assist the nurses and be the women's eyes and ears.[78] She will not tell Sheng that she is going. Yet he catches sight and scent of her as he passes through the general's quarters and wonders, jealously, why she has been there. In this romance, Mayli is frequently thinking of Sheng. She is assigned to work with Dr. Chung Liang in a regiment, under an officer named Pao Chen. The army has been ordered not to surrender under any circumstances.

Preparing for service, Mayli meets several of the nurses. They will be the watchers of the wounded. One of them is Han Sin-chen, who escaped the rape of Nanking by the Japanese army because she was away at school when her family was murdered. There is also a wealthy girl from Tientsin who had lost her mother and father, and has lost her brothers in battle. A third is a woman who was a soldier and was captured and escaped. Mayli becomes a leader among these women. A grace carries her through much difficulty.[79] Her hair is cut short. The women follow the troops on a long, tiring, confused march across a beautiful landscape. Mayli meets Charlie, an engineer who becomes a scout, following enemy troop movements in the countryside.

Sheng's men have walked thirty miles a day. Buck points to the specific objects they carried or wore: "rifle, bayonet, bamboo hat, helmet, three day's food, water bottle, spade, bullets, and two grenades." Sheng wants to know why a foreign leader is heading the operation. They watch aerial battles overhead. They conclude that the Americans are young men like children playing with magic. They have come with steel from furnaces in Pittsburgh. U.S. airmen are flyers like winged eagles in monster machines.[80]

Buck brings us into the setting of the Burma Road and alternates chapters between Sheng and Mayli. Mayli and Sheng are within miles of each other, but they do not meet—at least, not yet. The historical context of the relations between China and Burma lie behind this story, along with the colonial role of the English and Burmese discontent with it. The English soldiers are "massed along the Salween River."[81] The radio announces, in Japanese: "Rangoon burns! Today our forces bombed the city without mercy!" Japanese propaganda attempts to persuade the Burmese that they are their liberators.

The general insists on fighting. The One Above responds to his urgent note by saying that "in this war we are only one among others."[82] Yet, it is decided that Sheng will lead his men over the border on a dangerous mission. Mayli leads the women at an inspection, and she meets the One Above and his lady, who have arrived by plane. She senses that Sheng is very near. The chapters alternate between Sheng's anticipation of battle and Mayli's experiences, as some of the women sing for the injured soldiers. Buck draws out the longed-for meeting between them. In the darkness, Sheng passes by the doctor. Then he passes by Mayli, but does not see her. She hears his voice and stops and stares as he hurries away.[83] Mayli is sleepless on the night before battle. She wonders if, facing the threat, she can fulfill her duty in leading the nurses, or might be killed. In the morning Charlie Li returns from his scouting mission and reports on the condition of the U.S. and British armies, who appear "hard pressed."[84] Soldiers have fallen in battle, and Mayli argues with the doctor, who is deciding who should be treated and who should be left to die. She is troubled by the pain and injury she sees around her: "But Mayli had seen men like these in their own countries, carefree, and full of merriment, well-beloved in comfortable homes, and they were not strange to her. It was piteous to see them here, outwitted and betrayed, cut off and trapped."[85] They are faced with dismal losses and retreat: "Defeat was in the smell of the air, in the dust, in the heat."[86] She speaks in English to the soldiers and they are surprised. She sings an English song to a dying young man, and it is the last thing on earth that he hears. It is at this moment that she sees Sheng, who has recognized her singing, and he lifts her to her feet.

JOHN HERSEY: *A BELL FOR ADANO* AND *HIROSHIMA*

John Hersey was born in Tientsin, China. Like Pearl Buck, he was the son of missionaries. He became a foreign correspondent for *Time* magazine in 1939 when he was assigned to China and its wartime capital on the upper Yangtze River. He became a reporter and novelist during World War II, traveling widely to document the war in Europe and in the Pacific. Hersey reported on Guadalcanal and the war in Sicily. He gathered evidence of the Holocaust in Poland and the Baltic, and interviewed survivors following the atomic bombing of Hiroshima. Indeed, his most famous book is *Hiroshima*, a brief and quite accessible volume of survivor accounts. *Hiroshima* was first published in 1946 in an issue of the *New Yorker*. Hersey's novels include the Pulitzer Prize–winning *A Bell for Adano* (1943), for which he drew on his experience in Italy, and *The Wall*, a searching story of the Holocaust set in the Warsaw ghetto in Poland. He began writing *The Wall*, one of his longest novels, following his observations in Poland in 1945. Upon returning to China, he witnessed the rise of communist rule in that country. For *Life* magazine and the *New Yorker* he wrote about Peking (Beijing) and Shanghai, and about the nationalist army.

Hersey's nonfiction is rather straightforward. It is the work of a journalist, a compassionate man inclined toward realism rather than toward stylistic innovation, psychological probing, or philosophical musing. He began writing fiction by creating novels of contemporary history or observation that transpose journalism into fictional form. Initially, Hersey's work as a journalist for *Time* was written anonymously, without a by-line. He became involved in a long-distance relationship with Frances Ann Cannon, the daughter of a cotton goods manufacturer in Charlotte, North Carolina. Following his many flights from the Far East to be with her, they married on April 27, 1940.

Hersey obtained his job with *Time* three years earlier, partly because he was familiar with China. He had worked in 1937 as Sinclair Lewis's secretary, and actively pursued work at *Time* magazine where Henry Luce was the owner. Luce had also been born in Tientsin of missionary parents. The conflict in China necessitated journalistic coverage, and Hersey was sent in 1939 to the Chungking news bureau, supervised by Theodore H. White.

In June 1942, John Hersey's first book, *Men on Bataan*, was published. *Time-Life* reports on the war in the Philippines supported this book, which also included interviews and accounts from General Douglas MacArthur's men. The book appeared at a time when men who had fought in the Philippines had been imprisoned and Corregidor had been surrendered. Hersey writes objectively, as a reporter, alternating chapters on MacArthur with chapters on his men. In about fifty brief stories, he offers images of heroes in a book that seems intended to lift the morale of the public at home.

John Hersey was an eyewitness to battles on Guadalcanal, where he joined a military patrol, and on the Solomon Islands. In the battle of the Matinikau River on Guadalcanal in October 1942, his life was in the balance as Company H under the command of Captain Charles Rigaud engaged the enemy. In his book *Into the Valley* (1943), Hersey recalls his own ignorance about the peril and pain of war. The company was surrounded and under fire by Japanese artillery and snipers. Surviving this, he later wrote his account less objectively than he had done in his earlier work. He attempted to discover the lives and feelings of the men who had been involved in this confrontation. This compassion for the experience of people would mark his work on *A Bell for Adano*, *Hiroshima*, and *The Wall*.

John Hersey gradually became a novelist, and his work provides a barometer of the decade. He was a man who was in the right place at the right time. Indeed, Hersey seemed to be almost everywhere. In 1943, he covered the daring landing and violence of the Sicilian campaign. His encounter with the military governor of Licata, Italy, became a springboard for his novel *A Bell for Adano*. Hersey watched the war unfold from several vantage points and asked an essential question: How was he to make some sense of it? What comes across clearly in his work is humanitarian concern. Hersey is connecting the dynamic unfolding of the news of the day with storytelling. He is a feature article writer with a broad geographical scope, a chronicler of contemporary history in journalism and fiction.

A Bell for Adano

A Bell for Adano began in 1943 with an article that Hersey expanded into a story. The people he met became characters in that story. There is Major Victor Joppolo, who arrives on the shore of Sicily, touching the dock, wondering at the land of his ancestors. He is a New Yorker of Italian background who sets up with the occupying force in an office in Adano, above the great hall. He wants to accomplish much that will extirpate the influences of fascism that have prevailed in the town. As he comes into town, he notices that the bell tower is now vacant and had been replaced by a fascist slogan: "The Italian people who built the Empire with their blood, will make it fruitful with their work and will defend it against anyone with their arms."[87] Zito, the doorman, says that the war has disrupted the town. People have been without bread and are hungry. The town authorities have run away. The spirit of the town has been shattered and the dead need to be buried. The seven hundred-year-old bell has been stolen.

Bells ring often in the cities of Italy today. In this novel, the bell's absence is felt keenly as an emptiness in the town, a loss of its tradition and soul. "When the bell spoke, our fathers and their fathers far back spoke to us," says Matteo Cacopardo, an elderly sulfur merchant. Zito claims that it provided a calming tone for the town, signaling the towns-people to their meals and ordering the rhythm of their lives. "All life revolved around it," says Father Pensovecchio.[88] Recognizing their loss, Joppolo intends to get another bell for the town.

Jopollo meets Mercurio Salvatore, a town crier, the messenger of the village, who is a former fascist. He must read the orders that are posted. Father Pensovecchio says Mass in the morning. The major has been discussing the town's lost bell with Zito and realizes that he must hurry to Mass. A blond woman is in the congregation, and he notices her—and does a double-take. The priest tells the people that the Americans have come there as liberators. In the fourth chapter we see Gargano, the police chief, entering a bakery shop. People object to his disregard of them as he goes to the head of the line. Carmelita argues about this, and Gargano arrests her and brings her to Joppolo. Joppolo is sympathetic and finds Gargano insensitive, but wants to keep him in his position. He requires Carmelita to serve a one-day sentence and then suspends it. He talks about the foundations of democracy. We can read here Hersey's concern for people, for acts of mercy as well as rules for order. In Joppolo's response to Gargano, we see the rejection of the insensitivity of a man who thinks that his position gives him privilege and power over others, while he claims to be doing his duty in managing the crowd. The woman who was in the church is Tina, the daughter of Tomasino, a star fisherman. The major finds her attractive and wishes to meet her.

General Marvin, a character based upon General George S. Patton, enters the story as he is riding down a road approaching Adano. A man with a cart and a mule is blocking the way and the general yells out: "goddamn you goddamn cart get out of the road!" The man is asleep, and the general orders that the cart be thrown over into a ditch. The mule cries out and the general orders that it be shot. The man wakes up and begins to cry, and the general continues with his convoy down the road to Adano. When he arrives, he orders that all donkey carts be prohibited from the roads. Then he is told that the water supply depends upon these carts for transportation of the water. He rescinds the order.

General Marvin is not exactly the epitome of human sensitivity. The narrator mentions his popular reputation for heroism. From that perspective, he appears as "the genial, pipe-smoking, history-quoting, snappy-looking, map-carrying, adjective-defying divisional commander" who shoots off twelve rounds from a captured Luger pistol every morning. However, this portrait of this heroic "deliverer of Italian soil" is what the "Sunday supplements" tell you; the "boys who have come home and finally limp out of hospitals" won't tell you straight either because "even then the truth is bent by their anger." The narrator says, "But I can tell you perfectly calmly that General Marvin showed himself during the invasion to be a bad man, something worse than what our troops were trying to throw out."[89]

Hersey makes use of a widespread rumor that General Patton indeed had a mule shot and a mule cart thrown off a bridge. He had heard that Patton slapped around two men who were shell-shocked by battle. The character he creates is not that of a military hero who broke through German forces at Normandy and marched across France to the Rhine. General Marvin is a lover of war and a despiser of peace, and becomes Major Joppolo's adversary. The novel is carried along by Major Joppolo's decisions and actions. Cacopardo is so busy telling General Marvin off that he neglects to tell him where the German forces are.

It was a bold move to caricature one of the war's most illustrious generals. General George Patton may be best known for his army's sweep across France, and was noted for tough words and raising hell. Following the D-Day victory, Patton landed near Omaha Beach and visited the Allied commanders. His new objective was to push toward the Rhine and to attack what was called the Siegfried Line. This would lead to the Battle of the Bulge. With the bridges all destroyed before them, Patton's army reached the Rhine on March 7, 1945, and crossed the Rhine on March 22. A photo shows his first act: he pissed on German soil.

Long before the Second World War, Patton had distinguished himself as a tenacious fighter, and made his mark as an Olympic athlete. Upon graduating from West Point in 1909, he married Beatrice Banning Ayer and accepted an assignment to a cavalry troop in Sheridan, Illinois. He was then assigned to Fort Myer in Virginia, near Washington, DC. Patton became a fencing instructor and learned cavalry tactics. It was perhaps an unusual beginning for a military man who would lead armored divisions. When the First World War broke out, Patton considered making a request to fight in the French army. Permission was denied; the U.S. Army wanted him. He was engaged in field duty at Sierra Blanca in Mexico. War correspondents reported on his heroism. When the United States entered the First World War, Patton commanded a tank corps in Langres, France. The tank was a new weapon of war. Injured in battle and recuperating at Dijon, he was dubbed "Hero of the Tanks," and was recommended for promotion to colonel. He also received the Distinguished Service Medal. He was thirty-three years old.

Between wars, Patton was a staff officer and executive officer of cavalry at Fort Myer. He was posted to Hawaii in May 1935, and then returned to the mainland. George C. Marshall was named Army Chief of Staff in the spring of 1939 and stayed with Patton that summer. The September 1 attack on Poland by the German army made it glaringly obvious that cavalry was outmoded. In July 1940, Patton was assigned to Fort Benning, Georgia, and the Second Armored Division to train the army stationed there. General Marshall appointed Patton to lead the I Armored Corps. In this capacity, he planned the expedition to North Africa and desert training. One hundred ships carried twenty four thousand troops toward November 8, 1942, landings: one about 150 miles below Casablanca, and another at Fedala, 15 miles north of the city. Patton attacked Casablanca and secured the Axis surrender. At the North Africa camp, seven or more Allied divisions landed along ten miles of shore amid wind and waves. The campaign in North Africa raged fiercely. After Tunisia, the Allies' next goal was Italy. The initial plan was for General Bernard Montgomery's troops to land around Catania, and Patton's troops to move toward Palermo. Patton sought to take Agrigento, and he aimed at Messina and Palermo. The *Monrovia* was the flagship of Admiral Hewitt's fleet. On board, Patton joined ninety thousand men for the first assault on Sicily.

A Bell for Adano was one of the first major novels of the Second World War. It was followed by *A Walk in the Sun* by Harry Brown in 1944 and the best seller *Mister Roberts* by Thomas Heggen in 1946, and then by Irwin Shaw's *The Young Lions*, Norman Mailer's *The Naked and the Dead* (1948), and James Jones's *From Here to Eternity* (1951). Hersey's first novel received the Pulitzer Prize for fiction on May 8, 1945, announced in the *New York Times* in a little box on page 1 on the same day that the newspaper's headline declared the end of the war in Europe.

Of course, Hersey's active career as a war correspondent continued with a stretch in Moscow and a tour of the concentration camps of Poland. His most notable and lasting reporting came when he returned to China and when he reported from Hiroshima in the spring of 1946. Hersey interviewed people in the devastated city about their experiences at the time of the "noiseless flash" that shook the city. He portrayed them sensitively through clear, understated reporting. The *New Yorker* published Hersey's account in one issue on August 31, 1946.

Hiroshima

One of the most momentous events of the Second World War was the invention of the atomic bomb and its detonation over Hiroshima and Nagasaki. In her review of John Hersey's *Hiroshima* in *The Nation*, Ruth Benedict observed that "the calmness of the narration throws into relief the nightmare magnitude of the destructive power the brains of men have brought into being." Hersey said of his writing: "The flat style was deliberate." He wished to give his readers a direct experience of the people whose stories he was telling on the page. His goal was to allow readers to draw their own conclusions and moral or political responses.[90] Gertrude Stein asked if the nuclear bomb was even a worthy subject for literature. In "Reflections on the Atom Bomb" (1947) she wrote: "I could never take any interest in the atomic bomb," and added that she believed that it was a negation of literature. Almost two decades later, Susan Sontag, in "The Imagination of Disaster" (1965), called popular productions "naïve" commercial art amid "the most profound dilemmas of the contemporary situation."[91] Others have wondered if harrowing incidents like the explosions of the atom bomb over Hiroshima and Nagasaki can even be written about in popular literature or depicted in popular film.

John Hersey's *Hiroshima* gave a momentous event a human face. His work began as an article in the *New Yorker* in August 1946. It was read aloud on radio broadcasts by ABC Radio across four days. It then was published in book form. Hersey's journalistic account is developed through a series of profiles that gives voice to survivors of the atomic bomb.

The dropping of the atom bomb on August 6, 1945, changed the world. During the coming years there was much anxiety about the potential for nuclear annihilation. We tend to think about it less today. However, as *60 Minutes* and other sources have been reporting, Russia has been ramping up its nuclear arsenal. North Korea continues testing its rockets, as if in a brash flexing of the muscles of its nuclear program. Iran is suspected of designs to develop a nuclear weapon despite agreements with the United States. The Trump administration has declared that they will give attention to the buildup of nuclear arms. Meanwhile, the world faces the problem of nuclear material falling into the hands of terrorists.

Hersey's book created a public conversation. The Atomic Energy Act preceded its publication by a few days, and called for limitations on sharing nuclear information. Reports on nuclear bomb development were guarded after the war. Of course, people wanted to know about this weapon and what had occurred in Japan to bring the war to a close.

John Hersey's journey to Hiroshima was financed by the *New Yorker*. His narrative, which told the story of six survivors, brought the foreign enemy into focus as fully human. The weight of knowledge of the bombings and their devastation was balanced in Hersey's text with straightforward, sympathetic portrayals of these six individuals. The *New Yorker* recognized the historical importance of the event and their responsibility to provide some perspective on it by publishing the work. The magazine had two hundred thousand subscribers, and another three hundred thousand copies of the issue were sold at newsstands.[92]

Part 1, "A Noiseless Flash," introduces us to the six people who will be the focus of Hersey's narrative. They are Dr. Masakazu Fujii, the widow Mrs. Nakamura, the German priest Father Kleinsorge, Dr. Sasaki of the Red Cross Hospital, Methodist pastor Kiyoshi Tanimoto, and Miss Toshiko Sasaki, a clerk at the East Asia Tin Works. Hersey adopts a reportorial tone, and his narrative provides images. First, there is a group picture of ordinary people whose lives have been disrupted. Hersey focuses upon what they experienced in those first moments of the noiseless flash. Their recollections of that morning bring us into their lives. We follow Tanimoto as he goes to Mr. Matsuo's house to deliver a cabinet. Within one long paragraph we witness action and are given the geography and general features of the city. An explosion pulls apart the house, and Matsuo leaps under bedrolls. Tanimoto hides between large rocks in the garden.

Each portrait draws us closer to the individual who is the focus. Mrs. Nakamura is busy caring for her children. One of the doctors and the priest are in their underwear on the hot August morning, reading as the bomb falls over the city. The building comes toppling down around Dr. Masakazu Fujii as he reads the newspaper, and he loses his eyeglasses. Exposition unfolds the drama of these characters. We see them in action and we are given their perceptions. In Part 2, The Fire, these stories become more poignant and the pathos increases. Hersey evokes the struggle and the trauma with images of the wounded "hurrying across the bridge in an endless parade of misery."[93] Yet, what is "unforgettable," as the *New York Times* put it, is how this book speaks for humanity. Most importantly, John Hersey's *Hiroshima* combined documentary reporting with compassionate imagination and empathy. "There has never been a time in history when the character of human imagination wasn't important," writes Thomas Friedman.[94] Hersey certainly applied that imagination to contemporary history in *A Bell for Adano*, *Hiroshima*, and *The Wall*.

By Part 4, twelve days after the bomb, we are given a scene through the eyes of the German priest. He sees a rice field "streaked with brown," houses destroyed, windows broken, and "collapsed city blocks."[95] However, what is more troubling is what is invisible: the radiation that begins to cause "peculiar sensations," inflammation, hair loss, malaise, fever, and nausea. The disease, says Hersey, "would later come to be known as radiation sickness."[96] By the third or fourth week after the explosion, people concluded that the bomb had spread a poison.

American servicemen believed that their lives were saved by the detonation of the bomb. In their view, it secured Japan's surrender and prevented the loss of thousands of lives in an invasion of Japan. At the time, polls showed that about 85 percent of the American public supported the decision. That was before widespread public awareness of radioactive fallout. Some individuals note that the Japanese were devoted to the emperor and to tenacious fighting to the death. They argue that there would have been firebombing of Japanese cities and further fighting on Pacific islands that would have caused a greater number of casualties than occurred in Hiroshima and Nagasaki. Dissenting voices have increased across the more than seventy years since the atomic bombs were dropped on those cities. Some of those critics suggest that there were alternatives, such as a demonstration of the force of the bomb at sea. Others have argued that Japan was in effect defeated by August 1945. Surrender was being considered, although not unconditional surrender. The charge has also been made that the United States wanted to intimidate the Soviet Union by displaying the awesome power of the new invention. Once the bomb was built, others say, it was necessary to justify the great cost and effort that went into making it. That is a bit like Anton Chekhov's assertion that if a gun appears in a story, we must expect that it will be used.

On April 25, 1945, the United Nations Charter was created. Less than one hundred days later Hiroshima was devastated by the most powerful human-created explosion in history. The cities of Kyoto and Hiroshima were on the list of targets chosen for the atomic bomb. The B-29 raids had not hit those cities. Hap Arnold, commander of the Air Force, argued that Kyoto, a large city of 743,000, had a strong manufacturing capacity and should be considered a significant military target. Secretary of War Henry Stimson argued against targeting Kyoto, an important religious center. Hiroshima, Niigata, Nagasaki, and Kokura were chosen as targets. On April 12, 1945, President Roosevelt appeared for the business of the day wearing a red tie and a gray suit. By 1 p.m., he was complaining of a terrible headache, and fell over in his armchair. Dr. Howard J. Bruenn, summoned to the president's side, recognized this as a cerebral hemorrhage. At 3:35 President Roosevelt died: yet another loss for wartime America. At 5 p.m., Vice President Harry S. Truman received a call while he was in Senator Sam Rayburn's office. He had been asked to go to the White House. At 7:09 p.m. he took the oath of office as the thirty-third President of the United States. Harry S. Truman had inherited a war, and the plans to unleash the atom bomb.

Following the bombing, in the heat of the moment, Japan's Emperor Hirohito told his nation, by a radio broadcast, that they must be strong and accept the horrible. The American public was relieved that the bomb had brought the war to an end. The 85 percent U.S. support for the bomb's use in 1945 dwindled, and in a 1994 poll, about 39 percent of Americans opposed the use of the atomic bomb at Hiroshima, and 6 percent of respondents to the question remained unsure. There remains the moral challenge concerning the issue of strategic bombing that had dire consequences for a civilian population.

In 1945, the Joint Chiefs of Staff developed a strategy that included a campaign of blockade and bombardment that would precede any invasion. Admiral Leahy insisted that the blockade would have to be effective. Truman had called a meeting on strategy on June 14, 1945, and another on June 18. Preparations were made to build a potential attack force. Secretary of War Henry Stimson and his aide Edward L. Bowles commissioned scientist William Shockley to develop an estimate of probable Japanese losses and American losses. Stimson had been told previously that operations in the Pacific might be expected to result in more than a million casualties.[97] Shockley estimated that there would be more than 1.7 million U.S. casualties and between 400,000 and 800,000 deaths. However, no one could know how long the fighting would continue or how many men and women would be lost. Truman later wrote in his memoirs that the bomb saved "half a million [American] boys."[98]

In the end, a Soviet invasion was not decisive in the surrender of the Japanese. Indeed, the Japanese could say with some pride that their military was not defeated in the fight. The atom bomb did it. Some critics have claimed that the Nagasaki bomb was gratuitous, and that the devastation at Hiroshima was surely enough. This, however, implies that surrender would have been inevitable upon the Japanese seeing the damage of the first bomb. The detonation over Nagasaki made it clear that the Americans had more than one bomb. Of course, that reality was a frightening one. With the Soviet testing of an atomic bomb in 1949, the presence of nuclear arms became an ever-more anxiety-provoking reality. Humanity had entered the nuclear age.

On May 26, 2016, former Vice President Walter Mondale spoke with Chuck Todd (MSNBC) about America's strong relationship with Japan. "This is one of the biggest events in modern Japanese history," said Mondale, speaking about President Barack Obama's visit to Hiroshima. Mondale, a former ambassador to Japan, called the atomic bombing "a big issue that hasn't been subject to much discussion." He cautioned against any use of nuclear weapons, saying that "we've got to put nuclear weapons in another category" and must "prevent any repetition" of the use of nuclear arms: "the most hideous weapon possible."[99]

5

LIFE ON THE HOME FRONT

Saul Bellow, Ayn Rand, John Dos Passos, Theodore Dreiser, John O'Hara, John P. Marquand, and Others

Across America, the war was in the thoughts of people in hundreds of communities. With hints of heroism and reports of misfortune, it came and rested uneasily in America's consciousness. After the news of Pearl Harbor, the nation was at war. Winter 1942 passed, and spring sunshine lit the lawns of dozens of small towns. The warmth returned, but the sounds of play on the baseball fields receded. The young men had gone and the fields were left to their younger brothers and sisters, the kids who collected scrap and bottles for the war effort. The war was a presence, an act of imagination. In New York, air-raid drills and curfews made some children uneasy. In America's Midwest, the battle seemed far away, but patriotism lay at the core of daily life.

When families sat down for dinner, they remembered the boys who had gone to war. Those young men knew about teamwork. They grew up pitching baseballs and used that skill to pitch grenades. In 1940, the *Sporting News* called for flag observances at baseball fields. Others hoped that the National Anthem would be played before games. In October, players registered for the draft. The leagues hosted "I Am an American Day" and "Defense Bond Day." Phillies pitcher Hugh Mulcahy reported for duty on March 8, 1941. The 1940 MVP, Hank Greenberg, was drafted on May 7, 1941. He served until December 5, and after Pearl Harbor, on December 7, he reenlisted. America was now at war, but the commissioner of baseball argued that the game must go on. Baseball would be preserved as a feature of American culture that would maintain public morale. FDR wrote to Commissioner Landis on January 15, 1942: "I honestly feel that it would be best for the country to keep baseball going."[1]

So, the games continued. When 1942 began, sixty-one major league baseball players were in the armed services. Once the season ended, there were 243.[2] Cleveland Indians star pitcher Bob Feller played military baseball for the Norfolk Naval Training Station. Forty-three major league players played for Great Lakes Naval Training Center in Illinois. Among them were six All-Stars and two future Hall of Famers.[3] Major League Baseball donated money to the military for the purchase of equipment for military baseball. There were war bond drives at the baseball parks. Military servicemen received free admission to games. The major leagues continued, but the minor leagues were devastated. Many minor-league players entered military service, and 128 of them died in the war. Two major-league players also lost their lives.[4] Attendance at major-league games dropped from 18.5 million in 1939 to 8 million in 1943. Baseball did not turn to the Negro League for players; rather, former players came out of retirement to return to major-league teams. However, arguments against Nazi racism and totalitarianism may have opened the way for black baseball players in the major leagues.

In 1942, the film *The Pride of the Yankees* brought audiences the story of Lou Gehrig. The film was released a year after the baseball star's death from amyotrophic lateral sclerosis (ALS), a paralyzing, debilitating disease now often called Lou Gehrig's disease. Gary Cooper, who played Gehrig, was a film star of the era who had also recently played the hero-soldier in *Sergeant York* (1941). Cooper delivered Gehrig's memorable farewell speech about being the "luckiest man" with great dignity. The director and cameramen had to adjust to the fact that Cooper could not comfortably swing the baseball bat left-handed, as Gehrig did. What Cooper could do well was portray an American hero. During that first year of America's involvement in the war he represented hundreds of young heroes who had gone overseas. It was a time for heroes. The world needed them.

SAUL BELLOW

When Tom Brokaw wrote *The Greatest Generation*, he linked together a variety of different individuals who were connected by the common experience of an era. The stories they told suggest resolve, self-sacrifice, and patriotism: a vision of America's role in the world, a sense of the spirit of the times. That sense of a cultural zeitgeist emerges in the work of American writers of the 1940s. We can celebrate a major author like Saul Bellow for his insight and his recognition of this connection, as well as for his awareness of the disjunction that the war created in many lives. In Bellow's *Dangling Man* (1944), we meet a man who is certainly not heroic. We are soon brought into Joseph's meditations. This private man, in his musings, recognizes his connection with other people of his generation: "Because I was involved with them, because, whether I liked it or not, they were my generation, my society, my world. We were figures in the same plot, eternally fixed together."[5] Joseph gazes out a window at a snowfall, chimney smoke, cars passing, and he thinks about life. Are not the outward features of humanity's material world expressions of our interior, psychological lives? These lives are organized around these homes and these ways of life. Yet, people could not be only "a reflection of the things they lived among." Beyond "their business and politics, their taverns, movies, assaults, divorces, murders" he has tried "to find clear signs of their common humanity."[6]

In *Dangling Man*, the journal entries begin on December 15, 1942. They are filled with thoughts on the ordinary daily business of a man's life. Chicago and its suburbs act as a backdrop in which Joseph, an almost solipsistic man with a philosophic turn of mind, lives his life. As he gazes out the window, looking upon the physical world, there are thoughts of the distant war in Europe and what his own commitment to that cause might be. The mists that "faded and spread and faded" on the windowpane are reminders for him of the appearances and dissolutions of moments in history, ages that we may have read and interpreted incorrectly: "In all principal ways the human spirit must have been the same," he concludes. The times shift. The world changes and we do not always get "the world we bargained for."[7]

Joseph waits in the December whiteness, released from caring for his aging in-laws, Mr. and Mrs. Almstadt. He does not want to talk with old man Almstadt about why he has not enlisted in the army, or why he is otherwise idle. Mrs. Almstadt is absentminded, and is likely suffering from dementia. She pours him a glass of orange juice that has a feather floating in it from the decimated chicken next to it. When he is back in his apartment, he hears sounds from neighboring apartments. He hears his landlady's daughter and Mr. Vanaker's alcoholic cough. On December 18, Joseph writes about himself in the third person, as a man with a block of hair and a little mustache that makes him look older than he is. He was once a communist, but now dresses conservatively to avoid the appearance of nonconformity. He studied history at the University of Wisconsin and, five years later, is now married. He still surrounds himself with books about historical periods: early ascetics, the Enlightenment, "Romanticism and the child prodigy."[8] He imagines himself as a visionary who is also "hardheaded," although he insists that hardheaded judgment is secondary to wonder and speculation about people who are all "bearing the imprint of strangeness in the world."[9] There is for him an inexplicable "feeling of strangeness" that causes him to dangle as if not quite belonging to the world, while observing himself as if from under a cloud. So, he clings to the "splendors, the shifts, excitements, and also the common, neutral matter of existence."[10] For some sense of a common ground, he holds fast to the images of passersby, to brothers and sisters, parents, friends and wives, and the sense of connectedness that they provide.

Saul Bellow's *Dangling Man*, depicts a character's struggle to find a place in the community while asserting his desire for a higher life as an individual. Feeling the need to be independent, Joseph asserts that the world encumbers him, so he must evade it. To be fully human, Joseph decides, one must participate in a "colony of the spirit," of people who defend themselves against the world. Joseph rejects the Army as a threat to his individuality. Yet, he finds that he cannot feel fulfilled in isolation while the war and life around him on the home front is going on. He must join with others. The dangling man is disconnected; he is detached from the flow of life, so he asks the draft board to call up his number so he can enter the army.

The problem here is that Joseph has no community to turn to. He cannot find a living connection with other people. To escape his condition of "dangling," he swings from one extreme to the other. He gives up his individuality altogether. Bellow is implying that we must not give up our individuality. Rather, as we gain confidence in our abilities, we can better participate in and contribute to the human community. The society is strengthened by a person's contribution, and his life expands in freedom because of his commitment. This is a theme that runs like a thread through most of Bellow's subsequent novels. The desire for service, which Henderson and Herzog display in Bellow's later novels, shows us where Bellow's sympathies are. Bellow is not explicit about the moral relation of the individual to the community. However, he does speak of a person attaining a higher consciousness of connection with other persons. Life, Bellow's novels suggest, is about compassion. It is about "feeling, outgoingness, expressiveness, kindness, heart."[11] To attain higher consciousness and a more complete life, one seizes upon service.

Safely at home in Chicago, Joseph writes that, except for the sight of an occasional solider and a military truck in the street, "we are insulated from the war."[12] He is dangling, waiting to be called for active service. His journal begins with a critique of the "hardboiled" stoic extroversion he says has become commonplace in America. People might criticize his keeping a journal as self-indulgent, but this solitary man insists on distinguishing himself from the busy, tough, outward folks who "fly planes, fight bulls or catch tarpon": the Hemingway male image.[13] He is a married man whose helpful wife Iva supplies him with books. Joseph observes the active man: Tad is flying to North Africa, to Algiers or Oran, or the Casbah. Joseph is a Canadian, so the process of induction into the U.S. Navy is longer for him than most. So he waits and he dangles.

AYN RAND

Ayn Rand prefers the active man who is an individualist, a nonconformist. Rand's rejection of collectivism, communism, and totalitarianism emerged from her own keenly felt response to family events and her personal experience in Russia. Her position is also a rational response to the New Deal style of government intervention in the economy, and an extension of her atheistic rejection of religion. Rand made a strong case for capitalism and free-market economy, and against government intrusion. She speaks for liberty, individuality, creativity, and a kind of rationalism. Consequently, she has become the darling of some libertarians. However, in Rand there is no transcendent vantage point. Humans are less interrelated souls than assertive agents in quest of their own ends. An opponent might critique Rand's atomistic worldview and how she approaches reason. One may assert that human beings are not self-encapsulated egos, and that an impulse toward altruism may provide benefits to a responsible community that respects individuality.

Ayn Rand drew criticism from both left (Sidney Hook) and right (Whittaker Chambers) on the political spectrum. In his review of *Atlas Shrugged*, conservative pundit William Buckley called the novel "excruciatingly awful" and "a remarkably silly book." Buckley suggested that the book would not have "lasting ill effect" but that "it is not a cure for anything."[14] Buckley was opposed to Rand's atheism, and saw Rand's assertion of individualism against collectivism as a religious struggle, like that of Christianity against atheism.[15] During the 1950s and 1960s Ayn Rand became a target in Buckley's *National Review*. Whittaker Chambers, in that publication, sharply critiqued Rand's novel in his article, "Big Sister Is Watching You." He called Rand's secularism naïve. Her position, he said, was near absolutist, and was marked by features of fascism. He saw in her version of capitalism distortion and a "heartless mechanism" because it lacked altruism and was not balanced by charity or faith. Rand was arguing for the free market, for a capitalism unfettered that was egoistic, and that Chambers believed was contrary to Christianity. This challenged the *National Review*'s approach to the conservative venture. William Buckley distanced himself from secular libertarianism. In later years, Alan Greenspan was attracted to Ayn Rand's ideas and acknowledged that her philosophy of Objectivism opened his thought beyond the technical realm of economics in which he was highly accomplished.

Ayn Rand's publications have entered popular culture in a bowdlerized form. Rand's emphasis on "the virtue of selfishness" has been subject to caricature. So too has her Nietzschean superman and her rejection of mass man. In the film *Dirty Dancing*, a character who is carrying a copy of *The Fountainhead* says: "Some people matter and others don't." Tobias Wolff's novel, *Old School*, satirizes Ayn Rand when its adolescent narrator discovers how he can assert his will beyond all moderation.[16]

The author of *The Fountainhead* signed a contract on December 10, 1941, for a manuscript that would become that book. The attack on

Pearl Harbor had quickly shifted America's attention to foreign affairs, and patriotic resolve and productive power began to gear up the wartime economy. Capitalist energy was the hope of the day. The publishing firm of Bobbs-Merrill provided a one-year time line for Rand to complete her book. Meanwhile, her story continued to expand, and she introduced her criticism of altruism—"the doctrine that demands that man live for others and place others above self."[17] Rand had begun her work on her novel of ideas with an indictment of the conformity of her fictional architect, Peter Keating. She contrasted this with her character Howard Roark, and his individualistic approach to life. The villain, Ellsworth Toohey, appears in the second part of the novel as he tries to undermine Gail Wynand's media business. At first Rand called her novel *Peter Keating* until editor Archie Ogden pointed out to her that she was featuring the character she completely disagreed with. Rather than minimize Howard Roark, it was important that she build up this character. She changed the title to *The Fountainhead*.

Howard Roark and Peter Keating are both architects, but they live in the world quite differently. Roark has a great creative drive, but will not conform to society's norms. Keating, whom Rand classifies as a "second-hander" rather than an original man, is employed by a big architectural firm, and he plays by its rules. Roark has a less prestigious, low-paying job, but he always insists on being his own man. Roark is assigned to develop a public housing project for Keating called Cortland Homes. He lets Keating use his creative design provided that no change will be made to the design. However, the government interferes, bureaucracy intrudes, and other architects add changes to the plan. Roark is extremely upset by this, and he dynamites the building.

Roark must defend himself in a trial with a grand speech. The hardworking men and women of the jury listen to him. Society's accomplishments have emerged from individuals like this, Rand argues. They are innovators out of the mainstream. Such creativity belongs to individuals, not to the collective. In contrast, government is about collectivism, and this affects independence and creativity. Ultimately, "the integrity of man's creative work is of greater importance than any charitable endeavor," she asserts.[18] Rand advocates selfishness and reason, and asserts that an individual's rights must be recognized above society's collective needs. This appears to position her squarely against utilitarianism's focus on consequences that result in "the greatest good for the greatest number." The jury votes to acquit Howard Roark. They have understood the principle of individualism. Wynand, who once believed that his newspaper could shape public opinion, now sees his media enterprise fall to public opinion. Dominique marries Howard Roark. She rises up in the elevator, in the Wynand Building, seeing the sun and the sky and Howard Roark.[19]

Rand's fundamental ideas become clear when we look back at the novel's origins. At first, she thought to call the novel *Second-Hand Lives*. These are people who live according to hand-me-down social conventions, and do not seize the day as unique individuals. They are something like Friedrich Nietzsche's notion of mass men, or the masses in Ortega y Gasset's *The Revolt of the Masses*. Nietzsche, in his quest for a new morality, sought to revitalize society, which he believed was trapped in a tedium of conformity and Christian proscription. Drawing on this, Ayn Rand cared about characters who would not care about the opinions of other people. It can be argued that a true superhero is one who is large enough to embrace others as well as self. However, for Rand it did not matter if this supposed superman did not care about others' needs.[20] Rand emphasized rationalism, even while Nietzsche was an "irrationalist." She was vigorously opposed to communism, and chose to point to Nietzsche's assertion of individualism while not pursuing the irrational.

Hollywood and RKO Pictures employed Ayn Rand, first as a filing clerk and then as the head of a department. She married actor Frank O'Connor and created a film script, *Red Pawn*, set in Russia. She wrote *Night of January 16* in 1933, and across the next years she wrote her first novel, *We the Living* (1936). This story was largely autobiographical, and it was set in Russia among the cultured classes. It featured the Argounovas and the Ivanovitches, who are tossed out and cast down by the Russian Revolution. They are ostracized because they do not belong to the Communist Party. Kira has an affair with the ruthless Andrei, who is connected with the secret police. He pays for Leo's time at a sanatorium, where Leo is recovering from tuberculosis. Kira tells him that she hates the ideals he stands for.[21]

Rand's political consciousness grew during this period. President Roosevelt's emerging coalition included workers and unions, liberal reformers and African Americans. Rand opposed the movement of the nation toward the political left. Her character Ellsworth Toohey represented what Rand viewed as the worst of left-wing politics and the leanings of some of the people she encountered in New York. Howard Roark, her exceptional heroic individualist, partly based upon Frank Lloyd Wright, was the shining light who opposed collectivism and conformity. He was an inventive and uncompromising individual, whereas Peter Keating was merely a copier: a mediocre second-hander. Dominique was the love interest, the sometimes dark, moody woman who could see that Howard Roark was doomed by a world that favored faceless, conforming people who dressed well and always played by the rules. Rand not only opposed Roosevelt's New Deal, she rejected what she saw as an overreach of state power into the realm of business. In 1937, Rand wrote a letter to the *New York Herald Tribune* protesting Roosevelt's court-packing scheme of adding liberal justices to the Supreme Court who would be favorable to his policy proposals. She argued that this was insidious: "No tyranny in history has ever been established overnight," she wrote.[22]

Rand's assertions in favor of free-market economics ran counter to the approach of economist John Meynard Keynes, which cast aside laissez-faire policies; Keynesian economics advocated government spending to stimulate the economy.[23] Rand joined the Wendell Willkie group and drew on arguments from Herbert Spencer and William Graham Sumner, whose positions tended toward social Darwinism. Meanwhile, Rand unequivocally asserted the value of a free-market economy.

The Fountainhead sold more than one hundred thousand copies in 1945 and was on the best-seller list. Readers appear to have been intrigued by the romance and risqué eroticism in the novel as much as by the ideas.[24] Roark is a strong male protagonist who meets Dominique when he works in her father's quarry. She asks that he be assigned to fix a marble fireplace. He smashes it up and gets another man to replace it. Dominique, on horseback, hits him with her riding crop. He comes in through her bedroom window. We witness the fortunes and misfortunes of their relationship. It is mostly at the final trial that Rand has a forum for Randian ideas and philosophical viewpoints.

The 1949 film version of *The Fountainhead* was directed by King Vidor; Rand wrote the screenplay. Howard Roark is played by Gary Cooper. Keating is portrayed by Kent Smith, Wynand by Raymond Massey, and Dominique by Patricia Neal. Rand had to shrink her seven hundred-page novel down into a manageable script. This led to unfortunate compromises for a novel that was about not compromising.[25] Rand had remained in contact with Hollywood throughout the 1940s, and in the spring of 1941, she was working for Paramount Pictures when she wrote her *Romantic Manifesto*. After writing *The Fountainhead*, she wrote two film scripts in 1945: *Love Letters* and *You Came Along*. During this time, Nathaniel Branden arrived in her life as an Ayn Rand enthusiast, and wrote extensively on Rand's Objectivism. Rand continued to believe that fiction could have important political consequences. These "sprang from her Russian background and her careful observation of the New York left."[26]

Critics of Ayn Rand point out that Rand's individualism lacks an embrace of social responsibility. It does not sufficiently recognize our relatedness and connection as social beings who learn from each other and owe something to each other. One may say that Rand herself has been given much by her intellectual forebears: Nietzsche, Spencer, her own father, and other influences. A critic may also ask if Rand's elitism is not inconsistent with democracy. Does this elitism predispose advanced capitalism to rule by a class of expert supermen or technocrats? To speak of a "democracy of superiors," as Rand does in her journals, appears to be a contradiction.[27]

JOHN DOS PASSOS

The swing of the political views of John Dos Passos from socialism toward conservatism puzzled some of his readers. His works following his U.S.A. trilogy, which concluded with *The Big Money*, suggest a somewhat gradual movement of his politics to the right. Social transformations and personal experience appear to have contributed to this shift. World War II America brought cultural changes, as did the subsequent postwar period. Americans like Dos Passos were forced by events to question their earlier views. In the 1940s, Dos Passos suffered personal losses. During this time, he appears to have fervently embraced his role as historian as well as novelist. The naturalist and modernist innovations of his previous work, those he is most remembered for, lay behind him now. He continued to write fiction and social critique in a more conventional style. In the late 1940s, his essays turned toward U.S. history, in search for America's values and traditions.

Readers may have wondered why Dos Passos seemed to take a sudden interest in Thomas Jefferson, or in Roger Williams. Why was he writing about Benjamin Franklin, John Adams, Joel Barlow, and Alexander Hamilton? Yet, there it was—a history of pivotal figures and founding fathers that Dos Passos no doubt hoped would speak to his readers in 1948–1949. He believed that these courageous individuals had set forth the constitutional principles and moral framework on which rested the nation and its future. Dos Passos asserted that, in times of crisis, we turn to history for precedents and clues to action, to seek answers to the questions of today. *The Ground We Stand On* (1948) bore the subtitle "The History of a Political Creed." Dos Passos begins this book by affirming "the use of the past," and in his first sentence, he declares: "Every generation rewrites the past." Then he immediately asserts that the crisis of the Second World War has created urgency for sure historical foundations, for, "in times of danger, we are driven to the written record by a pressing need to find answers to the riddles of today."[28]

Certainly, our present time is different, but the people who instigated and fostered the United States "were not very different from ourselves," Dos Passos reminds us.[29] We may ask how much of their past achievement is still part of our lives; their efforts, successes, and failures are "only alive in so far as some seeds and shoots of it are still stirring and growing in us today."[30] Dos Passos claims that poor history teaching has turned off people to history, yet he believes that a grasp of our past is essential. For example, looking back at the period immediately following the First World War, Dos Passos is critical of Woodrow Wilson and his "failure to pull anything worthwhile for America or for the world out of the peace."[31] Considering his contemporary situation, he sees both communism and fascism arising out of this incomplete resolution of that war, and he opposes both ideologies.

John Dos Passos crafted his innovative U.S.A. trilogy in the 1930s, looking back at an earlier time in American life. *The 42nd Parallel* (1930), *1919* (1932), and *The Big Money* (1936) present the lives of a few characters whose stories are told in a more complex fashion than in his earlier novel, *Manhattan Transfer* (1925). Devices like "Camera Eye" and "Newsreel" bring us the perspectives of film and newspapers, subjective consciousness and social awareness. Dos Passos gives his readers episodes that seem fragmentary, but are drawn together in the overall canvas of his trilogy. In his later trilogy, titled *District of Columbia*, Dos Passos affirms democracy. He launches a diatribe against communism in *Adventures of a Young Man* (1939), against fascism in *Number One* (1943), and against the New Deal in *The Grand Design* (1949). By this time, Dos Passos had become more conservative in his views and more traditional in his approach to the novel.

The interest that John Dos Passos took in Thomas Jefferson should not strike anyone as strange. His U.S.A. trilogy is a contemporary history in which he weaves notable figures with his fictional characters. In *The Ground We Stand On*, he studies Jefferson, Roger Williams, and Joel Barlow. He makes passing comments on Franklin, Adams, and Hamilton. The U.S.A. trilogy gathers news clippings, quotations, slogans, and songs, and uses phrases of the early decades of the twentieth century to capture the spirit of the American people in a moment in history. In *The 42nd Parallel*, Dos Passos included brief biographies of Luther Burbank, Eugene Debs, William Jennings Bryan, Big Bill Heywood, and references to the Wright Brothers. The figures he chose had become myths of the collective imagination.[32] This mythical gallery is entwined with Dos Passos's use of the devices of narrative, "Newsreel," and "Camera Eye." As the literary critic Alfred Kazin pointed out, this becomes a method of "turning even the individual life into a facet of history."[33]

The power of John Dos Passos's U.S.A trilogy was acknowledged by Norman Mailer when he called it "the most successful portrait of America in the first half of the twentieth century."[34] Implicit in this is Mailer's own wish to successfully portray America in the second half of the century, as J. Michael Lennon points out.[35] Dos Passos was fine for showing when people "are more the prey of social forces than the active element that changes society," Mailer told Paul Attanasio in a 1981 *Harvard Crimson* interview.[36] In that interview, Mailer asserted that fiction was a noble pursuit that transformed how people looked at their experience. He later wrote that he believed that he was expected to use his own eyes, his own words, to see the world "by the warp or stance of my characters."[37] Mailer's assertion about his work might have come from Dos Passos, however different their politics.

By the late 1940s, Dos Passos had traveled some distance from the positions he had once held as a writer on the political left in the 1920s. During those years he examined the modern condition and issues of the

First World War. He sought a new language, a path of artistic response to deal with this. This art, observes Kazin, was "the only possible new language—it would capture the discontinuities of the modern world."[38] With *One Man's Initiation* (1919), *Three Soldiers* (1921), and *Manhattan Transfer* (1925), Dos Passos was a dissenter, an experimental artist who commented on the violence of war, the rhythms of modernity, and the situation of the common man and woman amid the modern postwar world. The U.S.A. trilogy (*The 42nd Parallel, 1919, The Big Money*) was an inquiry into recent history, an innovative work of storytelling, and a call to conscience. Just as a poet like William Carlos Williams looked to ordinary language for the American idiom, Dos Passos was seeking a new style that would correspond to the fragmented modern world that was rushing headlong into the future.

The trilogy is set in the first decades of the twentieth century. *The 42nd Parallel* begins in 1900. The second volume, *1919*, is a searing indictment of the First World War. *The Big Money* reasserts that bureaucracy, industry, and commercial forces unleashed by the modern world are too much for the common man and woman. By the 1940s, Dos Passos is already onto another theme, which he repeats in *The Ground We Stand On*. He asserts that democracy needs the guidance of people of character whose skill and insight extends beyond the limits of the masses. The models for future leaders are to be seen in the founding fathers of the past. As he embraced this view, he continued to write both fiction and nonfiction. There was *Number One* (1943); *State of the Nation* (1944), which is set on the American home front and considers America's burgeoning industrial growth; and *Tour of Duty* (1946), set in Hawaii, the Marshall Islands, tours of the Pacific during the war, and later Berlin at the time of the Nuremberg trials.

In 1947, Dos Passos was shaken by a car accident in which his wife, Katharine Smith, died. *The Ground We Stand On* may be, in part, his regaining of his own personal ground in the steadiness of tradition. He eventually remarried, to Elizabeth Hamlyn Holdridge, and they settled in Virginia in 1950. The writer's turn toward the political right resulted in his support of the democratic conservatism of Harry F. Bird in Virginia. In *The Grand Design* (1949), a satiric novel, Dos Passos critiques the growth of bureaucracy from the New Deal. *The Prospect Before Us* (1950) examines the dominant ideologies in Europe and looks abroad to England and South America for ideas for the United States. His interest in Thomas Jefferson continued with *Washington, DC: Adventures of a Young Man* (1952). This appeared with *Number One* and *Grand Design* in a three-volume set. *Adventures of a Young Man* features a character named Glenn Spotswood, who is in Spain during the Spanish Civil War. This reflects Dos Passos's time there.

Appearing in 1949, *The Ground We Stand On* is a call for effective democracy. "How shall self-government work?" he asks.[39] History provides us with reference points. The founders of the American Republic subscribed to a vision of liberty, religious toleration, and rule of law. Dos Passos asks, "today in the nineteen forties, have we anything left of that world picture of 1776?"[40] His question remains relevant for us today for, as he says, "we do need to know which realities of our life yesterday and our life today we can believe in and work for."[41] By understanding the ground we stand on, we can recall the national identity that unites us.

THEODORE DREISER

Theodore Dreiser's moral evaluation of American society began with his novel *Sister Carrie* (1899), and his final works appeared in the 1940s. He was a writer from another era, one of the great naturalists and realists whose novel, *An American Tragedy* (1925), had probed the dark side of the American dream. His 1946 novel was a work of magnitude. *The Bulwark* traces the story of a Quaker family's decline in the face of capitalist materialism. The family moves from Maine to a place just outside Philadelphia, where society's search for wealth has begun to replace virtue and the simple spirit of Quaker life. Solon Barnes is caught between Quaker faith and spiritual discipline and an aggressive fortune-seeking capitalism in which a person's integrity may be lost. He observes nominal Quakers around him abandoning their values. Solon is determined to raise his five children as Quakers, but he watches as they drift off and follow their own paths in the new society. His principles are tested, but he ultimately endures. He is "one of the nation's bulwarks": a man of faith and kindness, a strong, moral, good man who will be an inspiration to the future. Dreiser followed this novel with *The Stoic* (1947), which focused on Frank Cowperwood's quest for power. In contrast with Solon Barnes, Frank is a man who lives for self-gratification. With these novels Dreiser concluded a trilogy that he had begun two decades before.

Dreiser passed away in 1945, a representative writer from an earlier age. Norman Mailer, whose work was just emerging following the war, later took up the thesis that American novelists do not write well about a class that is not their own. He referred to Dreiser and pointed to Marxist arguments of the 1930s that middle-class writers were not able to write effectively about the working class. There is a claim in the United States to a largely classless society, he observed. Earlier twentieth-century writers were rooted in immigrant ancestry, and were ineffective in representing upper-class characters or social contexts. Dreiser "came closer to understanding the social machine than any American writer that ever lived," wrote Mailer. In his hands, the novel could serve as a guide to "smash down doors now locked to him," but Dreiser could not describe these classes well. He would call a rich girl charming, but could not make her charming, says Mailer.[42]

Yet Dreiser was clearly a reference point for Mailer, whose fiction brought a new voice, a twist beyond Dreiser's style of naturalism and realism. In Lionel Trilling's critique of Dreiser in "Reality in America" (*The Liberal Imagination*), Trilling links Dreiser with Vernon Parrington, saying that they are both limited in their perspectives. They showed more the concrete "real" than the "electric qualities of mind" of "a complex and rapid imagination."[43] Trilling points to Henry James as an example of someone who had this kind of vivid imagination. Dreiser is considered more a writer of solid, steady work than one engaged in the play of intellect. Trilling asserts that Dreiser held political beliefs that were too incomplete for a complex modern era. When Mailer writes of Dreiser, it is much more positively. Mailer reflects on how literary reputation since 1945 is affected by response from "the academic community," says Donald Pizer.[44] Mailer says that Dreiser had the desire to transcend working-class realities. He was familiar with their many long hours of labor and limited leisure, and envisioned opportunity for a broader life. From a German immigrant family, Dreiser scrutinized the Horatio Alger myth of success and upward mobility with a keen eye to an individual's moral compass. That perspective on success and advancement in America seems to have never left him.

JOHN O'HARA

On the Broadway stage, the decade started off with the energy of the Rodgers and Hart musical *Pal Joey* (1940). The book for the musical was based on the short stories of one of the finest popular short-story writers of the 1940s: John O'Hara. "The United States in this Century is what I know and it is my business to write about it to the best of my ability," wrote O'Hara in 1960; "The Twenties, the Thirties, and the Forties are already history, but I cannot be content to leave their story in the hands of the historians and the editors of picture books. I want to record the way people talked and thought and felt, and to do it with complete honesty and variety."[45] This is exactly what John O'Hara did. It is what makes him—a popular writer perhaps more than a literary one—such an important barometer of his times. O'Hara, a fine writer of dialogue, catches what the poet William Carlos Williams called "the American idiom": the voice and pulse of America.

John O'Hara was from Pennsylvania, and he was drawn toward New York City when he attended Fordham Prep to prepare for admission into Fordham University. In the 1920s, this section of the Bronx was quite different from the busy, multiethnic world of Fordham Road that is near the university today. Fordham University was a relatively quiet enclave of gray stone buildings and trees and shrubbery, where the Jesuits lived and taught. O'Hara's Irish Catholic family preferred to send him to a Catholic school, and wanted to send him to the best one possible within their means. That meant a liberal arts education in the Bronx, where his classmates were often the children of Italian and Irish immigrant families. O'Hara, however, did not last at Fordham Prep. He was a rebellious soul and resisted the strictures and limitations of his social life there. He felt bored and alienated, and he broke with the Church and headed back to Pennsylvania. He was sent to work by his family as a laborer, a worker in the mines, and a porter at the Railway Express office. O'Hara developed a taste for bars, saloons, and dance halls. He associated with rough-edged working men who were employed in the mills of Schuylkill County. He took the trolley to meet young women in the dance halls, where big band music played. His education would be one of hard work on the job, jazz and drink in the evenings, and reading whatever he wanted to read. Yet, at eighteen, this was not enough. He decided to make another try at college. His family sent him to Niagara Prep. Niagara University is a Vincentian school near Niagara Falls, a Catholic university whose mission is grounded in the liberal arts and in St. Vincent de Paul's concern for the poor. John O'Hara still did not subscribe to the religious approach of his new school, but he did find it more to his taste than the prep school of his previous experience. Or, perhaps he had grown a bit and could deal with this new environment a little better than the one he had experienced at Fordham. At Niagara, O'Hara excelled at English, and became the class valedictorian.

O'Hara's biographer, Frank MacShane tells us that O'Hara often drifted through the town of Lewiston, New York, with a book and a pipe. O'Hara was coached in the art of drinking and smoking by an Irishman, Foxy Cole, at Fort Niagara. The self-discipline that O'Hara devoted to his studies did not necessarily extend to other areas of his life. On the night before his parents arrived to see their son as the class valedictorian, John O'Hara got uproariously drunk and was escorted back to his dorm by two state policemen.

The man who would write the stories that became the famed Rodgers and Hart musical *Pal Joey* was self-educated, creative, and iconoclastic. He went back home and worked as a journalist for the *Pottsville Journal*, the local newspaper. He filed a report that a man had shot his father to protect his mother. His editor William Kehoe insisted that he get his facts and details right, notes MacShane. It is something that O'Hara never forgot.[46] The drama of real life could be imaginatively developed and shaped into stories. O'Hara would seek to get at the stuff of experience, the stories of people's lives, the heartbeat of his times.

O'Hara moved to New York in the late 1920s. He lived for a time with relatives in East Orange, New Jersey, and commuted into New York City. He inquired into jobs with the *New York World* and the *New Yorker*, and landed a job with the *New York Tribune*. Mostly he was a rewrite editor, but journalism helped O'Hara focus on life, events, and people's stories. It was also a social occupation that connected with his natural sociability and his taste for bars and nightclubs. He became one of the first writers for *Time* magazine, and he fancied himself a late Jazz Age writer, sending stories to the *New Yorker*.[47] In 1929, O'Hara went to work for a Hearst newspaper, the *Daily Mirror*. In 1930, he was working with the *Morning Telegraph*, a popular-culture newspaper focusing on sports and entertainment.[48] He married Helen Ritchie Pettit, and they lived briefly in Brooklyn and then in Manhattan. Money was tight, and the marriage was a victim of financial strain, Helen's discontent, and O'Hara's drinking. In 1933, things fell apart.

Pittsburgh was the next site of John O'Hara's news gathering and prose. The *Bulletin Index* had become a society paper, and O'Hara became busy exploring Pittsburgh society. However, that did not last, and back to New York he went. There he lived in a small apartment on East 51st Street and hobnobbed with Dorothy Parker, Ira Gershwin, and other writers. Meanwhile, he wrote a novel set in Pennsylvania, which he called *Appointment in Samarra* (1934). His story of Jazz Age characters was partly inspired by F. Scott Fitzgerald, whom he met in New York. With America already deep in the Great Depression, O'Hara wanted to write a story of striking realism. It is a story set across three days in the lives of Julian English and his wife, Caroline. In it, Pottsville, Pennsylvania, becomes the fictional town of Gibbsville. Life for this couple is far from happy; Julian owes money to Reilly, and in anger he tosses a glass of whiskey into his face, bruising his cheek with the ice cubes in his drink. He becomes a social outcast in the town, and tensions with his wife escalate. He flirts with a mobster's girlfriend, and fights with Caroline, who says she is leaving. Julian shuts the garage door and turns on the ignition to his car: the last desperate act of his troubled life.

Julian English's experience parallels that of Scott Fitzgerald's admissions in "The Crack Up." As MacShane recognizes, O'Hara's character is of an age just following the Jazz Age generation: a generation to which prosperity came more easily, but then was affected by the Depression. Fitzgerald, MacShane points out, recognized a "widespread neurosis" that was wrecking his own generation.[49] Julian does not have the inner resources to confront depression, and has not developed the sensibility and values to cope with life's hardships. People in Pottsville did not like O'Hara's book, but Hollywood did. Or, at least a few people there saw promise in O'Hara; they invited him to work for Paramount Pictures. He was thirty years old and he threw his efforts into writing scripts.

O'Hara's time at Paramount was brief. By the mid-1930s, he was back in New York City. Adele Lovett, who met him at Dorothy Parker's apartment, was instrumental in introducing him to many writers in New York, like the songwriters Howard Dietz and Hoagy Carmichael, writers Russel Crouse, Robert Sherwood, and Robert Benchley, and financier Averell Harriman. O'Hara turned his attention to Broadway, to dramatic dialogue, and to writing more short stories. He published *The Doctor's Son* (1935), a book of short stories. The following year he was back in Hollywood. It was a fitful time, during which he was seldom sober. Among his screenwriter friends were Nunnally Johnson, Joel Sayre, and Budd Schulberg, who encouraged his interest in politics.[50]

In 1936, John O'Hara was approached with the prospect of adapting John Steinbeck's *In Dubious Battle*. Steinbeck's novel was about an agricultural workers' strike. Steinbeck liked some of O'Hara's stories, and he liked O'Hara, but preferred to work alone. John O'Hara did not care for what was then being called proletarian fiction. They met at Steinbeck's home in Pacific Grove. O'Hara was going to write a draft of a screenplay, but the script never happened.

Sometimes real life is stranger than fiction. Imagine meeting the love of your life at the Newark International Airport. That's what happened for John O'Hara. Actually, Belle Wylie was near him on the plane, exchanging glances with him. It wasn't until the plane landed for a stopover in Wichita, Kansas, that O'Hara finally spoke to her. Once in Los Angeles, O'Hara was invited to a party by Lucilla Potter, wife of director H. C. Potter. O'Hara attended the party, and across the room he saw a familiar face: the girl he had seen on the plane. Belle Wylie was Lucilla's sister. Small world, isn't it? Some might call it grace, or call it serendipity, synchronicity. Maybe some things are meant to be?

Hope of Heaven (1938), a California story about Peggy Henderson who works in a Beverley Hills bookshop, is rich in dialogue. However, the story did not do well critically or commercially. John and Belle Wylie O'Hara went overseas to Europe on an extended vacation. The change of atmosphere was exhilarating, but what he saw developing in Europe was ominous.

During difficult times, what people need is often not the kind of seriousness that O'Hara wrote into *Appointment in Samarra*. In hard times, people need entertainment; they need slices of life that are vibrant—social comedies, romance, and fun. Back in Hollywood with Belle, O'Hara went to work for RKO Studios to fix the dialogue in a film titled *In Name Only*. He then worked on screenplays for Twentieth Century Fox, during the time when Nunnally Johnson was adapting Steinbeck's *The Grapes of Wrath* for that motion picture company.[51]

While writing in Hollywood, he spent time with F. Scott Fitzgerald, who was living in Encino. O'Hara later recalled the pathetic quality of the relationship between Fitzgerald and Zelda, and how he took care of her as she deteriorated mentally. "The loneliness of his private hells was so enormous," O'Hara said.[52]

Years before, Fitzgerald had shared with O'Hara his manuscript of *Tender Is the Night* (1934). O'Hara knew that amid Fitzgerald's efforts at screenwriting in the late 1930s, he was at work on *The Last Tycoon* (1941). It was his final novel, one that Fitzgerald never finished. Edmund Wilson would call it "his most mature work." There were only six chapters of *The Last Tycoon*, and some drafts and a synopsis when Fitzgerald died. Perhaps it is, as Wilson said, "far and away the best novel we have had of Hollywood, and the only one which takes us inside."[53] In the story we meet Monroe Stahr, a film producer, who might lead film into a golden age, a new era. The story is narrated by Cecilia Brady, who is the daughter of an executive at Stahr's studio. Stahr is still remembering his deceased wife when Cecilia takes a fancy to him. Fitzgerald's notes suggest that Stahr was going to be involved in a power struggle between money and art, represented by Cecilia's father on the one hand and the screenwriters and directors on the other.

O'Hara, meanwhile, welcomed the money side of that equation, and he had become a well-known popular writer. He was given the go-ahead to write a script for *Moontide*, a film that was produced shortly before the 1930s came to a close. Shortly afterward, *Pal Joey* (1940) made a celebrity of O'Hara. Stories he had written for the *New Yorker*, George Oppenheimer told him at a party, would make for a delightful musical. They did.

The team of Richard Rodgers and Lorenz Hart Jr. that turned O'Hara's stories into a musical was one of the most successful in Broadway musical theater. Between 1935 and 1940 they created nine musical comedies—and then came *Pal Joey*. The play opened on Christmas evening at the Ethel Barrymore Theatre, and it starred a new dancing sensation: Gene Kelly. The hit song, "Bewitched, Bothered, and Bewildered," came from the lively score by Rodgers and Hart. Even if the lyrics were too risqué, the song was a keeper, and the show was an indisputable hit. John O'Hara's vision of humanity was realized onstage.

When the United States entered the Second World War, John O'Hara applied for a commission with the Navy, but was in unacceptable health. Meanwhile, at night the East Coast hunkered down in blackout for protection from U-boats or potential air raids. In Quogue, Rhode Island, where O'Hara spent summers, no one was permitted on the beach at night. Windows of homes with beachfront property were blacked out on the ocean side. Watching the war from the sidelines was not enough for O'Hara; he thought he might have his services engaged as a war correspondent. He took a job in the film section of the Office of the Coordinator of Inter-American Affairs, which was focused on Latin America. He became chief storyteller in a job that got no further overseas than Queens. He was then trained for the Office of Strategic Services (OSS) in Virginia. He grew a beard and called himself Doc, but nobody was fooled. He was a writer in poor health, and it showed. So much for becoming a spy!

John O'Hara finally became a war correspondent in 1944 for *Liberty* magazine. He was sent to Honolulu, where nightclub social life and beer drew more of his attention than war correspondence. However, he was soon on board the USS *Intrepid*, an aircraft carrier that now welcomes visitors where it is docked on the Hudson River in Manhattan. The *Intrepid* was bound to meet with the *Franklin* at Eniwetok in the Marshall Islands when a Japanese plane fired on it. The carrier returned fire with its antiaircraft guns. It was O'Hara's first and only taste of military action during the war. He was a correspondent for about two months and wrote little more than an article he called "Nothing from Joes," about soldiers and sailors who wrote letters home. These men were concerned that censors might read their letters, or that one of their letters might be their last. The SS *Kaskaskia* brought him to San Francisco, and from there he headed back home to New York.

O'Hara produced about twenty stories during the war years, amid days that were clouded in drink. He wrote the introduction to the *Portable F. Scott Fitzgerald*, which was edited by Dorothy Parker. Privately, he recognized how drinking might have abbreviated Parker's career and damaged Fitzgerald. Meanwhile, he continued to write for the *New Yorker*, although his relationship with the magazine was beginning to unravel. His sharp social observation continued to receive attention from readers.

Pipe Night (1945) appeared as O'Hara's fourth collection of stories. The stories are a varied bunch, ranging across the social strata and environments that O'Hara had exposure to—the upper class of Manhattan and Rhode Island, the economically deprived sections of Harlem and the Bronx, and the lives of hardworking men and women. There are characters who are judged by others according to their social class, characters who are emotionally oppressed, strangers in bars and clubs, people facing privation who sustain hope. O'Hara writes with sympathy for the downtrodden. A too-young college boy falls for a college girl at a tennis club. He waits in the parking lot for her, but then sees that she is being visited by a local cop on a motorcycle. The policeman is not one of the good ones, however. He forces the girl to see him, and the college boy must respond. In "Bread Alone," a black man takes his son, Booker, to a Yankee game. A foul ball flies toward them, but mysteriously disappears. After the game, Booker takes the ball out from under his shirt and presents it to his father. "You got it? The ball?" the father exclaims. "Sure. It's for you," Booker says. In "Graven Image," a pompous undersecretary is condescending toward a doorman. The undersecretary seeks to leave his car at the entrance to a Washington hotel. His action shows his diminished stature as a human being. In "Civilized," a woman is offered a heavy leather chair by the attorney who will work out her divorce settlement. The chair affects "comfort and warmth"; the attorney doesn't.

O'Hara's daughter Wylie Delaney O'Hara was born in the year those stories appeared. A proposed screen adaptation of a Sinclair Lewis novel fell through. O'Hara wrote a script for a story that was suggested by the actor Burgess Meredith, about a reporter asking questions and always getting different answers from people. The play was designed for Henry Fonda and James Stewart. O'Hara flew to Los Angeles and met the actors in Bel Air. He wrote a comedy sketch set in a jazz contest won by a female trombonist. Burgess Meredith obtained a deal from United Artists, and Fred MacMurray and King Vidor were assigned to direct the film. George Stevens and John Huston also contributed to *On Our Merry Way* (1948).

Pipe Night was published by Duell, Sloan and Pearce. O'Hara's *Hellbox* (1947), a collection of twenty-six stories, was then published by Bennett Cerf, who started Random House with Donald Klopfer. O'Hara made use of the Quogue setting in several of his *New Yorker* stories reprinted in his story collections. The stories suggest that relationships in this summer community were superficial. There is a man falling apart from alcoholism, a widow who wants to live through young people, a wartime doctor abandoned by his patients when the original town doctor returns from the war. Stories that O'Hara set in Hollywood include "Drawing Room B," the story of a Hollywood actor who was once wellknown but is now down on his luck. He shows his anger at an aspiring actor on a train. In "The Three Musketeers," three childhood friends are drawn into a conflict when the fiancée of one of them is put upon by the other two. There is a dark overcast tone to some of these stories. They deal with postwar characters that include navy flyers, students, people lacking friendship, and places lacking community. The stories demonstrate O'Hara's strength with dialogue, his sense of human sympathy, and his keen eye for contemporary social life. John O'Hara's stories are filled with social observation and images of the times.

JOHN P. MARQUAND

So Little Time (1943) by John P. Marquand is a novel set in the period immediately before the Second World War. Marquand envisioned a trilogy of novels with the war as their background: So Little Time, Repent in Haste (1945), and B. F.'s Daughter (1946). So Little Time's protagonist is Jeffrey Wilson. The story is set in a time of anticipating war. The original manuscript was 1,040 pages long, and was cut to 675 pages. Henry Seidel Canby had told Marquand, "You know this is in no sense a novel."[54] So Little Time was a Book of the Month Club choice and sold 469,000 copies through BOMC; the novel became a bestseller for several weeks alongside Lloyd Douglas's The Robe.

Early in the novel, Jeffrey's wife Madge complains, "You never tell me anything at all." Her comments suggest that she wishes for a broader life, one beyond home and friends. She wants to know of Jeffrey's business, to be part of his professional world. This suggests the separation of the spheres, a divide between the commercial and the domestic that was prevalent in the 1940s and 1950s. Jeffrey reasons, "[Y]ou could not share your whole life with anyone else in the world."[55] He recognizes that he and his wife have different perspectives and experiences.

Yet, Madge surprises him. Sometimes he thinks that she does not know anything about him. Then suddenly he discovers "she knew just what I was thinking."[56]

In reading Marquand today, one must get used to "darling": a term of endearment used often by his characters. In *So Little Time*, Madge calls Jeffrey "darling" five times in the first five pages. (Colloquial speech includes words like "swell.") Another feature of the novel is that chapters are each given titles. We begin with "Why Didn't You Ever Tell Me?" and the Joycean sounding "Portrait of the Artist as a Young Man." Madge's questions about their marriage are insecure and deeper than casual ones. She tells her husband: "Oh, don't worry so much about the war. You can't do anything about it, Jeffrey."[57]

The opening scene suggests that *So Little Time* will be an exploration of contemporary manners. The story is set in New York City, where Jeffrey and Madge have a view of the Chrysler Building and the changing light of the skyline. Yet the couple's breakfast could be taking place in any suburb or small town in America. There is casual normalcy, almost a tedium, to their conversation. Jeffrey says that he doesn't get into his day until about eleven o'clock. The backdrop of the war appears when Madge mentions the arrival of Walter Newcombe, a war correspondent back from the evacuation of Dunkirk who has written the book *World Assignment*. Jeffrey tells her that he is no friend, and that she wouldn't like him very much.[58]

Madge sounds the first discordant notes that suggest that things may not be so settled in the couple's relationship: "Even now these little things come out. It makes you like a stranger; it's like waking up and finding a strange man in the bedroom; it isn't fair."[59] By the time Jeffrey is finished with his breakfast, a reader may have already caught these underlying shadows. He is always leaving the newspaper twisted up, she says. All she can read are the obituaries. He has to put more money into the bank account so that the bills can be paid. He puts off social affairs.

The narrative moves smoothly into flashbacks, one of John Marquand's surest techniques. We are with Jeffrey on a train to Boston back in 1919, after the First World War. He recalls the stranger who sat down next to him and offered him a swig from a bottle of whiskey. "Is this seat taken, Bud?" the man asked him. The character appears in his mind like a sudden snapshot. The voice is colorful and quirky. He is a veteran who had tuberculosis, so they tossed him out of the army. But he can fight better than anybody, he insists. He is a prizefighter; note the blue spread eagle tattooed on his chest. That unexpected kind of encounter happened when Jeffrey was on his way to the telegraph room in Boston. That is where he met Walter Newcombe, he tells his wife (their conversation follows with four more expressions of "darling"). We follow the drift of Jeffrey's mind as he tries to return to the present from this recollection: "It's funny how people pop up when you least expect it," he says.[60]

Marquand's story points to one of the realities of American consciousness in the 1940s: "You could get away from the war for a little while, but not for long, because it was everywhere, even in the sunlight. It lay behind everything you said or did."[61] The narrative viewpoint implies that we are being given Jeffrey's perspective. Marquand places his social commentary in the mouths of his characters. Madge tells Jeffrey that most people don't like ideas: "They don't expect them from you—only from a celebrity, and you're not a celebrity."[62] Then Walter Newcombe, a journalist, becomes our center of focus during the next two chapters. "By thunder!" his boss, Mr. Jenks, exclaims. "I slept with that girl once in Berlin in 1885." The naïve young reporter responds: "But how could you? She's a statue, Mr. Jenks."[63] Yes, it is a wonder that Walter Newcombe has ever become a notable journalist. He has been to Dartmouth, but clearly he is no Jake Tapper of CNN. While Tapper, with his fine reporting, interviewing, and commentary is a credit to his profession, Marquand's Dartmouth graduate Newcombe is a puzzle to everyone. This signals that Marquand's social satire has subtly begun.

Marquand begins to take measure of American popular-culture heroes. There had been a shift in emphasis on the business icons of the twenties to the white-coated doctors of *The Microbe Hunters* and Dr. Kildare, and then to the glamorous role of foreign correspondents, who were viewed as men of the world. Of course, Marquand's tone is satirical, and we are told that this new hero is "just like you and me."[64] Yes, Walter Newcombe is an ordinary guy who the Book of the Month Club has made famous; the foreign correspondent who has been said to vibrate to the world is just like anyone else who "smoked cigarettes or drank milk . . . loved dogs and roly-poly children."[65] Walter is not a cultured individual; rather, he is one of "gullible acceptance" and "guileless simplicity."[66]

Jeffrey lives a different kind of life than does Walter, whom he soon encounters. He has a sense of imagined community. He considers organizations like Rotary, Lions, and the Elks, and he attends the Bulldog Club Dinner. He imagines that there are dozens of similar banquet dinners around the United States, and wonders if there is a comfort in doing the same thing, a companionship in which people together realize "a grim uncharted future."[67] The awkwardness of the festivities is underscored as the club president struggles with the microphone, which gets stuck, collapses, and causes a quick movement of his hands, which tip over a glass of water. The public address system is dreadful, and his voice booms throughout the room. This calls attention to his comments, which are satirically referred to as "solemn and world shaking."[68] Chairs fall over. Throats are cleared. Walter Newcombe is introduced, and he steps forward looking like Ichabod Crane in a windstorm. He wears a shirt with pointed lapels and high-waist trousers. His nasal voice rings out with a report of spring 1940 in England, and the current battle against Nazi Germany. When he claims that Germany is surrounded by "a ring of steel" and is "harassed [by the] economic forces of the French and the British Empire," it is clear that he is spouting propaganda. One attendee rises to ask Mr. Newcombe if he really believes any of this. The man is gaveled down, silenced by the club president, who thanks Newcombe for the fine and hopeful picture he has given everyone.[69]

Jeffrey joins Newcombe at the Waldorf. He recognizes that Newcombe represents impermanence, like a stay in a hotel room. A door swings open, and we meet a girl of about twelve or thirteen years old: Walter's daughter, Edwina. Her mother, Nancy, a nurse, skipped off one day with a Greek, leaving Edwina alone with Newcombe. The theme of marital problems returns. Newcombe has been reading of a different kind of war in Tolstoy's *War and Peace*, which he has never read before. His enthusiasm for the novel seems to betray that he is unaware of its enduring fame as a classic work of literature. "More people ought to know about that book," he says.[70]

Jeffrey insists on learning what is really going on in Europe. "You know better than to ask me that," Walter says. "Thank God we're here in America."[71] He passes through a city of taxicab drivers, doormen, and elevators, St. Bartholomew and Times Square.[72] The sidewalks are filled with people and he says that "the weight of their numbers made it impossible for you to think of them as individuals.[73] On Lexington Avenue, reaching for a key, he is home.

We meet Jeffrey's children, Jim and Gwen. The appearance of Jeffrey's college-aged son in chapter 6 shows us a difference in the perceptions of the father and the son in regard to the war. Jim views the First World War as a terrible mistake, a matter of "mass hysteria" and British propaganda.[74] Jim's reflections are interrupted as Gwen enters the room with her mother. Jeffrey observes his family, wishing he had never read any Sigmund Freud. Daddy is a "darling" too. He asks his wife about their daughter: "Where did she get that Daddy darling stuff?"[75]

A central character is Minot Roberts, who is arriving to pick up Jeffrey for the Air Squadron dinner. Minot is described as a "static" type of man who is lost in another time. He is "a little like the face of a clock that no longer ticked."[76] Minot is a World War I veteran who is addicted to humming little tunes that Jeffrey finds irritating. A well-off man, Minot is a godfather to Jim and gives him a fifty-dollar bill.

This is a novel of the home front: the daily life of New York East Siders, who are somewhat troubled by the news as the war creeps in. The headlines declare that the Nazis have laid siege to Denmark and Norway, landing in Trondheim and Narvik. It is winter 1940, and America's entry into the war is still months away. Walter Newcombe's cheery picture of some grand strategy to force Germany into Norway could hardly be right. Now, as the narrator says, "The show was on."[77] Jeffrey, at the theater with Marianna, calls the hotel for Walter Newcombe and gets Edwina on the phone. Walter has gone to London, and Jeffrey wonders how he lives that restless life. We follow Jeffrey and his wife to Westchester, Connecticut. On an October morning in 1940 Jeffrey notices that Wendell Willkie is campaigning for president.

Marquand spices up his novel with lines from popular songs. Beckie, in Connecticut, memorizes Shakespeare and reads the *New York Times Book Review*. She resists the Book of the Month Club, and asserts that she will make up her own mind about the books that she will read.[78] The chapter ends with Jeffrey's meditation that maybe he and his wife don't belong there. There is an image of tombstones, and Jeffrey says: "It was as if we were all dead and didn't know it."[79]

Marquand is at his best as he seamlessly transitions into flashbacks. Memories from the Great War return to Jeffrey, of his plane going down, his writhing on his left side on the grass, gasping for breath as he watched the plane burn.[80] He and Stan Rhett had to bail out. The memory comes back to him as if it is happening again—a German soldier appears, a rifle shot sounds. Jeffrey carries Stan on his shoulders. He stumbles and falls into the safe arms of a rescuer. In the light of a single candle, a major sees Jeffrey. "What about the other one?" he asks.[81] No, Stan didn't make it.

At 59th Street, Jeffrey decides to catch a taxi near the Plaza Hotel. At the park entrance is a statue of General William Tecumseh Sherman in gold, with a gold angel at his horse's head and the statue of a nude lady "basking in the sun."[82] Minot Roberts will be at the Clinton Club. In autumn 1940, across the Atlantic, the Battle of Britain rages in the skies. Jeffrey thinks it unimaginable to consider the recent fall of France.

Shadows from the Great War influenced John Marquand's attitude toward the Second World War. Throughout the war years, he remained very conscious of the war overseas. He enlisted and became involved with military intelligence, although he was too old to fight in the Second World War. John Marquand was of the generation of Hemingway and Fitzgerald. He was from a New England family who had been in America since 1732. Marquand was in college by 1911, and had a relationship with Christina Sedgwick, whose Uncle Ellery edited the *Atlantic* magazine. He served in the National Guard with the Massachusetts Field Artillery. While he was in the National Guard, he developed his ability to tell stories, often aloud. He also developed the flashback technique that he would use in his fiction. Later, he was in an officer's training camp in Plattsburg, New York. He was sent to France, and saw action in the bloody battle of the Vesle River and the Argonne.

In 1921, someone suggested to Marquand that he did not have the temperament for a business career. He had begun writing for the *Saturday Evening Post*, and became a client of the Brandt and Brandt literary agency. Marquand returned to France, among the expatriate writers of the 1920s. Back in the United States in the 1930s, he began his novel *The Late George Apley* (1937), a satire about a man in Boston, where life proceeded in expected patterns through each generation. The story was serialized in the *Saturday Evening Post*. The novel won the Pulitzer Prize in 1938, and later became a Broadway play and a film. (Ronald Colman played the title character in the film.) Marquand married Adelaide Ferry Hooker in 1937, and they had a child when Adelaide was thirty-seven and he was forty-seven. Adelaide's sister Blanchette was married to John D. Rockefeller II, and the Rockefellers became his in-laws.

Marquand is perhaps best known for his Boston trilogy: *The Late George Apley*, *Wickford Point*, and *H. M. Pulham, Esquire*. He satirized New England class consciousness, and critiqued society and its loss of traditions. The novels are reflective of a wider cultural sphere than Boston. *The Late George Apley* sold about fifty thousand hardcover copies; *Wickford Point* sold less well. His editor, Alfred McIntyre, speculated that serialization might have diminished sales rather than expanded them. During this time, Marquand traveled to Asia and explored Peking, China, and the Gobi Desert.

Marquand drew on his Asian experience for his popular Mr. Moto series. His story "No Hero" (1935) was supported by his adventures in Japan and Shanghai. He had been in Peking in March 1935, and met his second wife, Adelaide Hooker, in China. In his first Mr. Moto novel, K. C. Jones, a pilot, gets involved with an intelligence agent from Japan, Mr. Moto. Five more Mr. Moto stories followed; each one was a spy thriller that began as a serialized story and then became a book. The series included *Thank You, Mr. Moto* (1936), *Think Fast, Mr. Moto* (1937), *Mr. Moto Is So Sorry* (1938), *Last Laugh, Mr. Moto* (1942), and *Stopover Tokyo* (1957). *Thank You, Mr. Moto* focuses upon Peking (Beijing); *Think Fast, Mr. Moto* presents a character from New England, Wilson Hutchings, in a dramatic encounter in Honolulu with Mr. Moto. *Mr. Moto Is So Sorry* is about two Americans, Sylvia Dillaway and Calvin Gates, who are brought into issues between Japan and Russia while in Mongolia. These stories became a series of films with Peter Lorre in the main role. The character was discontinued during the war with Japan. Mr. Moto returned years later in *Stopover Tokyo*.

Diana Trilling, in *Harper's*, questioned popular fiction in "What Has Happened to Our Novels?" Americans were buying more books than ever in spite of a paper shortage. She argued that the quality of novels had declined since the 1920s. Pointing to Marquand's *So Little Time*, she asserted that Little, Brown had overused promotional tactics for a poor book by a hardworking author.[83] Marquand rejected Trilling's derision of the Book of the Month Club and became a BOMC judge in 1944, and was associated with middlebrow writing. He placed a literary cocktail scene in *So Little Time* because he disliked those occasions. His story "The End Game" appeared in *Good Housekeeping* in March 1944; *Repent in Haste* appeared in two installments in *Harper's*. *Point of No Return* was serialized in *Ladies' Home Journal* (1948).

Edmund Wilson compared Marquand's work unfavorably with Sinclair Lewis's novels, which "however much it may be open to objection, is at least a book by a writer—that is, a work of the imagination that imposes its atmosphere, a creation that shows the color and modeling of a particular artist's hand. But a novel by J. P. Marquand is simply a neat pile of typewritten manuscript."[84] In November 1945, *B. F.'s Daughter* was a selection of the Literary Guild Book Club. However, the Literary Guild editors, considering the romantic plot, wondered what Polly's future might be.[85]

After Pearl Harbor, Marquand believed that the war would be fierce. In 1941 and 1942, he spent time in Los Angeles for the filming of *H. M. Pulham, Esquire*. His critique of Hollywood emerged in *So Little Time*. He was in Washington, DC, in the winter of 1942, visiting Camp Dietrich. In 1943, he asked the War Department if he might work as a foreign correspondent overseas. He requested to go to China, and was attached to the company led by General James S. Simmons, an expert in disease control with the Surgeon General's office. Marquand entered the war effort in 1944 as a consultant to the Secretary of War, which meant that he had to be in Washington, DC during 1944 and 1945, an experience that led to his work on *B. F.'s Daughter*. He was briefly a war correspondent in the Pacific in 1945. Marquand collaborated with George S. Kaufmann on a play version of *The Late George Apley*, which was produced in 1946. *Repent in Haste* was serialized in *Harper's*, and was published as one of his shorter novels.

Repent in Haste (1945) is set in the Pacific, with Lieutenant Jimmy Boyden and William Briggs, a war correspondent. Boyden is from East Orange, New Jersey, which is a little more like Newark than suburban West Orange. Marquand was not likely familiar with this largely working-class town, and his fictional place falls short of realism. Jimmy is from a kind of middle-class neighborhood that does not exist in East Orange quite in the way that Marquand depicts it—as a place of "bad taste." *B. F.'s Daughter* features a female protagonist, Polly Fulton. There is the man she loves, Bob Tasmin, and the one she marries, Tom Brett, a public relations man. Her father, B. F., is a domineering, rich industrialist. She gradually discovers that she is much like him. Her husband has a mistress, Winifred James, a secretary. Discovering this, she confronts the woman. Winifred claims that Tom needs love, not someone with "so many perfect standards." Polly seeks out Bob Tasmin, who refuses her advances.

Point of No Return (1947) is one of Marquand's finest novels. This is a sociological study of a town affected by change. Charles Gray is from Clyde, Massachusetts, and he works at the Stuyvesant Bank. *Point of No Return* was written across three years. Marquand is sometimes remembered for this novel as a fiction writer about business, although he did not know a lot about business when he started writing it. To create a banker, he had to ask advice from a friend who was one. In the novel, money drives Charles Gray. He cannot make the money that the Lovells can make. He is at first not a convincing business character; Charles Gray needed some revising.

Marquand closed his writing of the 1940s by beginning a novel about a soldier with a code. *Melville Goodwin, USA* (1951) is narrated by a radio host, an unreliable narrator who ironically reveals aspects of American experience. *Melville Goodwin, USA* was his story of a military man who has a passing romance with Dottie Peale, a publisher's widow. The character was different from Hemingway's Richard Cantwell of *Across the River and Into the Trees*; he was also unlike Norman Mailer's General Cummings in *The Naked and the Dead*, through whom Mailer critiqued the power and authority of such officers. Herman Wouk, in contrast, supported authority and naval discipline in *The Caine Mutiny* (1951). In 1952, the Pulitzer Prize for fiction was awarded to Wouk's novel, which sold 236,000 copies. The National Book Award went to James Jones's *From Here to Eternity*, which sold 240,000 copies. Marquand remained popular; in the 1950s, he produced *Thirty Years*, a volume of short stories, and the novels *Sincerely, Willis Wayde* (1955) and *Women and Thomas Harrow* (1958).

JOHN STEINBECK, *CANNERY ROW*

Cannery Row (1945) was a comic response to several hard years of war. After Steinbeck's *The Grapes of Wrath* (1939) won the Pulitzer Prize for its searing critique of the farmworkers' situation in California, Steinbeck made an expedition down the coast to the Sea of Cortez with his friend Ed Ricketts, a marine biologist. He was then engaged in propaganda for the U.S. government war effort, and went overseas as a correspondent. *Cannery Row* was a sharp turn away from all this seriousness into the playful story of a sympathetic group of workers in Monterey, who want to make enough money to give a party to their friend Doc.

Cannery Row brings us to Lee Chong's grocery and to the Palace Flophouse, where Mack, Hazel, Eddie, Hughie, and Jones will live. Mack is the central character, and he is the group's ringleader. Doc's Western Biological Laboratory is nearby. Doc has a library or music room, where he listens to classical music or plays it for his romantic dinners with women. His companions are "Dora's girls," the prostitutes who are managed by Dora, a woman with flaming orange hair who wears garish green dresses. Daily, Doc collects marine specimens in the Great Tide Pool at the tip of the peninsula, accompanied by Hazel, a young man who sometimes finds Doc's preoccupations peculiar. Mac insists that they should give Doc a party. To get money for a party, they borrow Lee Chong's Model T truck and head out to capture frogs. They will sell the frogs to Doc, whose payment to them will pay for his own party.

Cannery Row brought America some lighthearted laughter in 1945, the final year of the Second World War, when it was much needed. Steinbeck was now writing short novels like *Cannery Row*, almost as "exercises," in between his longer works. Soldiers had asked him to write something funny that wasn't about the war, and he responded by producing *Cannery Row*.

BERNARD MALAMUD

Bernard Malamud (1914–1986) wrote stories that were set somewhere between realism and fantasy. His first stories, published in little magazines, give us a glimpse into 1940s America in Brooklyn. Malamud was the son of a grocer; he attended City College, and then taught at Lafayette High School. He took a job recording the 1940 census in Washington, DC. While in Washington, Malamud wrote an article about the fall of France for the *Washington Post*, and a short story, "Armistice." After returning to New York, he attended Columbia University, where he wrote a masters' thesis on the poetry of Thomas Hardy. Malamud's stories, carefully crafted, came slowly to him. Readers could find them in *Assembly, Threshold, New Threshold, American Prefaces*, and other magazines that have faded away. He married Ann Chiara in 1945, and they had two children: Paul, in 1947, and Jenna, in 1952.

In the 1940s, Malamud applied himself to the familiar dictum, "write what you know," and his stories were etched with striking realism. One reads of Jewish life in Brooklyn, and the grocery store that his father operated. The first seventy-eight pages of *The Complete Stories* offer ten stories that were written from 1940 to 1950. After "Spring Rain" appeared in *PVS* in 1942, "Grocery Store" was also published in that magazine. There were many stories in 1943: "Steady Customer" and "Benefit Performance" appeared in *New Threshold* and *Threshold* magazines, respectively; "This Place Is Different Now" was in *American Prefaces*. Other classic Malamud stories appeared later in the decade. "The Cost of Living" was published in *Harper's Bazaar* in 1949. In 1950, "The Prison" was in *Commentary*, and "The First Seven Years" was in the *Partisan Review*.

This master of the short story abandoned his first attempt at longer fiction. He then wrote *The Natural* (1952), the baseball novel that is among his best known and enduring works. Malamud became one of America's most important writers between the 1950s and the 1980s. *The Assistant* (1957) won the American Academy and Institute of Arts and Letters Rosenthal Award. *The Magic Barrel* (1958), a short-story collection, featured the often-anthologized title story. Malamud wrote six more novels: *A New Life* (1961), *The Fixer* (1966), *The Tenants* (1971), *Dublin's Lives* (1979), *God's Grace* (1982), and *The People* (1989), which lay incomplete upon his death. He won the Pulitzer Prize and the National Book Award for *The Fixer*.

JOHN CHEEVER

The Chelsea Hotel was bankrupt in 1938. In 1939, it was purchased by new owners, and John Cheever (1912–1982) took a room there. The Chelsea was where Thomas Wolfe had lived on the eighth floor, and was where Cheever was just lonely and depressed.[86] The storied history of the 23rd Street hotel drew artists and writers to its rooms many years afterward. Dylan Thomas, ill with pneumonia, raged against the dying of the light. Jack Kerouac wrote *On the Road* there, and Arthur C. Clarke wrote *2001*. Maybe there was some inspiration in the air. In 1940, John Cheever's stories began appearing regularly in the *New Yorker*. In the summer of 1940, three of his stories were in the *New Yorker*, two in *Harper's*, one in *Collier's*. Novelist William Maxwell, for a time his editor at the *New Yorker*, encouraged Cheever toward revisions. Cheever read Anton Chekhov stories to focus his fiction.[87] "The Happiest Days" appeared in the *New Yorker*; "I'm Going to Asia" was published in *Harper's Bazaar* in September 1940, and was one of the stories in the O. Henry Award Prize Stories of 1941. Cheever married Mary Winternitz in New Haven on March 22, 1941.

Standing in Times Square on December 8, 1941, Cheever looked up at the banner lights on the Times building announcing the news. Life was about to change for millions of Americans. "All I know about war is what I saw in the movies ten years ago," he wrote to Josephine Herbst.[88] He enlisted, reported to Fort Dix, and was sent to Camp Craft in Spartansburg, South Carolina. In August 1942, his platoon was sent to Camp Gordon in Augusta, Georgia, and he began writing army stories. Cheever was moved to Special Services, and he edited a regimental newspaper, *The Double Deuce*. Meanwhile, he wrote stories about life in the army and the war's effect on civilian life. On leave in September, he visited his wife and family and met with Bennett Cerf of Random House, who would publish a volume of his stories. The short-story collection was called *The Way Some People Live*, and the first printing of 2,750 copies sold fewer than 2,000 copies. In January 1944, Cheever's regiment was sent overseas, first to England, and then cast into the fierceness of the European conflict. Now in the Special Services, Cheever did not join the 2nd Infantry Regiment. The men that Cheever had trained with were killed in action. He was a survivor.

He was assigned to the Signal Corps to create propaganda. In Astoria, Queens, Cheever wrote scripts for *Army-Navy* magazine at Paramount Studios. He took the subway there from his apartment on West 22nd Street. He worked alongside William Saroyan and Irwin Shaw, and cartoonist Charles Addams.[89] Money was tight when the Cheever family moved uptown. He thought about going overseas as a reporter, but Signal Corps kept him at work in New York. In April 1945, Signal Corps decided to send him to Guam and to Manila, which had been shattered by war. Biographer Blake Bailey points out that Cheever's brief time in the army as a Signal Corps writer was the only full-time job he ever had.

In 1945, Cheever moved to Sutton Place—one of his short-story settings. There the Cheevers were in the midst of well-off "dignitaries we can't afford to tip," wrote Mary Cheever. Cheever had a contract for a novel with Random House. The story he had begun, *The Holly Tree*, would later become *The Wapshot Chronicle*. During this time, Cheever appeared to be more effective with his short stories than with his effort in writing his novel, which drifted, floundered, and never quite landed. Cheever wrote "The Sutton Place Story," which was later selected to lead off *The Short Stories of John Cheever* (1978). In the story, Deborah Tennyson is a little girl who "knew about cocktails and hangovers." She is in the care of Renee, a sometime prostitute characterized by instability, drink, and depression. In "The Enormous Radio," Jim and Irene Wescott live on the twelfth floor at Sutton Place, with their two children. They love music and they love their new radio, and are surprised as its crackling sound brings the voices of their neighbors into their own living room. Irene hears "demonstrations of indigestion, carnal love, abysmal vanity, faith and despair."[90] Even when the radio is fixed, it gives the Westcotts the disturbing news of the world's tragedies and violence.

Blake Bailey tells us that Cheever observed in the suburbs that "improvised way of life" in their postwar expansion from the city.[91] He wondered how he might capture "the experience of his generation."[92] An attempt to rewrite Cheever's stories for the stage by Herman Mankiewicz and George S. Kaufmann in 1948 was not particularly successful. "Town House" closed after nine days (September 23 to October 2, 1948). Cheever's novels include *The Wapshot Chronicle* (1957), *The Wapshot Scandal* (1964), *Bullet Park* (1969), and *Falconer* (1977). His stories established him as one of the most significant short-story writers of the twentieth century.

MARY MCCARTHY

In the 1960s, Irving Stock referred to Mary McCarthy as "a sort of neoclassicist" who had a "satirical eye for the hidden ego in our intellectual pretensions."[93] In McCarthy, we recognize a writer who evidently enjoyed being antagonistic. In *The Company She Keeps* (1942), she gives us six chapters that were originally published as stories in magazines. She told the *Paris Review* that she had begun to think of these stories as one unified story. Stock points out that her character, Margaret Sargent, appears to be one that is filled with traces of McCarthy's autobiography. She struggles for truth, says Stock, "in the intellectual life of her time."[94] She begins her story collection with a satire on manners, and the portrait of a married woman with a secret: she is having an affair with a younger man. In "Rogue's Gallery," we see Margaret Sargent working for a rogue and con man at an art gallery. "The Man in the Brooks Brothers Suit" follows Margaret into an affair with a man on a cross-country trip. She has drunken sex with him, and she is hesitant to leave him. The stories that follow are titled "The Genial Host" and "Portrait of the Intellectual as a Yale Man." Jim Barnett becomes a radical political commentator. Margaret works for a conservative magazine, but still sends checks to the American Civil Liberties Union.

After Mary McCarthy married the literary critic Edmund Wilson, they bought a house in 1939, at Wellfleet on Cape Cod. Wilson encouraged her to begin writing fiction in those years between 1940 and 1945. The tensions between them inevitably became a concern in her life and her work. She went into psychoanalysis, and traveled for sessions to New York. Her pregnancy in 1942 resulted in a miscarriage. Wilson wrote some poetry while living on Cape Cod, and wrote book reviews for the *New Yorker* in 1943. A fellow critic, John Peale Bishop, who had settled in South Chatham at a home he called "Sea Change," died in Hyannis on April 4, 1944. Wilson and McCarthy separated in 1944. They were each married again to other partners by 1946. Mary McCarthy's "The Weeds" (1944), written during this time, begins with the figure of Persephone. In the myth, Hades has abducted Persephone, and Demeter can only partially rescue Persephone from hell. She returns for warmth of the spring and summer.

Mary McCarthy's reputation evolved as a liberal intellectual who focused on progressive politics, art, and education throughout the 1940s. She has been described as contentious, cerebral, and cutting. In 1947, McCarthy wrote that she saw American public intellectuals as "critical and rather unproductive."[95] In Hannah Arendt she saw "tremendous intellectual power with great common sense."[96] However, other thinkers did not appear to be offering the same level of inquiry and vigorous public contribution.

Mary McCarthy spoke her mind. William Barrett said that she wrote with "an acid pen."[97] She had "a tough critical outlook, an adversarial habit of mind," notes Beverly Gross, who has called McCarthy "our leading bitch intellectual," while others spoke of the "clinical, dispassionate, acerbic dissections Miss McCarthy performs on her fellow human beings."[98] Doris Grumbach simply said that she was "frank."[99] She became more prominent during the 1950s, and offered some autobiographical recollections in *Memories of a Catholic Girlhood, How I Grew* (1957). McCarthy was a satirist, a sexually sophisticated writer who broke through stereotypes and provided sharp social observations.

McCarthy's fiction also aroused some ire. Some critics charged her with drawing her fiction from life and real people. She was a novelist of manners and some saw in her work a lack of fully developed characters. Norman Mailer attacked McCarthy's novel *The Group* (1963) in an essay, "The Case against Mary McCarthy." He claimed that she failed out of "the accumulated vanity of being overpraised throughout the years for too little."[100] Some critics might direct Mailer's own comment at him. He and McCarthy were certainly fiery writers who could stir the cauldron and create a strange, troubled brew of critique and calamity.

6

POSTWAR AMERICA AND THE
AGE OF ANXIETY

There was an inch of snow on the ground at the inauguration, on Saturday, January 20, 1945. A red uniformed Marine band played "Hail to the Chief." Roosevelt rose in his leg braces, assisted by James Roosevelt and a Secret Service man. He shook hands with Harry Truman. Justice Harlan Stone stood with Roosevelt, who held to the rail beside him and took the oath. His speech was brief. "We have learned to be citizens of the world, members of the human community," he said, pointing to the nation's alliances, commitments, and future of global involvement.

Four months later, in May 1945, *Time* magazine summed up the violence and heartbreak of the Second World War by underscoring its moral significance:

> This war was a revolution against the moral basis of civilization. It was conceived by the Nazis in conscious contempt for the life, dignity and freedom of individual man and deliberately prosecuted by means of slavery, starvation, and mass destruction of noncombatants' lives. It was a revolution against the human soul. [1]

When it was over the soldiers and sailors came home. A girl crossing Times Square was swept up by a sailor in a celebratory embrace. There was music and they danced and they cried together. Americans started families. They built suburbs. They chased dreams and sought prosperity. The men and women of the United States had fought bravely on two fronts, in Europe and against Japan in the Pacific. Nearly three hundred thousand Americans had died in combat, serving their country in the Allied cause.

STORIES, ISSUES, AND TRENDS

They came home with their stories. Some they shared. Some they never told. They greeted their families of origin and started their own. There was work to be done. Yet there was also leisure: baseball, card games, the paperback book, and the new phenomenon of television. Popular fiction blossomed between the end of the First World War and the time of the Second World War. The 1940s saw a gradual climb in book sales, despite paper shortages. Book sales especially increased after 1945. Within the next fifteen years there was a 250 percent increase in book sales.[2] Paperback books had emerged with Pocket Books in 1939. In 1946, about 60 million paperbacks were published; this more than tripled by 1953.[3] In 1945, John Steinbeck's *Cannery Row*, set near Monterey, offered a light, comic diversion from war. John Hersey's *A Bell for Adano* became a feature film. *A Tree Grows in Brooklyn* (1943) continued to be popular. Joe was coming home to Stella in Pittsburgh in Lester Cohen's aptly titled *Coming Home*. Sinclair Lewis's *Cass Timberlaine* offered the dramatic story of a congressman turned judge, who has an affair with a younger woman. (Jinny, from a Minnesota town, then has an affair with another man.) Young readers were entertained by Nancy Drew and Hardy Boys mysteries. Their parents encountered the films that were being produced from the mysteries of Dashiell Hammett and Raymond Chandler. Issues of race appeared in Chester Himes's *If He Hollers Let Him Go* (1945). Meanwhile, the science fiction magazine story was beginning to be published in paper-bound books. These stories suggested how humanity might use science to meet with social and technical issues, alien beings, and civilizations that were set in remote places in the future. They often implied the concerns and dilemmas of the present.

In 1945, people were reading historical fiction that took them away from present harshness to other eras. The year's best sellers included Lloyd Douglas's *The Robe*, Thomas B. Costain's *The Black Rose*, and Samuel Shellabarger's *Captain from Castile,* set during the Spanish

Inquisition and the expedition of Cortez. There were also James Ramsey Ullman's *The White Tower*, and Kathleen Leiser's *Forever Amber*, an English seventeenth-century romance that was banned as pornography in fourteen states. Upton Sinclair's *Dragon Harvest* appeared as the latest installment in his historical fiction series. In a room at Columbia University, Jack Kerouac was writing *Orpheus Emerged*, a manuscript that lay hidden for years and was published in 2002. In Brooklyn, playwright Arthur Miller was writing his novel *Focus*, critiquing racism and anti-Semitism.

Chester Bowles's *Tomorrow Without Fear* (1946), a nonfiction book, raised questions about what would occur if Roosevelt had continued to pursue the New Deal. Bowles asserted that the war had changed the economy; it had improved America's standard of living. Government spending on public works, health, and education had given a boost to the economy. Bowles concluded that if the government could aim to provide full employment, willing consumers would follow.[4] Truman recognized these goals, and appointed several conservatives to his cabinet.

Meanwhile, the postwar transition rumbled throughout U.S. industry. Following the war, some eight hundred thousand aircraft industry workers were laid off. On November 20, 1945, General Motors employees went on strike and 225,000 workers walked out. Two months later, 800,000 steel workers and 174,000 electrical workers went on strike. The return of veterans from overseas, of course, was welcomed by their wives and girlfriends at home. However, demobilization affected working women. Women workers constituted about 25 percent of the auto industry during the war years. They were only 7.5 percent of the workforce as of April 1946. From September 1945 to November 1946, more than half a million women's jobs disappeared.[5] Pay for women remained lower than that of men.

Immediately after the war, women were often portrayed in film as "powerful, unpredictable, possessed of a mysterious power . . . that eluded control," says historian William H. Chafe. However, he observes, this reverted to a pose of innocence in the 1950s. A naïve Marilyn Monroe and a placid Doris Day replaced the feisty Katharine Hepburn and Greer Garson, Chafe notes. Male culture continued to emphasize "individualism, courage, strength."[6] The Marlboro Man came home to the sweet and conscientious homemaker. By 1950, nearly 60 percent of all eighteen- to twenty-four-year-old women were married. There had been 42 percent in this age range married in 1940. In the baby boom of the 1940s, the U.S. population grew by 19 million, or at more than twice the pace of the 1930s. In the 1950s, America added 30 million people.[7]

The GI Bill was created by Congress in 1944. Following the war, the soldiers and sailors went back to work. Trade school and college attendance increased. The suburbs began to grow and extend outward from America's major cities. Couples were having babies. Dr. Benjamin Spock's *Pocket Book of Baby Care* was published in June 1946, and sold 60 million copies within a year. Three times as many baby care books were sold by 1953.[8] In 1946, more than two hundred mass-market magazines appeared.[9] Radio bought music, news, and drama to listeners. Sponsors became a commercial force in radio in the 1940s as producers tracked audience response via the Hooper system, instituted in 1935. Before this, the impact of radio advertising had centered on popular magazines.[10] Television reached 6 percent of American homes by 1949; this rose to about 76 percent by 1956 and nearly 90 percent by 1960. (Today, of course, television is ubiquitous; its presence in restaurants and bars and waiting rooms is pervasive.)

The American economy began to take a turn toward increasing prosperity and industrial might. The Employment Act of 1946, as a safeguard, permitted a government role in the effort to avoid a postwar depression. The goal of the Employment Act was to create job opportunities. Following the war, military spending receded, freeing more federal funds. Economists like John Meynard Keynes and William H. Beveridge challenged Adam Smith's notion of the invisible hand and the self-adjusting economy, and sought government involvement. Beveridge advocated this in his book *Full Employment in a Free Society* (1945). He asserted that unemployment was a moral problem the nation had to overcome. The Farmers Home Administration Act (1946) emerged from the Dust Bowl concerns of the 1930s and the Resettlement Act of 1935. The development of price controls and farm loans evolved into the Farm Credit System.

Postwar Americans sought security, and economic growth brought a measure of that for many people. However, almost one-quarter of the nation could not survive on their limited income.[11] The richest in America welcomed a rise in their income from 19.3 percent to 25 percent of total U.S. income; the richest 1 percent held one-third of the nation's wealth. The disparity in income, which Senator Bernie Sanders argued about in the 2016 presidential primaries, was an issue then as it is now. The bottom 20 percent in income earnings held less than one-half of 1 percent of the nation's wealth. The GI Bill, Federal Housing Authority (FHA) loans, and Veterans Administration (VA) loans contributed to some upward mobility. Yet, the "other America" of Appalachia, the rural South, and urban areas was still a distressing reality.

The postwar period also brought looming concerns about the new forces of atomic power that had been unleashed upon the world. The Atomic Energy Act (1946), also known as the McMahon Act, established the Atomic Energy Commission to oversee and regulate uses of atomic energy. At first there was hope that the United States could keep atom-bomb science and technology shrouded in secrecy. A central body of lawyers and administrators were the regulators, rather than scientists. In hindsight, attempts at secrecy were ineffectual, and this approach to regulation had to be adjusted. Concerned that fissionable materials could be diverted to other states or individuals, Congress sought protections and licensing.

PRESIDENT HARRY S. TRUMAN

Harry Truman was underestimated by some people. Most saw him for the practical politician that he was: a no-nonsense man from Missouri. Truman was a thinking man and a voracious reader, a man with an inclination toward books. President Truman had a good grasp of foreign affairs and world geography. He read Shakespeare, the Greek historians Herodotus and Thucydides, classic novels, and Cicero in Latin.[12] Harry Truman came from a household of books, and he read constantly. His daughter Margaret, who became a novelist, was surrounded by books, and recalled her father being immersed in reading.[13] A presidential aide commented that Truman was "a prodigious reader" who would absorb a great deal of material.[14] That reading habit continued throughout his lifetime. Margaret Truman said that her father's idea of heaven would be a comfortable chair, a reading lamp, and lots of books he wanted to read.[15]

In the 1940s, America began reading about Harry Truman. The senator traveled in his car to inspect military installations to make sure that they were well equipped and using tax dollars wisely. He became the leader of a Senate committee that studied the issue. President Roosevelt chose him as his running mate. Vice President Truman succeeded him in April 1945. He faced the consequential decision of whether to use the atom bomb in the war against Japan, and he had no regrets about the dropping of the bombs. *Time* named Harry S. Truman Man of the Year for 1945.

As the Second World War expanded U.S. global involvement, Truman remained focused on domestic concerns as well. Harry Truman was the first American president of the twentieth century to take a strong stand on civil rights. He had come from a Missouri background in which the vernacular we hear in Mark Twain's novels was prevalent.[16] Yet, he firmly upheld initiatives for civil rights for all Americans. Truman arrived with the Missouri delegation to the Democratic convention in Chicago on July 14, 1940. Earlier, he had told the black audience at the National Colored Democratic Association Convention in Chicago that creating educational opportunities for African Americans would be beneficial for all Americans.[17] Truman won his seat in the Senate by close to 8,000 of the 665,000 votes cast in the election, including a strong margin in the African American vote.[18] Later, as president, Truman sought stronger statutory protection of the right to vote. He also sought laws to stop discrimination in employment and in travel across state lines by bus, train, or airlines.

Truman's civil rights actions went beyond the African American population and their significant issues and concerns. In Chicago on April 14, 1943, Harry Truman spoke out in support of Europe's Jews, who he said were being "herded like animals." Rabbi Stephen Wise of the American Jewish Congress and Judge William J. Campbell were the keynote speakers for the conference at which Truman spoke. "Merely talking about the Four Freedoms is not enough," Truman said, referring to Roosevelt's inaugural speech. "This is the time for action." Truman argued that the people of Europe "must be made free" and not rudely subjected to the "mad Hitler." He declared the need to save people from "systematic slaughter" and pointed to the need to secure a democratic future. It was, as biographer David McCullough points out, a remarkable speech. Perhaps it can be said to be one that anticipated his presidency. (The theme of securing a democratic future in Europe, as well as asserting the need for the containment of communism in Asia, would be central features of his presidency.) Truman said that "we must do all that is humanly possible to provide a haven and a place of safety for all those who can be grasped from the hands of the Nazi butchers."[19] The way to do this was to draw on "our traditions of aid to the oppressed and our great national generosity."[20] Truman had begun to speak of the international responsibilities of the United States. It would be the role of the United States to assume leadership in the postwar world. His nation, he said, could not possibly "avoid the assumption of world leadership after the war."[21] He wanted Congress to investigate and respond to the wartime confinement of Japanese Americans. In 1948, the year of the United Nations Declaration of Human Rights, Truman insisted that the U.S. Constitution and the Bill of Rights could act as guidelines for social justice.

Truman was tenacious in the political arena. In the fall 1946 election, Republicans gained control of the Congress, with 246 to 188 members in the House and 51 to 45 members in the Senate. (There were 48 states at the time.) In 1948, many political pundits wondered if there would be a split in the Democratic Party. Much of the South would follow Strom Thurmond and the States Rights Party. The new Progressive Party had Henry Wallace as their champion. In 1946, Wallace had called for free trade in Eastern Europe and accommodation with the Soviet Union. Truman vetoed the Taft-Hartley Act in 1947. He addressed the anticommunist sentiments that had begun to be felt more broadly among the American public. He focused upon the New Deal and civil rights to bring along his liberal constituents.

The 1948 Democratic National Convention took place in Philadelphia from July 12 to July 14. Harry S. Truman was nominated, with Alben W. Barkley of Kentucky as his running mate. The convention is notable for the strong pro-civil rights speech that was made by Hubert Humphrey, then the Minneapolis mayor. Humphrey argued that the American people should "get out of the shadow of states' rights and walk forthrightly into the bright sunshine of human rights." The civil rights plank was adopted in a fairly close vote that required overcoming some Dixiecrat opposition from the Mississippi delegation, who walked out of the convention. Hubert Humphrey was elected that year to the U.S. Senate. The incumbent, Harry Truman, received more than 75 percent of Democratic National Committee votes, and was nominated without any difficulty.

On July 26, 1948, Truman signed Executive Order 9981 ending racial segregation in the military. This was a strong acknowledgment of the commitment of African American soldiers and sailors who fought for their country in the Second World War. On August 25, the House Un-American Activities Committee (HUAC) held a televised hearing on the confrontations between Whittaker Chambers and Alger Hiss, which had become a contentious issue.

Truman was a man of the people, an individual who could identify with the factory worker, the shop owner, the independent farmer, the mother buying groceries and raising her family. William Safire records Truman's campaign speech in Elizabeth, New Jersey: "The big fundamental issue in this campaign is the people against the special interests." Of course, Truman was arguing that those special interests were principally what the Republican Party then stood for. Presumably the country was "enjoying the greatest prosperity it has ever known" because of Roosevelt's policies. What American needed was 61 million people at work, and to establish fair prices, affordable housing, Social Security, and fairly distributed income.[22]

The 80th Congress of the United States met from January 3, 1947, to January 5, 1949. Republicans had gained a majority in both chambers, acquiring 13 more Senate seats and 57 seats in the House of Representatives. Truman called this the "do-nothing Congress," despite the fact that that Congress passed 906 bills. The 80th Congress passed the Taft-Hartley Act, which Truman spoke out against on his train whistle-stop campaign tour.

Truman posed a strong argument against the Republican congressional majority that focused upon a populist message: "Did the Republican leaders care what happened to you in the Depression?" he asked. "Did the Republican administration provide the jobs you needed?" His Republican opponents were "driven by the forces of reaction," he said; what was needed was a "forward looking" government.[23] His train-stop tour and his appeals to the American people resulted in his close margin of victory.

Most Americans will be familiar with that memorable photo of a smiling Harry Truman holding up the newspaper headline "Dewey Defeats Truman." Many political pundits predicted that Truman would not win the 1948 election. Truman proved them wrong. On November 2, Truman won the general election and the Democrats regained control of the House of Representatives. They held this until the Republican "revolution" led by Newt Gingerich brought widespread Republican victories in 1994. Truman had begun to forge what Godfrey Hodgson called "the liberal consensus."[24]

THE COLD WAR

On March 5, 1946, speaking at Westminster College in Fulton, Missouri, Winston Churchill declared that an Iron Curtain had fallen upon Europe. The world had been plunged into the Cold War, an anxious stalemate between the Soviet Union and the United States and allied nations. The war and its aftermath brought new tensions between the Soviet Union and the Allied powers. The modern thriller, the spy novel, and the apocalyptic science fiction story would all be outgrowths of this anxiety and concern.

The war in Europe had entered its final shattering weeks when President Roosevelt died and Harry S. Truman became the President of the United States. Into Germany the armies came from the ends of the earth: Americans and Soviet Russians. They met on April 25, 1945, at the edge of the Elbe at Torgau, an East German city. Berlin lay in ruins. Hitler was dead, and Nazi Germany had been torn in two. The nations were already at odds; the Americans and Russians were soon to be great rivals pursuing the goals of two incompatible political systems. The war was nearly won, and already the alliance was unraveling. Historians recognize that the Russians played a significant role in ending the war. They have observed that Josef Stalin did not respond to the Nazi suppression of the Warsaw uprising, even though the Red Army was within striking distance of the city. Soviet forces had already occupied Bulgaria, Romania, and Hungary by October 1944, when Churchill and Stalin reached some agreement on Soviet influence in those nations. This concession by Britain was something of a trade-off for Greece. The United States was not consulted in the bargain. The Red Army was brutal in its occupation of East Germany, seizing property, raping women, pillaging homes. This barbarism increased the antipathy of the people against the Soviet Union. The Russians would soon strengthen their hold on East Berlin.

The Soviet Union had seen devastating losses of its population in the war; some 2.7 million Soviet citizens had died. The war had left a shattered countryside and devastated towns and industries. Stalin hid well his cruelty while making clear his demands. The man with the paunchy belly, pockmarked face, and stubble mustache insisted that Russia had suffered greatly and deserved the spoils of victory. A nation that gave its blood, its energy, and its resources must regain the territory that had been taken in the nonaggression pact with Germany in 1939. Russia set its sights on the Baltic, parts of Finland, and Poland. The Soviet Union asserted its claim to a sphere of influence, access to the sea and to the Turkish straits. It established a grand vision of regional domination. In these objectives, the Soviet Union sharply clashed with the goals of the United States. At Yalta, British and U.S. leaders pushed for free elections in Poland, in Eastern Europe, and in the Baltic states. The states of Eastern Europe would be bound to the Soviet Union, and their elections would seldom be free.

On Wednesday, March 12, 1947, at 1:00 p.m., Harry S. Truman stood on the marble steps at a podium facing the members of Congress. The American flag was draped behind him as he addressed the nation. In a speech that was broadcast on radio, Truman told his audience that an extremely critical situation had emerged. He was setting forth what came to be known as the Truman Doctrine. It would be U.S. policy "to support the cause of freedom" wherever it was threatened. He called for 400 million dollars in aid for Greece and Turkey, and asserted the need for global commitments. His speech, in essence, signaled the start of the Cold War. Recognizing that there was now an "iron curtain" that divided democracy from the communist bloc, American diplomats in the State Department—George Kennan, Dean Acheson, and General George C. Marshall—argued that the United States must assume leadership and take a stand against Soviet aggression. Kennan spelled out the idea of containment, which would later be known as the domino theory: that if one nation fell to communism, others would follow. (Dwight Eisenhower called this "the falling domino principle.") Meanwhile, the National Security Act of 1947 created the Central Intelligence Agency (CIA). Congress was concerned about agents working in the United States to spy on U.S. citizens. The House Un-American

Activities Committee (HUAC) sought out communist sympathizers, and initiated an atmosphere of suspicion.

Critics of the Truman administration have questioned whether the president's advisors promoted the domestic threat of communism for political reasons. They suggest that they sought to shore up Truman's 1948 campaign against claims that he was soft on communism. The Democrats had lost control of Congress in 1946, and they hoped to regain seats in the 1948 election. The HUAC investigation of Hollywood in 1947 resulted in the blacklisting of directors, writers, and actors, and set the stage for Joseph McCarthy's Red Scare investigations. Other critics ask if the Truman administration set the United States on course for later involvement in Vietnam. However, there was reason for concern about communist infiltration, and the Soviet Union generated anxieties in the United States and in Western Europe. Truman's administration created alliances with NATO and with the Marshall Plan that rebuilt Europe. To promote economic stability, officials met to create the World Bank and the International Monetary Fund. Meanwhile, the Truman administration began to rebuild the armed forces and expand the military establishment. The Department of Defense became further involved with defense contractors, industrial management, and research and development.

In his State of the Union Address of January 6, 1947, Truman pointed out that America was now on the path to prosperity. He encouraged the building of homes, good labor and management relations, international nuclear controls, and proposed the idea of a national health insurance, while calling for a balanced budget: "Progress in reaching our domestic goals is closely related to our conduct of foreign affairs," Truman said. He affirmed the value of recent peace treaties forged in Europe, but noted the painstaking effort that had been involved in hammering them out because of "the difficulty of reaching agreement with the Soviet Union." Truman asserted that America's policy toward the Soviet Union and all other countries would be based upon "the principles of international justice." He held out the expectation that both the United States and the Soviet Union would "return to production and reconstruction" and he addressed America's participation in the world and the need for "collective security."[25]

George C. Marshall was sworn in as Secretary of State on Tuesday, January 21, 1947. It was one of the most important moves of the Truman presidency. Marshall, as a general, offered a perspective on foreign affairs, and was well respected by Republicans in Congress. With Dean Acheson, he faced the problem of Britain's withdrawal of economic and military support for Greece and Turkey. The Soviets were pressuring the Baltic States and swallowing up Eastern Europe. George Kennan addressed the new reality in the eight thousand-word "Long Telegram." Kennan argued that there now could be no "peaceful co-existence" between the United States and the Soviet Union. The political culture of the Soviet Union was such that authoritarianism would persist. The Soviets were fundamentally insecure following a long and arduous commitment to war. Kennan concluded that Soviet tendencies were expansionist. America must prevent further expansion in developing regions, or there would be a domino effect. If one nation fell to communism, others surely would follow.

The business of economic aid to Europe was viewed as a postwar necessity. To rebuild Germany economically appeared to be a key to a stable international order. Global security would be enhanced by the $17 billion European aid economic package sent to Congress. The National Security Act and the National Security Council would create the Department of Defense, provide that the Air Force would become a military service branch, and recognize the formation of the Central Intelligence Agency. The North Atlantic Treaty Organization (NATO) was another initiative that remains relevant in our time. The United States and Canada joined with ten nations in West Europe to affirm that an attack on any one of them would be viewed as an attack on all of them. NATO would act as an alliance to preserve the peace through mutual support throughout the Cold War. This international commitment of cooperation functions today to maintain global security. Foreign affairs professionals today assert that nationalist calls to retreat from the alliance into isolation are inadvisable.

The Marshall Plan was created for the restoration of economic and agricultural productivity in Europe. "I need not tell you gentlemen that the world situation is very serious," Secretary of State Marshall said in an address at Harvard. This will require "substantial additional help" to Europe in order "to end poverty, desperation and chaos," he asserted. The goal, he said, was to permit conditions "in which free institutions can exist."[26] General Marshall had been the head of the U.S. Army during World War II. In his Harvard address, he proclaimed a need for "nominal economic health in the world." To preserve stability and peace, "the revival of a working economy" was necessary. Truman made a request to Congress for $17 billion in aid for Europe. The Marshall Plan indeed fostered stability, but it was not entirely altruistic. It ultimately provided a market for U.S. goods and an environment for U.S. investment as well as for the maintenance of peace. The Soviet Union would not participate in this plan to rebuild Europe, and prevented Poland and Czechoslovakia from being included in this program. In 1948 there was a blockade of Berlin, and unsuccessful Soviet efforts to get the United States to leave West Berlin. Supplies had to be airlifted into the city.

SCIENCE AND SCIENCE FICTION

The prestige of science increased during the Second World War, and technological research and development moved to the center of American culture. During this time, scientific innovation and speculation intersected with the development of science fiction. The years from about 1938 through the mid-1940s have been called the first "Golden Age" of science fiction, although perhaps Robert Silverberg is right to argue that science fiction's true golden age occurred in the 1950s.[27] Hugo Gernsback brought science fiction to the pulps in the 1930s. John W. Campbell produced *Astounding Science Fiction*. The Second World War erupted while American youth were entranced by the heroism of Flash Gordon, who first appeared in 1934, when many of the men who fought in World War II were boys absorbed in comic books. The space-opera comic book hero, along with Buck Rogers, was one of the most popular imaginary heroes of the day. Who can say how many future soldiers had been fans of the films *Flash Gordon* (1936) and *Flash Gordon Goes to Mars* (1938), or how Flash Gordon contributed to their notions of heroism? In the United States, *Flash Gordon Conquers the Universe* (1940) was a popular film drawn from the comic book and radio series. Perhaps a deadly ray from Mars, a magic time machine, and long-range rockets suggested a growing interest in the wonders of science.

During the 1940s, science fiction gained greater psychological depth and was often anchored in hard science. Isaac Asimov's fiction was now appearing in book form, with his classic *Foundation* series and his in-fluential three laws of robotics. Significant writers like Asimov were joined by authors like Robert A. Heinlein. Heinlein's *Orphans of the Sky* (1941) comprises two novellas that first appeared in *Astounding Stories: Universe* (May 1941) and *Common Sense* (October 1941). These stories were followed by *Rocket Ship Galileo* (1946) and *Red Planet* (1949), which features a boarding school set on Mars. *Sixth Column* (1949) is notable for Heinlein's commentary on racism, following a time when America's Japanese enemy was being characterized in racial terms.

Science was at war. When the United States entered the conflict, Heinlein's fictional imagination was put to use by the U.S. Navy. He was called on to identify and recruit engineers for government work, and he assisted efforts to improve technologies such as sonar, radar, and electronics. The Combat Information Center (CIC) assisted at Leyte Gulf by evaluating information as the battle was in progress. Yet, Heinlein was also a critic; he asserted, "Our civilization has not yet even dreamed of applying science to itself" and that "solutions do not exist in the technology of 1943."[28] He criticized the officer class as too self-satisfied.[29] Like Albert Einstein, Heinlein envisioned a world government. He wrote in a letter: "Hang it all, why don't the powers that be realize that the only way we'll attain lasting peace is to have every nation give up some of its sovereign power and have a world federation of countries."[30] Heinlein started a "think tank" in his apartment in the fall of 1945 with John Campbell, Theodore Sturgeon, and occasional visits from L. Ron Hubbard.

The growing popularity of science fiction coincided with the increasing importance of science in American life. The Second World War instigated transformations in science and technology policy that became salient features of postwar life. The formation of the Atomic Energy Commission was one such response. In July 1945, Truman and his cabinet received recommendations that the Atomic Energy Commission be managed under civilian control. There were many research programs commissioned during World War II, ranging from military to industrial research. These projects involved university laboratories at places like the California Institute of Technology and the Massachusetts Institute of Technology, and research and development at corporations like DuPont and General Electric. In the United States, research and development in medical science was partly focused in Bethesda, Maryland, where officials proposed the National Institutes of Health.

In 1940, there were 2.9 million people involved in professional and technical operations in the United States. That number greatly increased in the next two decades. The overall number of factory workers fell as clerical jobs increased. The trend from an industrial and manufacturing economy toward today's postindustrial service economy was under way.[31] When the GI Bill made higher education available to more Americans, graduate schools began to become more selective. The return of veterans coincided with a focus on diversity and the rise of measurement through the Graduate Record Examination, recommendation letters, and transcripts.[32] Emphasis on "scientific" management and specialization grew within corporate business and government. With this transition came a new managerial class, characterized by C. Wright Mills in *The Power Elite*.[33] The 1950s brought the phenomenon of "organization man," diagnosed by sociologist William Whyte.

The first computer for general use emerged in 1944 from a collaboration between IBM and Harvard. The MARK I was fifty feet long, eight feet tall, and three feet deep. It took up most of a big room. It had 765,000 parts and 530 miles of wire. The world was still many years away from Bill Gates and Steve Jobs, or the microchip and Silicon Valley. The system known as ENIAC made this MARK I computer obsolete within two years. In 1950, with government funds, John Neumann built the first stored program computer. Prior to this, computers were used for military industrial research and development, or scientific projects. The linkages between government and scientific research and development increased across the next decades.

Concern with science and technology education as an engine for national prosperity and international development has more recently pushed emphasis on STEM programs in American schools. Telecommunications and computer technology have caught the imagination of society and have created a more convergent, shrinking world. Microchip technology and microprocessing contributed to this enthusiasm and mass consumer transformations. The age of information dynamically arrived in personal computers, interactive networks, the World Wide Web. The 3-billion-dollar Human Genome Project sought to sequence human genes and map the human genome. Such technological developments have created greater ethical and political pressures. In the 1940s, these were science fiction dreams, at best.

Scientific discovery and hard scientific fact was the groundwork for Isaac Asimov's considerable accomplishments in the science fiction genre. It was Asimov who came up with the laws that robots inevitably would follow in most subsequent science fiction stories. Asimov combined expertise in chemistry and in-depth knowledge in physics with a stunningly prolific imagination. Many of his stories appeared in *Astounding Science Fiction*, and his Foundation series drew together his fiction into an enduring classic work. Asimov, Robert Heinlein, and Sprague de Camp, newly commissioned as a lieutenant, were interviewed on the day after D-Day in June 1944 for *Air Scoop*, the bulletin for the Naval Air Experimental Station (NAES). The publication explored "the creative thinking of science fiction writers brought to the war effort."[34] A month later, Heinlein reviewed Willy Ley's "Rockets: A Prelude to Space Travel" in *Astounding* (July 1944) as the Germans launched V-1 rockets across the English Channel. Asimov continued writing the Foundation stories and other short stories, like "The Mixed Man." He was drafted as the war came to an end in the Pacific. His story "The Mule" appeared in the November–December 1945 issue of *Astounding*.

In the 1940s, science appeared in American fiction and nonfiction in genres other than science fiction. The environment was not a broad public concern in the 1940s, but several American authors integrated their appreciation of the natural world in their work. John Steinbeck's writing in *The Log from the Sea of Cortez* (1941) was informed by concerns that might be called ecological. Louis Bromfield, who won the Pulitzer Prize for his novel *Early Autumn* (1926), was another pioneer in this regard. Upon returning from France, Bromfield bought 1,000 acres of land in Ohio and created there a self-sustaining organic farm. Bromfield developed soil conservation practices and tended to the land without any use of pesticides. Now a conservationist, he wrote nonfiction. His farm became known as Malabar Farm, and was later designated a state park. During the 1940s, Bromfield wrote *Night in Bombay* (1940), *Wild is the River* (1941), *Mrs. Parkington* (1943), *The World We Live In* (1944), *Pleasant Valley* (1945), *A Few Brass Tacks* (1946), *Colorado* (1947), *Kenny* (1947), and *Malabar Farm* (1948). Aldo Leopold published the *Sand County Almanac* (1949). During this time

Rachel Carson was developing her best-selling book *The Sea Around Us* (1951). Her book *Silent Spring* (1962) would bring sharp attention to environmental issues.

Nuclear weapons became a regular feature of science fiction stories from the late 1940s into the 1950s. Some writers appear to have anticipated the nuclear age. In 1940, Robert Heinlein wrote "Solution Unsatisfactory," which sees radioactive dust developed into a weapon. Before this, Stephen Vincent Benet's "By the Waters of Babylon" depicted a world destroyed by nuclear disaster. His story appears to imply that radiation was a factor, as a young explorer from a surviving tribal civilization sets forth on a vision quest and dares to cross into the devastated land beyond the river: a world, the story suggests, that might be gradually restored. When a 1944 story told of a chain reaction nuclear blast, the FBI investigated the author for a potential security breach.

The atomic age brought anxieties, and science fiction spread apocalyptic fears. Scientists were genuinely terrified by their discoveries and their achievement of the bomb. They wrote to tell the public of their concern. Doomsday myths became part of popular consciousness. Theodore Sturgeon wrote "Thunder and Roses" (1947). Damon Knight wrote "Not with a Bang" (1949). Ray Bradbury appeared on the scene with "There Will Come Soft Rains" (1950), in which an automated house continues to function even though the people have vanished in a nuclear holocaust. Cultural anxiety underpinned stories like *On the Beach* (1957), *A Canticle for Liebowitz* (1959), and *Alas, Babylon* (1960).

Science fiction sometime embraced and recommended the prospects of new technologies. However, it also presented a critique of modernity and cautionary narratives. It created an apocalyptic genre of utter catastrophe. Dystopian fiction "became a mass phenomenon . . . replacing New Deal liberalism as a popular interpretation of history," observes Andrew Feenberg. There was a secularized eschatology of end-of-the-world scenarios that were technically possible.[35]

Grounded in science, the science fiction genre moved beyond the pulp magazines into the new world of paperbacks. There were heroes solving problems, facing extraordinary dilemmas, other worlds, and threats to humanity. This was a fiction of possibility. In 1946, science fiction was a genre at which those oriented toward literary modernism looked askance. Immediately after the war, "to most people science fiction seemed lurid, fantastical and nonsensical trash," writes Adam Roberts in *History of Science Fiction* (2016).[36] Yet, in that period's science fiction, it is the human rather than the machine that is always "the essence of the story."[37]

The sensational and the fantastic are familiar elements of science fiction. Dramatic conflict and spectacle drive these stories. Stories that set events in distant dimensions, far-off places, may speak of our own cultural anxieties, and aliens may address our own alienation. Drama and spectacle are also staples of the evening news, which has been known to increase anxiety. When broadcast news journalists declare that U.S. Intelligence has identified sources of computer hacking at high levels of the Russian government, the shadows of the Cold War return. A new round of anxieties focuses upon Crimea, the Ukraine, Syria, nuclear buildup, or the U.S. president's relationship with Russia, and these events foment concerns about a new Cold War. Even before the news of cybersecurity issues, CNN (October 19, 2016) recognized an "outright conflict." The BBC asked, "Where Did It All Go Wrong?" (October 17, 2016). The *London Telegraph* (October 23, 2016) suggested that we have entered a new Cold War, and the *Los Angeles Times* (October 28, 2016) was reporting "The New Cold War Is Already On."

Anyone pondering the future might consider the terrors and cautions expressed in science fiction, and begin to read an apocalyptic strain that appears across many other texts. Critic David Ketterer once stated that he was not satisfied with the term *science fiction*. He placed it in the larger category of apocalyptic fiction: "Apocalyptic fiction is concerned with the creation of other worlds which exist, on the literal level, in a credible relationship . . . with the 'real' world, thereby causing a metaphorical destruction of that 'real' world in the reader's head."[38]

There has long been an apocalyptic tendency in American literature, which has been addressed by American critics. R. W. B. Lewis, in his chapter "Days of Wrath and Laughter" in *Trials of the Word* (1965), traced this from the time of the Puritans through the nineteenth century. Douglas Robinson holds that "the very idea of American history is apocalyptic."[39] While we can trace apocalyptic narrative to the first explosion of the nuclear bombs over Hiroshima and Nagasaki, its precursors lie in earlier texts. One may look at Michael Wigglesworth's Puritan verse in *The Day of Doom*, or at Nathaniel Hawthorne's stories, or read of Herman Melville's fierce white whale and Ahab's vengeance in *Moby Dick* in the mid-nineteenth century. Apocalyptic anxiety reappears nearly one hundred years later in Robert Frost's poem "Once by the Pacific." War novels attempt to diffuse it, trying to make sense not only of the war but of the influences of technology and the problems of bureaucracy, racism, and an anxious postwar culture. Rewriting the war enabled writers and readers "to gain a sense of emotional mastery over the events," say Sharon Baker and Wendy Martin.[40] The Second World War itself is "reworked" and "redefined," and veterans' anxiety about "fitting in" is mediated in postwar literature.[41] The soldiers and sailors in Norman Mailer's *The Naked and the Dead* or in Thomas Heggen's *Mister Roberts* fight for integrity against dehumanization.

THE AGE OF ANXIETY

"The sources of anxiety are to be found in basic trends in our culture," notes Rollo May. In *The Meaning of Anxiety* (1950), he wrote that at such times as the postwar period, "people grasp at political authoritarianism in their desperate need for relief from anxiety."[42] One of his reference points for this observation was his friend the theologian Paul Tillich's experience of the emergence of Nazi Germany. Tillich wrote: "First of all a feeling of fear, or more exactly an indefinite anxiety was prevailing."[43] However, May also cited Albert Camus and W. H. Auden, who spoke of an age of anxiety, and noted that Leonard Bernstein set to music Auden's poem *The Age of Anxiety* (1949). In American literature between 1920 and 1950, May observed, there would be "symptoms of anxiety rather than overt anxiety itself."[44] The writing of Thomas Wolfe, for example, suggested that "you can't go home again." That sense of homelessness was only beginning to emerge. In contrast, the emergence of anxiety as an explicit problem was a significant phenomenon. W. H. Auden's poem, *The Age of Anxiety*, was "an overt statement"; Auden interpreted the inner lives of four people during wartime. May views them as dealing with loneliness and "not being able to love and be loved," as they question their personal worth and their values.[45] May's comments on Auden's characters might be transposed to our time. Auden writes that we move hurriedly along as the wheel pulls and pushes us in a "stupid world where gadgets take on reality like little gods—even as we remain alone, unattached."[46] We must experience life, May concludes, not merely live through gadgets and hurry. We must have meaningful communication.

The famous photograph of a sailor embracing a woman in Times Square celebrated the end of the war and communicated hope. The photography in *Life* depicted an era, and the magazine's owner declared that the world had now entered "the American century." Story intertwined with image in films, in periodicals, and in the emerging new technology of television.

In 1940, James Agee wrote in *Now Let Us Praise Famous Men* that with a camera "everything is to be discerned for him who can discern it." Visual culture could reveal America; Agee wrote that the "keen historic spasm of the shutter" would serve "to portray America" and respond to the writer's inability to go beyond his material."[47] A picture might "speak a thousand words," but words on the page remained essential in communication. During the Second World War a flood of news journalism and social reports was complemented by books "which pandered to public excitement," writes Alfred Kazin.[48] However, books also embodied the cultural record. John Dos Passos wrote that books served as a historical lifeline across the "scary" present. There were books that engaged in the art of memory, stories that recollected traditions, heartfelt values, and the legacy of the past. Kazin wrote: "Yes, the pressure of the times is too great; it bears upon us. Literature today lives on the narrow margin of security that the democratic West, fighting for its life, can afford, and that margin may grow more narrow every day."[49] Literature sought this security during this time, which John Steinbeck called "the era of crisis."[50] It bolstered confidence at home and depicted bravery overseas. Kazin concluded his 1942 book with: "The world seems to be waiting, waiting for its new order . . . in everything we do, explorations of the human imagination, we reach for the same old truth, we have yet to see it all, our words, our voice, our dream, and what it may become."[51]

7

LOOKING TO THE FIFTIES

The Future of the Book

Typewriters clicked. Teletype clattered. Skyscrapers rose in steel and mortar, and the news was written on paper. From the factory floor came steam and steel, and trucks took books out to the suburbs. They landed on newsstands, at drugstores, and in groceries. They were stacked in warehouses and gathered in rows in bookstores and on library shelves. Books were sorted where the radio dial was turned up and the music was jazz, Tin Pan Alley, horns, and rhythm. The television under the rabbit ears of the antennae spilled light into the room. Its picture was black and white and grainy. Film and advertising and television were beginning to affect the ways that we read, and change some of the ways we communicate.

The 1940s was a time of transition, recovery, and expectation. It was, claimed Henry Luce in February 1941, the American Century: a time of industrial might and political strength and new responsibility in the world. It was, Luce asserted, no time for isolationism. This period of war and new global commitments also brought the promise of a new expansion of the book industry, despite wartime paper shortages. John Dos Passos wrote that books served as a historical lifeline across the "scary" present. There were books that engaged in the art of memory, stories that recollected traditions, heartfelt values, and the legacy of the past. George Orwell celebrated popular culture with his appreciation of "Boy's Weeklies" and detective novels while critiquing Western society and arguing for vitality and clarity in our public uses of language in "Politics and the English Language." While many literary critics held to the high standards of aesthetic appreciation, a more sociological critic like Orwell was concerned about fascism, communism, and the social impact of books. Alfred Kazin, as previously noted, pointed to popular books, "which pandered to public excitement."[1]

Public taste may be reflected in popular books. Whether written for "high" or "mass" culture, the book tells us something about the concerns and imagination of the period in which it was produced. Understanding more about the books of the 1940s and about their creators and readers will provide us with a way toward a social history of culture. In the early 1950s, the best-seller list showed reader interest in historical fiction (Mike Waltari's *The Egyptian*), mystery (Daphne Du Maurier's novels, *The Parasites* and *My Cousin Rachel*), and religion (Henry Morton Robinson's *The Cardinal*). Recollections of the war arrived in 1951 with *From Here to Eternity* by James Jones and *The Caine Mutiny* by Herman Wouk. As if signaling cultural bipolar disorder, the title *Joy Street* alternated with *Disenchanted* on the best-seller list throughout 1951. *The Silver Chalice*, by Thomas B. Costain, brought historical intrigue. *Desiree*, by Anne Marie Salinko, was turned into a film that made it a best seller. J. D. Salinger made his first appearance on the list, and John Steinbeck produced his novel *East of Eden*, which held the top place on the best-seller list from early November 1952 into the next year.

The public in the 1950s witnessed the first widespread introduction of television to the cultural mainstream. They experienced the impact of electronic media, as we do today in the digital information age. In our time, there has been a shift toward electronic media for news, information, and entertainment. Some people have suggested that the paper-bound book is going the way of the dinosaur. However, the printed book endures. Print, like a noble army up high behind the castle walls, effectively faces the challenge of other media because it provides a physical item that is visible, portable, and well made. The physical book is durable, and its production and sale can be controlled by publishers. Many people still like to hold a book in their hands. Even so, today we are witnessing a period of change for the book, just as the pressures of change were in the air at mid-century.

BOOKS AND PUBLISHING

The Second World War shook American publishing. Paper was rationed, and distribution was affected. However, a future of expansion in the publishing industry was waiting in ventures like Pocket Books and Penguin paperbacks, which opened an office in New York in 1939. New York was America's principal center for publishing. The city acted as a financial center, home to Broadway theater, and a communications hub. Its skyscrapers, built in the 1930s, had by the 1940s begun to form a distinctive skyline. New York markets reached out to the world. New York's harbor and Ellis Island remained the first port of call for thousands of immigrants, including immigrants who would make distinctive contributions to America's cultural life. News of the war in Europe appeared every day. The *New York Times* offered the most comprehensive coverage of the city's newspapers. Its rivals included *The Herald Tribune* and *The New York Daily Mirror*, a Hearst newspaper. *The Herald Tribune* supported Wendell Willkie in the 1940 election. Journalist Dorothy Thompson supported Roosevelt's reelection, and the newspaper forced her to resign. In Gay Talese's book about the *New York Times*, *The Kingdom and the Power*, he says that the *Herald Tribune* ran more ads during the war years, while the *New York Times* cut back on them. The *Herald Tribune* declined from 1947 into the 1950s, and the *Times* secured its position as the newspaper of record.

In the 1940s, *New Yorker* editor Harold Ross wired correspondent A. J. Liebling overseas, and he coached writers Mollie Panter-Downes, John Lardner, John Hersey, and E. J. Kahn. E. B. White wrote his "Notes and Comment" column for the periodical. "The war made the *New Yorker*," writes David Remnick, who points out that the magazine's circulation rose from 172,000 to 227,000 during the war years.[2] Uptown, Lionel Trilling, Mark Van Doren, and Jacques Barzun were among the luminaries on the faculty at Columbia University. The Physics Department there was formulating itself into the Manhattan Project. At City College, Nathan Glazer, Irving Howe, Daniel Bell, and Irving Kristol discussed politics and socialism in the cafeteria. Culture, politics, Marxism, and the events of the war stimulated their debate. Irving Howe joined the Independent Socialist League in 1947. He would become an important literary and social critic. Daniel Bell was to become a sociologist and professor whose major contribution was his study of post-industrial society. Irving Kristol would become one of the defining voices of modern conservatism. Nathan Glazer was a social critic who was the founder of the *Public Interest*. Literary critic Alfred Kazin, a Brooklyn Jew also at City College, held views that were a little more moderate than most of the left-leaning New York intellectuals of the 1940s. Kazin became friends with the social and political thinker Hannah Arendt not long after writing *On Native Grounds* (1942). Kazin, Howe, and Kristol were among the public intellectuals who made a career of commenting on books, politics, and American society.

While these thinkers from immigrant Jewish families were gaining influence, middlebrow fiction was on the rise. Pulp fiction, dime novels, and popular stories gained newfound respectability in mainstream publishing, as paperback formats increased in quality. Dell emerged in 1943, Bantam in 1945, and New American Library (NAL) in 1948. Paperback publishers acquired titles from the hardcover houses. For Norman Mailer's *The Naked and the Dead*, NAL paid a $35,000 advance. James Jones's *From Here to Eternity* received an advance of more than $100,000.[3] The postwar period was charged with industrial energy and material prospects. A baby boom brought the childcare recommendations of Benjamin Spock and the Kinsey studies of male sexuality. The GI Bill expanded the suburbs, stimulated higher education, encouraged specialized trades, and opened new prospects for veterans and their families. Across the Atlantic, a shattered Europe was drawn into a network of recovery. Upended by war, in some quarters individuals settled into a looming shadow of existentialist unease. Meanwhile, Americans grew conscious of the perils of the nuclear age. There was a search for security—in work, in therapy, in religion, and in family and community.

HISTORY AND BOOKS

Books had come a long way from the days when monks wrote on parchment in the scriptorium. In manuscript culture, scribes responded to the call for *lectio divina* (divine reading) in the Benedictine Rule. Their work in the field of the humanities was to inscribe the words of scripture. In 1300, Dante prophesied the future of literature by writing *The Divine Comedy* in the vernacular. By 1400, scriveners and clerks were copying Bible passages and pages for secular commerce, law, and government. In the mid-1400s, Johann Gutenberg's press created a revolution in book production. Five hundred years later, in 1948, the poet Thomas Merton became a monk for the modern age, recalling Dante in *The Seven Storey Mountain*.

With the appearance of *The Seven Storey Mountain*, Thomas Merton's autobiography, the time was ripe for his account of his spiritual search. In the generation that grew up during the Great Depression and confronted the Second World War, church attendance was high. Merton was a representative individual on a life journey who made the choice to enter a monastery and become a Cistercian monk. He wrote: "The life of each [person] is part of a mystery. . . . In one sense we are always traveling, and traveling as if we did not know where we were going."[4] The autobiography draws its title from Dante's Purgatorio in *The Divine Comedy*. Like Dante's influential poem, Merton's biography has three parts, and the narrative roughly follows a pattern of conversion from the things of this world to concern for matters of the spirit. The book was published on October 4, 1948, and became a surprise best seller.

Merton was a practicing poet throughout his life. His readers were curious about his religious commitment, and were drawn by his style. Part 1 of *The Seven Storey Mountain* covers Merton's life as a child, his time in France, his schooling in England, and the beginning of his studies at Columbia University. Part 2 focuses on the two years of his conversion and baptism. Part 3, from September 1939 to April 17, 1943, includes his application to be a Franciscan, which led him to Olean, New York, and St. Bonaventure University, where he worked as a teacher of English. He made a retreat to the Trappist Abbey in Kentucky, and embraced his calling to the Abbey of Gethsemane. He reflects on his first years in the monastery, and concludes with a poem to his brother, who died in combat in 1943.

World War II was a sign of the modern era that never quite left Merton's consciousness. Merton wrote a letter to the mayor of Hiroshima in 1962, recognizing that the people of the city had become "a symbol of the hope of humanity." This modern poet, who vowed to lead a medieval way of life, made a gesture that recalled the dawn of the nuclear age. He received survivors of the bombing at his Gethsemane hermitage on May 16, 1964. He wrote his poem "Original Child Bomb" to protest the use of the atom bomb on Hiroshima's civilians. Merton considered the atomic bombing as an act emanating from "abstract logic." He argued that those in power did not think in terms of human beings.[5] Those who supported the dropping of the atom bomb would argue that it had been necessary; Merton insisted that it was not. Although the Cistercian community led a tradition-focused lifestyle, Merton acknowledged that he wrote "as a man in the modern world."[6] He insisted that he was "personally involved" in twentieth-century events.[7]

Once the dust of war had cleared, several social critiques of American life began to appear. Books came from sociologists who diagnosed American society. David Reisman, in *The Lonely Crowd* (1950), asserted that "other directed" individuals were allowing their lives to be absorbed by peer group norms. William Whyte analyzed a trend toward conformity and uniformity in *The Organization Man* (1956). C. Wright Mills dissected the rise of *The Power Elite* (1956). After the war, men and women assumed traditional family roles, a trend that was exemplified by television shows like *Father Knows Best* and *Leave It to Beaver*. Robert Park observed the suburbs in *Human Communities* (1952). There were insights into female sexuality from the Kinsey Report (1953). Economist Kenneth Galbraith considered *The Affluent Society* (1958), and Gunnar Myrdal examined the formation of the welfare state in *Beyond the Welfare State* (1958). In presidential elections, Adlai Stevenson faced Dwight D. Eisenhower, and John F. Kennedy faced Richard Nixon. By the early 1960s, historian Richard Hofstadter was insisting that the common disposition of many people in the United States was toward *American Anti-Intellectualism* (1963) and that there was a *Paranoid Style of Politics* (1964).

Books were increasingly seen as a form of entertainment. With the paperback revolution, they also became more accessible. In 1940 a hardcover book sold for about $2.75 in 1940 dollars; that would be about $46 to $47 today. This tended to put these books somewhat out of the reach of most everyday book buyers. One could purchase a Pocket Book for a quarter. That meant that a paperback sold for a price that would comparable to about $4.25 to $4.50 in 2017. This is a good deal less than commercial paperbacks cost now, especially those issued in a larger format.[8]

The emergence of Pocket Books, started by Robert De Graff with Simon and Schuster on June 19, 1939, certainly did more than fulfill his early claim that it would transform New York reading habits. It revolutionized an industry. So too did other aspects of postwar economic and educational expansion. Academic publishing saw a surge in sales that lasted until trimmer budgets in the 1970s. Meanwhile, genre fiction was given a boost. Science fiction had previously appeared almost entirely in magazines; now mysteries and science fiction stories were increasingly collected in books for the new paperback market. Ian Ballantine issued paperbacks through Penguin Books, and then founded Bantam Books and Ballantine, which emphasized genre mysteries, westerns, and science fiction, including Ray Bradbury's *Fahrenheit 451* (1953). In 1952, Ace Books founded a line of science fiction paperbacks, with two novels packaged together in the same volume.

In the 1940s, the Book of the Month Club had begun to ask authors about their favorite reading. Radio programs brought commentary on books of the day; "The Author Meets the Critics" began on radio in Manhattan in 1943, and was on NBC radio and television in 1947. Guests included Bennett Cerf, Dorothy Thompson, and Henry Seidel Canby. "Of Men and Books" and "Invitation to Learning" were on the air in 1944. "Books on Trial" was sponsored by the Literary Guild. The television quiz show was something of an extension of these educational programs.

TELEVISION

Years before Marshall McLuhan observed that the medium is the message, the new audio-visual medium of television became a commonplace part of everyday American life. In 1953, Ray Bradbury's *Fahrenheit 451* not only cast concern about a society that would burn books; it also featured homes with flat-screen television sets, which are commonplace today. Since its public appearance in 1948, television has had a widespread impact on elections, news, and reading. Books have gone through their own changes in production, marketing, and distribution. There was a publishing boom in the 1950s and the 1960s, with increasing paperback sales, new series, and additional emphasis on genre fiction. Publishers' lists grew. The late 1950s saw a jump in the overall amount of product. *Publishers Weekly* recorded 14,876 titles in 1959. This was more than 1,400 titles over the previous year, and the figures rose to 15,102 titles the next year.[9] Of course, mass-market paperback sales could not be accurately counted until the international standard book number (ISBN) was instituted as the industry standard in 1981. There is also the question of what comprises a book; *Publisher's Weekly* categorized this as any volume of more than sixty-five pages.

By 1966, U.S. publishers were issuing some 30,000 titles a year. In 1996, that number had climbed to more than 63,000. Today, e-books, paperbacks, hardcover books, print-on-demand books, books on tape and CD, and other formats have pushed that number much higher. Between 2008 and 2010, e-books increased sales dramatically, but these have apparently reached a plateau. Pew Research indicates that more than half of U.S. readers have tablets: Kindle, Nook, or iPad, and the iPhone are pervasive. Fiction and drama continue to be adapted to film and broadcast media. Local book stores attempt to maintain a tradition of accessibility and personal attention, while trying to sustain themselves in an environment that includes online booksellers, the big chain stores like Barnes and Noble, and the mammoth Amazon.

Books tend to fall out of print, and many of the books of the 1940s have done just that. Some of the works of the authors mentioned in this book have at times been difficult to locate. The American novels of the 1940s are not frequently taught in America's schools. Longer novels, like those of Cozzens and Marquand, disappear from our bookstores. Hersey's *Hiroshima*, a brief and poignant book, may enter the classroom setting, while *A Bell for Adano* and *The Wall* do not. Great books are too easily forgotten. Yet, Richard Wright's *Native Son* is surely as relevant today as when the novel was written, and it merits a prominent place in American studies. Hemingway's *A Farewell to Arms* (1929) seems to be read more often than *For Whom the Bell Tolls* (1940). Steinbeck's *The Grapes of Wrath* (1939) is assigned more often than *The Moon Is Down* (1942) or *Cannery Row* (1945). We do get George Orwell's *1984* into the classroom quite often, but Graham Greene a good deal less so. There is perennial value to the novels of William Faulkner and Robert Penn Warren. One may be introduced to Faulkner through his short stories, and to Penn Warren through *All the King's Men*, or his poetry. You will find "The Worn Path" by Eudora Welty anthologized often, but what about her other stories? Where in a school curriculum might one sustain the works of Carson McCullers? What about the vigorous spirit in James Jones's *From Here to Eternity*?

Books like Ann Petry's *The Street* call out for rediscovery in our time. She raises questions that continue to bother us, and calls for reflection about women's rights and dignity. Yet, who will read her unless the book is assigned in a classroom, or Viola Davis and Oprah Winfrey are cast in a feature film?

Pew Research indicates that readership itself has declined. Those Americans reading even just one book dropped from 69 percent to 63 percent in one year, from 2014 to 2015. A National Endowment for the Arts (NEA) report of 2007, emphatically titled *To Read or Not to Read: A Question of National Consequence*, asserted that younger Americans were reading less than older generations. Dana Gioia, in the report's preface, wrote: "The nation needs to focus more attention and resources on an activity both fundamental and irreplaceable for democracy."[10] The document gathers together large national studies by federal agencies, with academic, foundation, and business support, and claims "startling consistency" across these sources and warns of the "long-term consequences" of a decline in reading.

Clearly, people read more in the 1940s. They read for information, and to put information to use. They read out of curiosity, to be informed, and for self-improvement. They also read for entertainment. It was a time before television and before computer screens. For drama or comedy, one had to go to the theater, see a movie, turn on the radio, or open a book. There was no Netflix, no DVDs. Computers lined entire walls in military and research facilities. There were no computer games. Bill Gates and Steve Jobs were not even born yet. A decade after the war ended, in 1955, Clifton Fadiman wrote an essay, "Decline of Attention," in which he asserted that most everyone had become producers and consumers and that personality and packaging were now at the center of public life. Journalists were trying to attract attention rather than engaging it, he said.[11]

It follows that the readers of the 1950s brought their previous habits and interests into the new communications milieu of the decade. It was a period in which there was an increasing intersection of books and reading, with public exposure to film and television. The distribution of cheap books and reprints to World War II soldiers had stimulated postwar reading and the emergence of book clubs. This led to the expansion of publishing and new channels of distribution. After World War II, chain bookstores like B. Dalton and Walden Books entered the merchandising field. The National Book Award was founded in 1950. The Book of the Month Club and the Literary Guild were joined by an array of other book clubs: the Labor Book Club, the Negro Book Club, the Catholic Book Club. There were close-knit groups of romance readers, as Janice Radway has shown in *Reading the Romance* (1984). One might even argue that sharing reading in groups like this kept society connected and cohesive, in the way that Robert Putnam in *Bowling Alone* (2000) has argued that bowling leagues once did.

The 2007 NEA report's observation of a decline in reading across the United States indeed has raised a question: "To read or not to read?" It is as if American culture, like Hamlet, is now facing some overwhelming question: a cursed spite that must be set right. "This is not an elegy for the bygone days of print culture, but instead a call to action," wrote Dana Gioia amid the disarming glare of the NEA report.[12] Reading it, one may wonder how enduring are the words of Franklin Delano Roosevelt that appeared in the 1940s and 1950s on posters in Midwestern libraries: "People die, but books never die . . . no man and no force can put thought in a concentration camp forever." The NEA report is a clarion call to educators to encourage reading. After all, reading is liberating. In John Hersey's *The Wall*, Noach Levinson and his friends broke out of the restricted area of the Warsaw ghetto into a library.

The fiction, drama, and poems of the 1940s remain valuable for us because they too are liberating. We may read the stories of the 1940s because they are still entertaining. Surely there are aspects of these stories that seem quaintly passé. However, an acquaintance with the concerns of the 1940s may bring us to reflect on the limitations of perspectives in our own time. To reread 1940s literature is no mere antiquarian pursuit, for the era of the 1940s is a pivotal one: a stepping-stone to our own. This is a mirror of our history, and we may see parallels and possibilities for our time in this era.

The historical position of the reader of 1950, following a momentous war, certainly had an impact on reading and the national imagination. Television and film were now significant aspects of popular culture that affected book production and reading. More people watched the film adaptation of *From Here to Eternity* than read James Jones's long novel (a process that for some readers today might feel like an eternity). Books and publishing thrived after the Second World War, even as

television absorbed some of the energy of drama and fiction and enlisted some of America's finest talent in the fifties and early sixties—
Paddy Chayefsky, Rod Serling, Gore Vidal. Television drew from theater and radio plays, film, visual art, musical scores, and the texts of
novels. Television offered game shows and lighthearted comedy. Soon
it evolved into a powerful medium for advertising. [13]

There were six television stations in 1946; one decade later, there
were 442 stations. [14] Television appeared commercially in 1948, and
stories gained a new broadcast medium. There was a consolidation of
networks: the Columbia Broadcasting System (CBS), the National
Broadcasting System (NBC), and the American Broadcasting System
(ABC). Advertisers found television much to their liking, and sponsored
shows. Their products became nationally familiar commodities. There
were also new television stars, like Milton Berle. Ronald Reagan hosted
Death Valley Days for the General Electric Theater. Jackie Gleason,
comedian and occasional jazz bandleader, became bus driver Ralph
Cramden, married to the wise, practical, and savvy Alice (Audrey
Meadows) whom he insisted he would send "to the moon" whenever
she got the better of him. They lived in a tight city apartment of a
couple of rooms, and were often visited by their bumbling and lovable
neighbor, Ralph's T-shirt wearing friend, Ed Norton (Art Carney).
Gunsmoke and *Bonanza* responded to the American audience's nostalgia and enthusiasm for the western, while *Father Knows Best* set the
tone for the 1950s family show.

Movie attendance fell from 90 million to 47 million from 1946 to
1956. Paramount, MGM, RKO, Warner Bros., and Twentieth Century
Fox produced most of Hollywood's movies. The House Un-American
Activities Committee investigated Hollywood writers in 1947, and in
the early 1950s, HUAC blacklisted writers and actors. Throughout the
entertainment industry, actors, directors, and writers were questioned
and urged to name names of communist sympathizers.

The postwar dreams of many women were reflected in the zany
antics of Lucille Ball in *I Love Lucy*, one the most popular situation
comedies of the 1950s. Lucy always displayed aspirations for a middle-
class lifestyle, or dreamed of an entertainment business break while her
husband Rickie worked as a local bandleader. With the return of the
veterans from the war, many of the women who had been in the wartime labor force shifted back into the home. Lucille Ball reflected the

image of a housewife sharing marital stresses and predicaments that were often prompted by her schemes and dreams. Upon establishing her career in the late 1940s, Lucille Ball became one of the great comic actresses of her time, and her television character was a symbol of the dream of success and upward mobility. Lucy's dutiful husband in that series was small-time band director, Desi Arnaz. They rented an apartment from Fred and Ethel Mertz, and Lucy schemed toward greater horizons. By 1952, about 10.6 million American families were watching *I Love Lucy*. The show struck a responsive chord and made people laugh. By 1954, the show had 50 million viewers.

Television is one of America's great vehicles of communication, and it is a source of news and entertainment for millions of people. It beams out over the bar in the family restaurant. It flickers behind the windows of homes. It is the modern hearth in millions of living rooms. Of course, television has not been without its critics. One critic, Marie Winn, called it "the plug-in drug." The medium has been commonly referred to by some as "the boob tube." Neil Postman cautioned against "amusing ourselves to death." Historian Daniel J. Boorstin once argued that with television we had entered an entrancing world of pseudo-events: "Vivid images came to overshadow pale reality."[15] In 2017, Donald Trump complained about "fake news" while shrewdly utilizing social media and the techniques of reality television. Critics concerned about passive television viewing have assumed television viewers' nonengagement. Others have argued that television watching need not be passive at all, especially today, when shows engage in multiple plotlines. One must take the historical comparisons into consideration, says historian Michael Kammen, who notes a change from the active audience for vaudeville at the beginning of the twentieth century, and says that "passivity has shown a steady increase with mass culture."[16] Even so, other critics applaud the wide variety of entertainment on television and the immense creativity that is involved in television production. As Charles Dickens once argued in 1850, about a hundred years before the advent of television, the amusements of the people are crucial for people who are among the hardest working on earth. Laughter, melodrama, stimulation, and folly all have their place in the world of entertainment and leisure.

In the years before the Internet, social media, or video games consumed our attention, sociologist Robert Putnam pointed to how

Americans, by the 1980s, had already become less engaged in public concerns. He observed that since the time of Stanley Kowalski in *A Streetcar Named Desire,* there has been a decline of the sociable sport of bowling. Putnam lamented our "bowling alone," and suggested that many Americans had withdrawn from civic involvement. Michael Kammen held that mass culture increased passivity. He pointed out that in 1947 some 18,500,000 people were involved in 33,000 bowling leagues in the United States, and that bowling, in the 1940s had become a $200 million a year sport.[17] By the 1970s this was no longer the case. The thesis of Robert Bellah in *Habits of the Heart* was that "with the rise of individualism we find it difficult to express the moral reasons for our social commitments."[18] This individualism does not support citizenship on behalf of the common good. The American society of the 1940s was one devoted to patriotism and self-sacrifice. There are many people across America today who hold those values; however, some critics suggest that media has been a contrary influence that marks a difference in the generations.

BOOKS AND CULTURAL MEMORY

We are all involved, drawn into the world like those men, women, and children of the forties chasing their idea of the American dream. The twentieth century and the first decades of the twenty-first century have brought to us an awareness of a bigger world, one we cannot shrink from—a global kaleidoscope of human activity that our communications bring into our living rooms. In our age of information, books remain an important part of the conversation. Stories still frame, interpret, and reimagine the world. Benedict Anderson proposed that reading newspapers and periodicals brought individuals widely separated by geography into an experience of belonging to an imagined community.[19] This is also true of the stories that we read.

A comment by literary critic Alfred Kazin bears repeating. In 1942 he wrote: "Yes, the pressure of the times is too great; it bears upon us. Literature today lives on the narrow margin of security that the democratic West, fighting for its life, can afford, and that margin may grow more narrow every day."[20] John Steinbeck called it "the era of crisis"; W. H. Auden called it "the age of anxiety."[21] Kazin concluded his 1942 book by saying: "The world seems to be waiting, waiting for its new order . . . in everything we do, explorations of the human imagination, we reach for the same old truth, we have yet to see it all, our words, our voice, our dream, and what it may become."[22]

Imaginative fiction appeals to possibilities. It argues for variety—for the many voices that are at play in a novel. The stories of the 1940s are for us a rearview mirror as we head down the road into our future. The signs appear around us: the digital age, the age of globalism, the clash of civilizations. And so, will America in 2018 be isolationist, like the America in the late 1930s when war began to break upon Europe and Asia? Or, is America to be a strong partner in shaping the realities of the twenty-first century, working in tandem with the nations of the world as was done in the years after the Second World War? Alongside a president's effort to "make America great again," will our stories also make America think again?

Again, the world is waiting. It waits in those thousands of people who arrived in Washington, DC, to witness the day of the inauguration of the forty-fifth president. It waits in the people who gathered the next day in cities to raise signs and raise their voices. Alfred Kazin's words from 1942 again seem relevant. We are waiting to see what may become.

We are also looking back—for foundations and principles, for the stories of those who helped sustain the dream. Like Noach Levinson in John Hersey's novel *The Wall*, we dig down into the library. We listen to the stories that people tell. And every record, every scrap of paper, contains a voice, a story that entertains, or a word of guidance for our time.

At one hundred years old, best-selling author Herman Wouk, expositor of the traditions of Judaism, writer of *War and Remembrance*, surely sat in a New York apartment not long ago looking out on a new era. In a unique way, this centenarian has lived as a repository of American dreams. He, like so many others, was witness to a profoundly transformative era. Today, part of making America great again is remembering what America has been. It is about recognizing the power of story. The stories of the 1940s are the stories, the American dreams, of what Tom Brokaw has called the greatest generation. In 1998, Mr. Brokaw wrote: "Wartime America was forced by necessity to confront the hypocrisy concerning equality under the law."[23] Today, one can only hope that the legacy of the book may teach Americans to overcome the gaps in our dreams of equality and justice, and to recognize the achievements of our forebears. We can look to the testament of their lives as we embrace our new reality.

NOTES

INTRODUCTION

1. Jonathan Rose, *The Holocaust and the Book: Destruction and Preservation*, 2.

2. Pierre Nora, *Realms of Memory*, ii.

3. David Wyatt, *Secret Histories: Reading Twentieth Century American Literature*, 135.

4. William H. Chafe, *The Unfinished Journey: America Since World War II*, x.

5. Michael Kammen, *American Culture, American Taste: Social Change in the Twentieth Century*, 58.

6. Paul Fussell, *Wartime: Understanding and Behavior in the Second World War*, 1989. First quotation, Preface, i, second quotation, 267.

7. Fussell is quoted by David Wyatt, *Secret Histories*, 136.

8. Thomas Friedman, *The World Is Flat: A Brief History of the Twenty-First Century*, 443.

9. Tom Brokaw, *The Greatest Generation*, 382.

10. Gore Vidal, "Writers and Critics of the 1940s," in *United States: Essays, 1952–1992*, 12.

11. Ibid.

12. Ibid., 13.

13. Ibid., 21.

14. Ibid., 17.

15. Ibid., 21.

16. Norman Davies says that a novel or a film set in a historically important context is a possible "point of entry" for understanding. Davies, *Europe: A History*, 430.

17. Kammen, 83.

18. Kammen, 88.

19. Eugenia Kaledin, *Daily Life in the United States, 1940–1959: Shifting Worlds*, 70.

20. Brokaw, *Greatest Generation*, 248.

21. Ibid.

22. Ibid., 137.

23. Ibid., 216.

24. *New York Times*, March 5, 1933, 4.

25. Roosevelt's first "fireside chat" was broadcast on radio on March 12, 1933.

26. Piers Brendon, *The Dark Valley: A Panorama of the 1930s*, 271.

27. Ibid., 270.

28. Ibid., 513.

29. Ibid., 690.

30. Ibid., 515.

31. Ibid., 517–20.

32. Franklin Delano Roosevelt, message to Congress, January 4, 1939.

33. Franklin Delano Roosevelt, radio address, September 4, 1939.

34. Ian Kershaw, *Fateful Choices: Ten Decisions That Changed the World*, 314.

35. David McCullough, *Truman*, 254.

36. Harold Ickes's letter to Roosevelt is quoted in Kershaw, *Fateful Choices*, 304. See also Harold Ickes, *The Secret Diary of Harold Ickes*.

37. Quoted in Kershaw, *Fateful Choices*, 322.

38. Ibid., 325.

39. Takeo Yoshikawa was a trained intelligence agent. Richard Kotoshirado had dual citizenship.

40. William F. Freidman was treated at Walter Reed Hospital for exhaustion and a nervous breakdown from overwork. The SIS was headed by Lieutenant Colonel Rex M. Minckler under the supervision of Colonel Oris K. Sadtler.

41. Hamilton Fish's comments appear in the *Congressional Record*, Vol. 87, Part 8, December 19, 1941, 10051.

42. On March 11, 1942, General MacArthur retreated with his forces to set up command in Australia.

43. *New York Times*, December 7, 1942, and December 8, 1942.

44. James Perloff, "Pearl Harbor Was Surprised, America Was Not," *New American*, December 7, 2016, https://www.thenewamerican.com/culture/history/item/4740-pearl-harbor-hawaii-was-surprised-fdr-was-not.

45. Robert B. Stinnett, *Day of Deceit: The Truth about FDR and Pearl Harbor*.

46. Ellen Nieves, "Some Upset by Twist on Pearl Harbor," *New York Times*, May 28, 2001, http://www.nytimes.com/2001/05/28/us/some-upset-by-twist-on-pearl-harbor.html.

47. CNN interview with Robert Dole, broadcast on Saturday, May 28, 2016, Memorial Day weekend.

I. SIGNALS FROM THE FIELD

1. Ernest Hemingway, *For Whom the Bell Tolls*, 17.

2. John Donne's "Meditation 17" is sometimes recalled by its well-known phrase: "No man is an island."

3. In the Spanish Civil War, cities and countryside were destroyed. Catholic clergy were decimated. Republican Loyalist leftists slew 5,255 priests, including 12 bishops, along with 2,492 monks and 283 nuns; they killed 55,000 civilians. Another 50,000 civilians died by Nationalist military guns.

4. Quoted in Jeffrey Meyers, "A Good Place to Work," *Commonweal*, February 7, 2015, https://www.commonwealmagazine.org/good-place-work.

5. Wilson and Trilling quoted in Jeffrey Meyers, *Hemingway: The Critical Heritage*, 245 and 274; Robert Spiller, *The Cycle of American Literature*, 206.

6. Quoted in Jeffrey Meyers, *Hemingway: A Biography*, 320.

7. Meyers, *Hemingway: A Biography*, 351.

8. Ernest Hemingway, *By-Line, Ernest Hemingway*, 329.

9. Meyers, *Hemingway: A Biography*, 361.

10. Ernest Hemingway, "Voyage to Victory," *Collier's*, July 22, 1944. See Stephen E. Ambrose, *D-Day, June 6, 1944: The Climactic Battle of World War II*, 478–79.

11. Ernest Hemingway, *Colliers*, November 18, 1944.

12. Ernest Hemingway, *A Farewell to Arms*, 184–85.

13. Michael Reynolds, *The Young Hemingway*, 17.

14. Michael Reynolds, *Hemingway: The Paris Years*, 56.

15. Ernest Hemingway, *Selected Letters*, 586.

16. Philip Young, *Ernest Hemingway: A Reconsideration*, quoted in Meyers, *Hemingway, The Critical Heritage*, 202.

17. Hemingway, *Selected Letters*.

18. Carlos Baker, *Ernest Hemingway: A Life Story*, 432.

19. Ibid., 438.

20. Ibid., 443.

21. Ibid., 454–55.

22. Ibid., 455.

23. Walter Lippman comments on Hemingway's perceptiveness of national limitations in *Public Opinion*.

24. Baker, *Ernest Hemingway: A Life Story*, 470.

25. Hemingway, *Selected Letters*, 715.

26. Jackson J. Benson, *The Short Stories of Ernest Hemingway: Critical Essays*, 47.

27. Quoted in Michael Reynolds, *Hemingway: The 1930s Through the Final Years*, 214.

28. A. J. Liebling, *World War II Writings*, 21.

29. Ibid., 37.

30. Ibid., 81.

31. Ibid., 88.

32. Ibid., 99.

33. Ibid., 108.

34. Ibid., 111.

35. Ibid., 110.

36. Ibid., 119.

37. Ibid.

38. Ibid., 122.

39. Ibid., 123.

40. Ibid., 136.

41. Ibid., 138.

42. Ibid., 141.

43. Ibid., 152. On December 7, 1941, Liebling was on a Norwegian boat that was in a storm. There is a thirteen-and-a-half-hour time difference between Britain and Hawaii, and Liebling was asleep when the report of the Pearl Harbor attack arrived.

44. Ibid., 218.

45. Ibid., 262–63.

46. Ibid., 263.

47. Ibid., 300–301.

48. Ibid., 306.

49. Ibid., 464–65.

50. Ibid., 465.

51. Ibid., 467.

52. Lippman, *Public Opinion*, 236.

53. John Dewey, *The Public and Its Problems: An Essay in Political Inquiry*, cited in Brett Gary, *The Nervous Liberals: Propaganda Anxieties from World War I to the Cold War*, 138.

54. Ibid., 140.

55. Lippman, *Public Opinion*, 14–15, 31.

56. Gary, *Nervous Liberals*, 29.

57. Ibid., 34–35.

58. Ibid., 36.

59. John Steinbeck, "Letter, September 20, 1943," *A Life in Letters*, 60.

60. John Steinbeck, *The Moon Is Down*, 1942, caption, Introduction, 1.

61. Ibid., 14. All quoted phrases are descriptions from the novel.

62. Ibid., 113.

63. John Steinbeck, "Introduction," *Bombs Away*, 2009, 2.

2. SOUTHERN VOICES

1. Louis D. Rubin Jr., *A Gallery of Southerners*, xi.

2. Quoted in Rubin, *Gallery of Southerners*, 84.

3. Richard H. King, *Southern Renaissance: The Cultural Awakening of the American South, 1930–1955*, 5.

4. Ibid., 10.

5. John Gardner, *On Moral Fiction*, 192–93.

6. Ibid., 145.

7. Richard Wright, "Inner Landscape," *New Republic*, August 5, 1940.

8. A. S. Knowles Jr., "Carson McCullers in the Forties."

9. Rubin, *Gallery of Southerners*, 21.

10. Bernard DeVoto, "Genius Is Not Enough," 3–4.

11. Thomas Wolfe, *The Story of a Novel*. Wolfe's work recalls Asheville, North Carolina. His father was from Pennsylvania. His mother was from North Carolina. He had relatives whose ancestors had been on both sides of the Civil War.

12. Richard S. Kennedy, "Thomas Wolfe and the American Experience," 153–54.

13. Thomas Wolfe, *The Story of a Novel*, 93.

14. Thomas Wolfe, *Of Time and the River*, 551.

15. Thomas Wolfe, *You Can't Go Home Again*, 699.

16. Ibid.

17. Ernest Hemingway, letter, November 14, 1945, in Ernest Hemingway, *Selected Letters*, 604.

18. Eric Sundquist, *Faulkner: A House Divided*, 133.

19. Frederick Gwynne and Joseph Blotner, *Faulkner in the University*, 84.

20. Original manuscripts are at the Alderman Library, University of Virginia.

21. Faulkner, *Go Down Moses*, in *Novels, 1942–1954*, 361.

22. Ibid., 137.

23. Sundquist, House Divided, 60.

24. Ibid., 61.

25. Faulkner, *Go Down Moses*, 361; Irving Howe, "Faulkner and the Negroes," in *Faulkner: A Collection of Critical Essays*, 46.

26. Faulkner, *Go Down Moses*, 361.

27. Ibid., 288.

28. Ibid., 270.

29. Ibid., 272.

30. Ibid., 275.

31. Ibid.,278.

32. Ibid.

33. Irving Howe, "Faulkner and the Negroes," 47.

34. Ibid.

35. Faulkner, *Go Down Moses*, 118.

36. David Wyatt, "Faulkner and the Burdens of the Past," *Faulkner: New Perspectives*, 116.

37. Howe, "Faulkner and the Negroes," 59.

38. Ibid.

39. Ibid.

40. Susan Willis, "Aesthetics of the Rural Slum: Contradictions and Dependency in The Bear," 178.

41. Faulkner, *Go Down Moses*, 117–18.

42. Katherine Anne Porter, "Introduction," in *Eudora Welty: Selected Stories*, xxi.

43. Ibid., xx.

44. Ibid., xviii.

45. Hemingway, *Selected Letters*, 680.

46. Eugene Armfield, "Short Stories by Eudora Welty," *New York Times Book Review*, reprinted in *The Contemporary Reviews*, ed. Pearl Amelia McHaney, 36; Katherine Woods, *Tomorrow*, reprinted in *The Contemporary Reviews*, 54; Jean Stafford, "The Empty Nest," *Partisan Review*, reprinted in *The Contemporary Reviews*, 46–47.

47. Diana Trilling, quoted in Pearl McHaney, *Eudora Welty, The Contemporary Reviews*, 84; Robert Penn Warren, "The Love and Separateness in Miss Welty's Fiction," 246.

48. David Wyatt, *Secret Histories: Reading Twentieth Century American Literature*, 191.

49. Diana Trilling, quoted in Pearl McHaney, *Eudora Welty*, 84.

50. Diana Trilling, "The Wide Net and Other Stories: Fiction in Review," 386.

51. Wyatt, *Secret Histories*, 92.

52. Ibid., 192.

53. Ibid.

54. Ibid., 204.

55. Eudora Welty, "The Key," in Eudora Welty, *Selected Stories*, 1954, 54.

56. Eudora Welty, "Old Mr. Marblehead," *Selected Stories*, 180.

57. Ibid.

58. Ibid., 185.

59. Ibid.

60. Ibid., 190.

61. Eudora Welty, "Why I Live at the P.O.," *Selected Stories*, 89.

62. Ibid., 92.

63. Ibid., 109.

64. Ibid., 93.

65. Ibid., 103.

66. Robert Penn Warren, "The Love and Separateness in Miss Welty's Fiction," 246–59.

67. Charles E. May, "Why Sister Lives at the P.O.," 44.

68. Eudora Welty, "Death of a Traveling Salesman," *Selected Stories*, 232.

69. Ibid., 232–33.

70. Ibid., 234.

71. Eudora Welty, "A Curtain of Green," *Selected Stories*, 212.

72. Ibid., 215.

73. Ibid., 216.

74. Ibid.

75. Katherine Anne Porter, Introduction, *A Curtain of Green*, reprinted in *Eudora Welty: Selected Stories*, 16.

76. Marianne Hauser, "A Curtain of Green," 6; Kay Boyle "Full Length Portrait, 707; Granville Hicks, quoted in Pearl McHaney (ed.), *Eudora Welty: The Contemporary Reviews*, 249.

77. Diana Trilling, "The Wide Net and Other Stories," 386.

78. Merrill Skaggs, "Enchantment in 'Frontier Home' and *The Robber Bridegroom*," 96.

79. Skaggs, "Enchantment," 96; see also Bruno Bettelheim, *The Uses of Enchantment*, 24.

80. Skaggs, *The Folk of Southern Fiction*, 58.

81. Lionel Trilling, *The Liberal Imagination*, 686.

82. Skaggs, *The Folk of Southern Fiction*, 621.

83. Noel Polk, *Faulkner and Welty and the Southern Literary Tradition*, 5–6.

84. Ibid., 21.

85. Ibid., 19.

86. Louis D. Rubin Jr., quoted in McHaney, *Eudora Welty*, 45. See also Louis D. Rubin and Robert Jacobs (ed.), *Southern Renascence: The Literature of the Modern South.*

87. Robert Penn Warren, *All the King's Men*, 311.

88. Ibid., 248.

89. Ibid., 299.

90. Larry A. Gray, "The Great Disconnect: Jack Burden and History in *All the King's Men*," 80.

91. Ibid., 81.

92. Warren, *All the King's Men*, 435.

93. Ben Railton, "'The Awful Responsibility of Time': Understanding History in *All the King's Men*," 103; James Perkins, "Jack Burden: Successful Historian," 97.

94. Robert Penn Warren, remarks at a meeting of the Southern Historical Society, November 1968.

95. Louis D. Rubin Jr. refers to Southern mythmaking in *Southern Renascence, A Gallery of Southerners*, and in several of his many articles. Also see Louis D. Rubin Jr., and James J. Kirkpatrick, eds., *The Lasting South: Fourteen Southerners Look at Their Home.*

96. Warren, *All the King's Men*, xv.

97. Robert Penn Warren, "A Note to All the King's Men," 182.

98. Michael J. Meyer, "The Many Faces of God," 238.

99. Ibid., 239.

100. Warren, *All the King's Men*, 13–14.

3. NATIVE SONS AND DAUGHTERS

1. Richard Wright, "How Bigger Was Born," xx. In this essay, Wright offers his reflections on the cultural significance of his character in *Native Son*. See also Henry Louis Gates and Kenneth A. Appiah (eds.), *Richard Wright: Critical Perspectives, Past and Present.*

2. Wright, "How Bigger Was Born," xx.

3. Ibid., xx–xxi.

4. Ibid., xxi.

5. Ibid., xxv.

6. Ibid.

7. Ibid., xx.

8. Ibid., xxi.

9. Ibid., xxiii.

10. Ibid., xiv.

11. Ibid., xiii.

12. Ibid.

13. Ibid., xiv.

14. Ibid., xv.

15. Ibid., xvi.

16. Ibid., xv.

17. Ibid.

18. Ibid., xxvi.

19. Ibid., xxvii.

20. Ibid., xxxi.

21. Ibid., xxxii.

22. Esther Merle Jackson, "The American Negro and the Issue of the Absurd," 132.

23. Wright, "Bigger," xxviii.

24. Ibid., xxviii–xxix.

25. Ibid.

26. Richard Wright, *12 Million Black Voices* (1941), "Our Strange Birth," 1969, 12.

27. Some 2 million African Americans moved between the 1890s and the 1920s.

28. Houston A. Baker Jr., "On Knowing Our Place," 208.

29. Wright, *12 Million Black Voices*, 129.

30. Baker, "On Knowing Our Place," 210.

31. Ibid., 203.

32. Ibid., 205.

33. Wright, *12 Million Black Voices*, quoted in Houston A. Baker Jr., *Twentieth Century Interpretations of Native Son*, 88.

34. Ibid.

35. Ibid., 115.

36. Baker, "On Knowing Our Place," 216.

37. Richard Wright, *Black Boy: A Record of Childhood and Youth*, 1.

38. Robert Stepto, *From Behind the Veil: A Study of Afro-American Narrative*, 236.

39. Ibid., 252.

40. Richard Wright, *The Outsider*, 156-57.

41. Chester Himes, *If He Hollers, Let Him Go*, 121.

42. David Wyatt points out that Himes has twenty-two jobs during the war years. Wyatt, *Secret Histories: Reading Twentieth Century American Literature*.

43. Himes, quoted in Wyatt, *Secret Histories*, 123.

44. Wyatt quotes from Ann Petry's *The Street*, in *Secret Histories*, 200.

45. Ibid., 201. See Wyatt's discussion of *The Street* in *Secret Histories*, 199–203.

46. James Baldwin, "Everybody's Protest Novel," *Collected Essays*, 15.

47. Langston Hughes, "Notes on a Native Son."

48. James Baldwin, "History as Nightmare," 11.

49. James Baldwin, "Too Late, Too Late," 98–99.

50. James Baldwin, "Autobiographical Notes," *Collected Essays*, 6.

51. James Baldwin, "The Image of the Negro," 378.

52. James Baldwin, "Smaller Than Life," 78.

53. James Baldwin, "The Dead Hand of Caldwell," 10.

54. James Baldwin, "Present and Future," 11.

55. James Baldwin, "Alas, Poor Richard," 147–49.

56. Maurice Charney, "James Baldwin's Quarrel with Richard Wright," 65–66.

57. Baldwin, "Alas, Poor Richard," 147, 151.

58. Ibid.

59. Baldwin, "Autobiographical Notes," 11.

60. James Baldwin, "Many Thousands Gone," in *Notes of a Native Son*, 35–36.

61. Baldwin, "Everybody's Protest Novel," 14–15.

62. James Baldwin, "Many Thousands Gone," in *Notes of a Native Son*, 30.

63. Baldwin, "Everybody's Protest Novel," 14.

64. Ibid., 14–15.

65. Baldwin, "Many Thousands Gone," 30.

66. Ibid.

67. Baldwin, "Alas, Poor Richard," 149.

68. Baldwin, "Many Thousands Gone," 27.

69. Baldwin, Everybody's Protest Novel"; Ralph Ellison, "The World and the Jug," 155–88. This was Ellison's response to Irving Howe's essay, "Black Boys and Native Sons," 165.

70. The office of President Barack Obama quoted James Baldwin in May 2015.

71. James Baldwin, "As Much Truth as One Can Bear," in *Cross of Redemption: Uncollected Writings*, 34.

72. James Baldwin, letter to Archbishop Desmond Tutu, 1985, in *Cross of Redemption*, 264.

73. James Baldwin, "The Artist Struggling for Integrity," in *Cross of Redemption*, 50.

74. Arnold Rampersad, *Ralph Ellison*, 142.

75. Ibid., 171.

76. Ibid., 174.

77. Richard Wright, *12 Million Black Voices*, noted by Ralph Ellison in a letter to Richard Wright, in Rampersad, 144. The letters are in the Richard Wright Collection, Beinecke Library, Yale University.

78. Ellison, letter to Richard Wright, in Rampersad, 145.

79. Quoted in Rampersad, 184.

80. Ibid., 92.

81. Ibid., 88.

82. Ibid., 186.

83. Ibid., 194.

84. Ibid., 157.

85. Quoted in Lucille B. Milner, "Jim Crow in the Army," 52.

86. In *Reporting Civil Rights*, 85.

87. George McMillan, "Race, Justice in Aiken," *The Nation* (November 23, 1946).

88. William Chafe, *The Unfinished Journey: America Since World War II*, 86.

89. Reprinted in *Jet*, January 2, 1958. Democrat Jim Folsom served as Alabama's governor from 1947 to 1951 and again from 1955 to 1959.

90. Jack H. Pollack, "Literacy Tests: Southern Style," 85.

91. Justice Earl Warren, *Brown v. Board of Education*, May 17, 1954.

92. Septima Clark, *Ready from Within*, 1.

4. WAR STORIES

1. John Horne Burns, *The Gallery*, 309 and 18.

2. James Jones, *World War II: A Chronicle of Soldiering*, 11.

3. Warren French, *The Forties: Fiction, Poetry, Drama*, 31.

4. Granville Hicks, *James Gould Cozzens*, 23.

5. James Gould Cozzens, *The Just and the Unjust*, 25.

6. Hicks, *Cozzens*, 28.

7. Cozzens, *The Just and the Unjust*.

8. Matthew Brucolli, *James Gould Cozzens: A Life Apart*, 186.

9. Orville Prescott, "Outstanding Novels," *Yale Review*, 382.

10. Noel Perrin, *Washington Post World.*

11. Louis O. Coxe, "The Complex World of *Guard of Honor,*" 157.

12. *Time* (September 2, 1957), quoted in Hicks, *James Gould Cozzens,* 42.

13. Ibid., 28.

14. Lucille B. Milner, "Jim Crow in the Army," 55.

15. Ibid., 54.

16. James Gould Cozzens, *Guard of Honor,* 5.

17. Ibid., 29.

18. Hicks, *James Gould Cozzens,* 40.

19. Cozzens, *Guard of Honor,* 238.

20. Hicks, *James Gould Cozzens,* 41.

21. Frederick Bracher, *The Novels of James Gould Cozzens.*

22. Hicks, *James Gould Cozzens,* 41.

23. Bracher, *Novels of James Gould Cozzens,* i–iv; see also Hicks, *Cozzens,* 45.

24. John M. Kinder, "The Good War's Raw Chunks: Norman Mailer's *The Naked and the Dead* and James Cozzens's *Guard of Honor,*" 193.

25. Ibid.

26. Kinder (193) adds that Norman Mailer drew on his own experiences of anti-Semitic prejudice, and rejected the practice of making Jews targets of ridicule and abuse. In *The Naked and the Dead,* Joey Goldstein writes that "it's hard to remember all the fine ideals. Sometimes even with the Jews in Europe I don't know why we're fighting." Mailer, *The Naked and the Dead,* 202.

27. Kinder, 187–88.

28. Ibid., 199.

29. H. H. "Hap" Arnold, *The War Reports,* 313.

30. Ibid., 310–11.

31. Ibid., 312.

32. Ibid., 315.

33. Ibid., 316.

34. Ibid., 317.

35. Ibid., 321.

36. Ibid., 331.

37. Ibid., 332.

38. Ibid., 334.

39. Ibid., 340.

40. Ibid., 341.

41. Ibid., 343.

42. Ibid., 466.

43. Milner, "Jim Crow in the Army," 53.

44. Ibid., 54.

45. Cozzens, *Guard of Honor*, 302.

46. Irwin Shaw, *The Young Lions*, 15.

47. Thomas Weyr, *The Setting of the Pearl: Vienna Under Hitler*, 1–2.

48. *Neue Freie Presse* (March 15, 1938), quoted in Weyr, *Setting of the Pearl*, 36. Hitler's proclamation is quoted in Weyr, 37.

49. Shaw, *The Young Lions*, 272.

50. Ibid., 275.

51. Ibid., 278.

52. Ibid., 286.

53. Ibid., 229.

54. Mailer, *The Naked and the Dead*, 303.

55. Diana Trilling, "The Radical Moralism of Norman Mailer," 49. Chester E. Eisinger calls *The Naked and the Dead* "one of the few successful novels of ideas written during the decade" in *Fiction of the Forties*, 21.

56. Mailer, *The Naked and the Dead*, 196.

57. Terry Teachout, "Norman Mailer, Literary Hustler," 57.

58. Ibid., 58.

59. Ibid., 57. See J. Michael Lennon, *Norman Mailer: A Double Life*.

60. Lennon, *Norman Mailer: A Double Life*, 46.

61. Norman Mailer, *Pieces and Pontifications*, 165.

62. David Cowart, "Norman Mailer: Like a Wrecking Ball from Outer Space." *American Adam*, by R. W. B. Lewis, looked at the American experience through the myth of America as a new Eden. Norman Mailer saw no new Eden of renewal, only conflict.

63. Norman Mailer, *Advertisements for Myself*, 384.

64. "In Another Country," *New York Review of Books*, July 22, 1971, reprinted in Gore Vidal, *United States: Essays, 1952–1992*, 583–94.

65. Dick Cavett, *Talk Show: Confrontations, Pointed Commentary and Off-Screen Secrets*, n.p.

66. James Michener, *Tales of the South Pacific*, 93.

67. Chester Kerr to Richard J. Walsh, John Day Company, quoted in Karen Leong, *The China Mystique: Pearl S. Buck, Anna Wong, May Ling Soon and the Transformation of American Orientalism*, 51; Herbert Agar review of "American Unity and Asia."

68. Ibid.

69. Buck, quoted in Leong, *China Mystique*, 31.

70. Pearl S. Buck, letter to Richard J. Walsh, quoted in Leong, *China Mystique*, 26.

71. Dorothy Canfield Fisher's letter to Harry Scherman nominating *The Good Earth* for the Book of the Month Club selection.

72. Buck, quoted in Leong, *China Mystique*, 44.

73. Ibid., 46; Buck's Harvard commencement address is cited by her biographer.

74. Leong, *China Mystique*, 48.

75. Pearl S. Buck, *The Promise: A Pearl Buck Reader*, 23.

76. Ibid., 33–34.

77. Ibid., 35.

78. Ibid., 36.

79. Section 3 of *The Promise* ends with the proverb: "Only heaven can fulfill promises."

80. Buck, *The Promise*, 51.

81. Ibid., 58.

82. Ibid., 68.

83. Ibid., 74.

84. Ibid., 77.

85. Ibid., 84.

86. Ibid., 85.

87. John Hersey, *A Bell for Adano*, 7.

88. Ibid., 8–9.

89. Ibid., 47–48.

90. Jonathan Dee, "John Hersey, The Art of Fiction No. 92," 211; Ruth Benedict, "The Past and the Future."

91. Gertrude Stein, "Reflections on the Atom Bomb," 27; Susan Sontag, "The Imagination of Disaster," 43.

92. Statistics on the *New Yorker* circulation in *The New Yorker Book of the 40s*, 38.

93. John Hersey, *Hiroshima*, 31.

94. Thomas Friedman, *The World Is Flat: A Brief History of the Twenty-First Century*, 443.

95. Hersey, *Hiroshima*, 86.

96. Ibid., 88.

97. Warren French, *The Forties: Fiction, Poetry, Drama*, 338.

98. Harry S. Truman, *Memoirs: The Years of Trial and Hope, 1946–1952*.

99. The Walter Mondale interview was broadcast May 26, 2016, on MSNBC.

5. LIFE ON THE HOME FRONT

1. President Franklin Delano Roosevelt, letter to baseball Commissioner Kennesaw Mountain Landis, quoted in *The Cambridge Companion to Baseball*, 87.

2. Ibid., 86.

3. Ibid., 87.

4. Ibid., 88.

5. Saul Bellow, *Dangling Man: Novels, 1944–1953*, 15.

6. Ibid.

7. Ibid.

8. Ibid., 17–18.

9. Ibid., 18.

10. Ibid., 19.

11. Saul Below, *Dangling Man*. New York: Library of America, 1–2.

12. Roosevelt, 124.

13. Bellow, *Dangling Man*, p.1–first paragraph. Joseph's comment on men who "fly planes, fight bulls, or catch tarpon" surely alludes to Hemingway.

14. William F. Buckley Jr., *Miles Gone By: A Literary Autobiography*, 309.

15. Jennifer Burns, *Goddess of the Market: Ayn Rand and the American Right*, 139.

16. Burns, *Goddess of the Market*, 68; Tobias Wolff, *Old School*.

17. Ayn Rand, "Roark's Speech," in *Selfishness*, Chapter 1, Part 2, *Ayn Rand Reader*, ed. Gary Hill and Leonard Peikoff. New York: Plume, 1999.

18. Ayn Rand, *The Fountainhead*, 684.

19. Ibid., 694.

20. Rand seems to have been moved by Herbert Spencer's Darwinian sense of fierce competition and Oswald Spengler's predictions of the decline and fall of the Western world.

21. Burns, *Goddess of the Market*, 80.

22. Ayn Rand, letter to the editor, *New York Herald Tribune*, quoted in Burns, 80.

23. See John Meynard Keynes, *General Theory of Unemployment, Interest, and Money*.

24. Jennifer Burns offers a variety of reader responses of their "awakening" to *The Fountainhead*; *Goddess of the Market*, 91–93.

25. John C. Tibbets and James M. Welsh, *Encyclopedia of Novels into Film*, 135.

26. Burns, *Goddess of the Market*, 93.

27. Ayn Rand, *Journals*, 74, quoted in Burns, 44.

28. John Dos Passos, *The Ground We Stand On: The History of a Political Creed*, 1.

29. Ibid.

30. Ibid., 2.

31. Ibid., 5.

32. Alfred Kazin, introduction to John Dos Passos, *The Big Money*, xiv.

33. Ibid., ix.

34. Norman Mailer, quoted in *Dictionary of Literary Biography*, 173.

35. J. Michael Lennon, *Norman Mailer: A Double Life*, 93.

36. Mailer quoted in Lennon, 23.

37. Norman Mailer, *Pieces and Pontifications*, 133.

38. Dos Passos, *The Big Money*, ix.

39. Dos Passos, *The Ground We Stand On*, 11.

40. Ibid., 12.

41. Ibid.

42. Norman Mailer, quoted in Donald Pizer, "Norman Mailer, Theodore Dreiser, and the Politics of American Literary History," 459.

43. Lionel Trilling, *The Liberal Imagination*, 11–14.

44. Pizer "Norman Mailer, Theodore Dreiser," 459.

45. John O'Hara, quoted in Frank MacShane, *The Life of John O'Hara*, 201.

46. Ibid., 27.

47. The *New Yorker* was founded in February 1925 by Harold Ross. He was succeeded by William Shawn.

48. MacShane, 54.

49. Frank MacShane cites F. Scott Fitzgerald, "The Crack Up."

50. Ibid., 86.

51. Frank MacShane points out that O'Hara had heard negative things about Darryl Zanuck, the producer at Twentieth Century Fox, but found that he liked him and could work with him. MacShane, *John O'Hara*, 101.

52. Ibid., 105.

53. See Edmund Wilson, *Literary Essays and Reviews of the 1920s and 30s*, 527; Ernest Hemingway, *Selected Letters*, 527.

54. Stephen Birmingham, *The Late John P. Marquand: A Biography*, 342.

55. Marquand, *So Little Time*, 12.

56. Ibid., 14.

57. Ibid.

58. Ibid., 7.

59. Ibid.

60. Ibid., 11.

61. Ibid., 15.

62. Ibid., 31.

63. Ibid., 17.

64. Ibid., 26.

65. Ibid.

66. Ibid., 29.

67. Ibid., 37.

68. Ibid., 38.

69. Ibid., 42.

70. Ibid., 53.

71. Ibid.

72. Ibid., 55.

73. Ibid.

74. Ibid., 64.

75. Ibid., 66.

76. Ibid., 69.

77. Ibid., 78.

78. Ibid., 100.

79. Ibid., 125.

80. Ibid., 229–38.

81. Ibid., 238.

82. Ibid., 240.

83. Diana Trilling, "What Has Happened to Our Novels?" 533.

84. Edmund Wilson's criticism of Marquand is quoted in a letter by Raymond Chandler, *Selected Letters*, 59.

85. Four editions, from 1947 to 1963, sold 771,000 copies.

86. Blake Bailey, *John Cheever: A Life*, 101–2.

87. Ibid., 111.

88. Ibid., 117.

89. Ibid., 131.

90. "The Enormous Radio" in *The Stories of John Cheever*. New York: Ballantine, 1978, 37–48.

91. Ibid., 183.

92. Ibid., 109.

93. Irving Stock, *Mary McCarthy*, 1.

94. Ibid., 15.

95. Mary McCarthy, "America the Beautiful," 116.

96. Mary McCarthy, "The Vita Activa," 156.

97. William Barrett, *The Truants*, 67.

98. Quoted in Paul Schleuter, "The Dissections of Mary McCarthy," 61, 64.

99. Doris Grumbach, *The Company She Kept*, 36.

100. Norman Mailer, "The Case Against Mary McCarthy," 138.

6. POSTWAR AMERICA AND THE
AGE OF ANXIETY

1. "Victory in Europe," *Time*, May 14, 1945, 17.

2. William Chafe, *The Unfinished Journey: America Since World War II*, 122.

3. Michael Kammen, *American Culture, American Tastes: Social Change in the Twentieth Century*, 181.

4. Chafe, *Unfinished Journey*, 75.

5. Ibid., 79. A total of 3.25 million women left their jobs, and about 2.75 million were hired.

6. Ibid., 128.

7. Ibid., 117–18.

8. Kammen, *American Culture*, 181.

9. Ibid., 32.

10. Ibid., 50.

11. Chafe, *Unfinished Journey*, 137.

12. David McCullough, *Truman* 58. Also see McCullough's essay in *Character Above All: Ten Presidents from FDR to George W. Bush*.

13. McCullough, *Truman*, 191.

14. Ibid., 557.

15. Ibid., 986.

16. Ibid., 588.

17. Ibid., 247.

18. Ibid., 251.

19. Ibid., 286–87.

20. Ibid., 287.

21. Ibid.

22. William Safire, *Lend Me Your Ears: Great Speeches in History*, 960–62.

23. These comments were repeated by Truman in Newark, Camden, Philadelphia, and Wilmington.

24. Quoted in Chafe, *Unfinished Journey*, 100.

25. Harry S. Truman, State of the Union Address. January 6, 1947.

26. George C. Marshall, speech at Harvard University, June 5, 1947.

27. Robert Silverberg, "Science Fiction in the Fifties: The Real Golden Age," Library of America, 2010.

28. William Patterson, *Robert A. Heinlein: In Dialogue with His Century*, Vol.1, 315, 317.

29. Heinlein is quoted in Patterson, *Robert A. Heinlein*, 342.

30. Robert Heinlein, letter to Ginny Gerstenfeld, a government engineer, quoted in Patterson, 332.

31. Daniel Bell, *The Coming of Post-Industrial Society*.

32. Leonard Cassuto, *The Graduate School Mess: What Caused It and How We Can Fix It*, 39.

33. See Chafe's reference to a new managerial personality. Chafe, *Unfinished Journey*, 110.

34. Patterson, *Robert A. Heinlein*, 326.

35. Andrew Feenberg, *Alternative Modernity: The Technical Turn in Philosophy and Social Theory*, 42.

36. Adam Roberts, *History of Science Fiction*, 287.

37. Ibid.

38. David Ketterer, *New Worlds for Old: The Apocalyptic Imagination, Science Fiction, and American Literature*, viii.

39. Douglas Robinson is cited in Ketterer, *New Worlds for Old*, viii.

40. Sharon Baker and Wendy Martin, "The Cold War Novel," 92.

41. Ibid.

42. Rollo May, *The Meaning of Anxiety*, 12.

43. Paul Tillich quoted in May, *Meaning of Anxiety*, 12.

44. Ibid., 4.

45. Ibid., 5.

46. Quoted in May, *Meaning of Anxiety*, 11.

47. James Agee, *Now Let Us Praise Famous Men, A Death in the Family, and Shorter Fiction*.

48. Alfred Kazin, *On Native Grounds: An Interpretation of Modern Prose Literature*, 495.

49. Ibid., 517.

50. Quoted in Kazin, *On Native Grounds*, 485.

51. Ibid., 517.

7. LOOKING TO THE FIFTIES

1. Alfred Kazin, *On Native Grounds: An Interpretation of Modern Prose Literature* (1942), 495. The comment by John Dos Passos appears in his introduction to *The Ground We Stand On*. The relation of fiction to reality is explored in Lionel Trilling's "Manners, Morals, and the Novel," in *The Liberal Imagination* (1950). Trilling says that a novel conveys "a culture's hum and buzz of implication" (194) and "our particular conception of reality" (203). The novel, he says, involves us "in the moral life" (209). In *When Books Went to War* (2014) Molly Guptil Manning describes the importance of books among World War II soldiers. Books were distributed to American soldiers in Armed Service Editions as propaganda, as well as for entertainment and to boost morale. George Orwell, "Politics and the English Language," *George Orwell Reader: Fiction, Essays, Reportage*. New York: Mariner Books, 1961.

2. David Remnick, "*The New Yorker* in the Forties," http://www.newyorker.com/books/page-turner/the-new-yorker-in-the-forties.

3. Beth Luey, "The Organization of the Book Publishing Industry," 29.

4. Thomas Merton, "Meditatio Pauperis In Solitudine," *The Thomas Merton Reader*, ed. Thomas T. McDonnell, 513.

5. Thomas Merton, *Hidden Ground of Love*, 460.

6. Thomas Merton, *Contemplation in a World of Action*, 144, 160.

7. Ibid., 161.

8. The American Publishing Association has noticed a fourteen-point drop in mass-market paperback sales since 2008. This is partly attributed to e-books.

9. For *Publishers Weekly* statistics see www.publishers weekly.com/pw.

10. Dana Gioia, preface, *To Read or Not to Read: A Question of National Consequence*, 6.

11. Clifton Fadiman, *Party of One*, 359–60. Considering transitions in print, orality, and literacy, Walter Ong proposed that modern communications introduce a "secondary orality," which calls upon the development of skills that are involved with interaction with television, film, audio recordings, and now computers; see Ong, *Orality and Literacy: The Technologizing of the Word*. Marshall McLuhan suggested that new media carry over the forms and patterns we already have in our reception of established media; see MacLuhan, *Understanding Media: The Extensions of Man*.

12. Gioia, *To Read or Not to Read*, 6.

13. Vance Packard wrote on the trends in advertising in *The Hidden Persuaders*.

14. William Chafe, *The Unfinished Journey: America Since World War II*, 123.

15. Marie Winn, *The Plug-In Drug*; Neil Postman, *Amusing Ourselves to Death: Public Discourse in the Age of Show Business*; and Daniel J. Boorstin, *The Image: A Guide to Pseudo-Events in America*, p. 13.

16. Michael Kammen, *American Culture, American Tastes: Social Change in the Twentieth Century*, 90.

17. Ibid., 92.

18. Robert Bellah, "Individualism and Commitment in American Life," lecture at the University of California, Santa Barbara, February 20, 1986, http://www.robertbellah.com/lectures_4.htm.

19. Benedict Anderson, *Imagined Communities: Reflections on the Origins and Spread of Nationalism*.

20. Kazin, *On Native Grounds*, 517.

21. John Steinbeck, *Steinbeck: A Life in Letters*, 485; W. H. Auden, *The Age of Anxiety: A Baroque Ecloge*.

22. Kazin, *On Native Grounds*, 517.

23. Tom Brokaw, *The Greatest Generation*, 386.

BIBLIOGRAPHY

Ackerman, Alan L. *Just Words: Lillian Hellman, Mary McCarthy, and the Failure of Public Conversation in America*. New Haven, CT: Yale University Press, 2011.

Adler, Mortimer, and Charles Van Doren. *How to Read a Book*. Reprint, New York: Touchstone, Simon and Schuster, 1972.

———. *Now Let Us Praise Famous Men, A Death in the Family, and Shorter Fiction*. 1940. Edited by Michael Sragow. Reprint, New York: Library of America, 2005.

Agar, Herbert. Review of *American Unity and Asia*. *Louisville Courier Journal*, 1942.

Ambrose, Stephen E. *D-Day, June 6, 1944: The Climactic Battle of World War II*. New York: Simon and Schuster, 1994.

Anderson, Benedict, *Imagined Communities: Reflections on the Origins and Spread of Nationalism*. London: Verso, 1983.

Anderson, Maxwell. *Candle in the Wind*. Washington, DC: Anderson House, 1941.

Arnold, H. H. *The War Reports*, Vol. II. Norwalk: Easton Press, 2006.

Asimov, Isaac. *Foundation*. Reprint, New York: Random House, 2004.

Auden, W. H. *The Age of Anxiety: A Baroque Ecloge*. 1947. Reprint, Princeton, NJ: Princeton University Press, 2011.

Bailey, Blake. *John Cheever: A Life*. New York: Vintage, 2009.

Baker, Carlos. *Ernest Hemingway: A Life Story*. New York: Charles Scribner's, 1969.

Baker, Houston A., Jr. "On Knowing Our Place." In *Richard Wright: Critical Perspectives Past and Present*, edited by Henry Louis Gates and Kenneth A. Appiah, 200–25. New York: Amistad, Penguin, 1998.

———. *Twentieth Century Interpretations of Native Son*. Englewood Cliffs: Prentice Hall, 1972.

Baker, Sharon, and Wendy Martin. "The Cold War Novel." In *A Companion to the American Novel*, edited by Alfred Bendixen, 90–108. Hoboken: Blackwell, 2012.

Baldwin, James. "Alas, Poor Richard." In *Nobody Knows My Name*, 147–49. 1961. Reprinted New York: Dell, 1970.

———. "Autobiographical Notes." In *Notes of a Native Son*, 6. Boston: Beacon Press, 1955.

———. *Collected Essays*. New York: Library of America, 1998.

———. *Cross of Redemption: Uncollected Writings*. Edited by Randall Kenan. New York: Pantheon, 2010.

———. "The Dead Hand of Caldwell." *The New Leader*, December 6, 1947, 10.

———. *Early Novels and Stories: Go Tell It on a Mountain/Giovanni's Room/Another Country*. New York: Library of America, 1998.

———. "From Harlem to Paris." *New York Times Book Review*, February 26, 1956, 26.

————. "'History as Nightmare': Review of *Lonely Crusade*." *The New Leader*, October 25, 1947, 11.

————. "The Image of the Negro." *Commentary*, April 1948, 379–80.

————. "Many Thousands Gone." In *Notes of a Native Son*, 27. Boston: Beacon Press, 1955.

————. "'Present and Future': Review of *The Person and the Good*." *The New Leader*, March 13, 1948, 11.

————. "'Smaller Than Life': Review of *There Was Once a Slave*." *The Nation*, July 19, 1947, 78.

————. "Too Late, Too Late." *Commentary*, January 1949, 98–99.

Barrett, William. *The Truants*. New York: Anchor, Doubleday, 1982.

Bell, Daniel. *The Coming of Post-Industrial Society*. New York: Basic Books, 2008.

Bellah, Robert. *Habits of the Heart*. Berkeley: University of California Press, 1985.

————. "Individualism and Commitment in American Life." Lecture, University of California, Santa Barbara, February 20, 1986. http://www.robertbellah.com/lectures_4.htm.

Bellow, Saul. *Dangling Man: Novels, 1944–1953*. New York: Library of America, 2003.

Benedict, Ruth. "The Past and the Future," review of *Hiroshima* by John Hersey. *The Nation*. December 7, 1946.

Benet, Stephen Vincent. "By the Waters of Babylon." *Saturday Evening Post*, July 31, 1939, 10–11, 59–60.

Benson, Jackson J. *The Short Stories of Ernest Hemingway: Critical Essays*. Durham, NC: Duke University Press, 1975.

Bettelheim, Bruno. *The Uses of Enchantment*. New York: Knopf/Doubleday, 1989.

Beveridge, William H. *Full Employment in a Free Society*. London: Allen and Unwin, 1944.

Biesen, Sheri. *Blackout: World War II and the Origins of Film Noir*. Baltimore: Johns Hopkins University Press, 2005.

Birmingham, Stephen. *The Late John P. Marquand: A Biography*. New York: Lippincott, 1972.

Blotner, Joseph. *Faulkner: A Biography*. New York: Random House, 1974.

Boorstin, Daniel. *The Image: A Guide to Pseudo-Events in America*. New York: Harper Colophon, 1962. Reprint, New York: Vintage, 1992.

Bowles, Chester. *Tomorrow Without Fear*. New York: Simon and Schuster, 1946.

Boyle, Kay. "Full Length Portrait." *New Republic*, November 24, 1941, 707–8.

Bracher, Frederick. *The Novels of James Gould Cozzens*. New York: Harcourt Brace, 1959.

Bradbury, Ray. *Fahrenheit 451*. 1953. Reprint, New York: Bantam Books, 1993.

————. "There Will Come Soft Rains." *The Martian Chronicles*. 1950. Reprint, New York: Bantam Books, 1979.

Brendon, Piers. *The Dark Valley: A Panorama of the 1930s*. New York: Alfred A. Knopf, 2000.

Briannes, Matthew M. *A Cultural History of 1940s Interracial America*. Princeton, NJ: Princeton University Press, 2012.

Brokaw, Tom. *The Greatest Generation*. New York: Random House, 1998.

Bruccoli, Matthew J. *James Gould Cozzens: A Descriptive Biography*. University of Pittsburgh Press, 1981.

————. *James Gould Cozzens: A Life Apart*. New York: Harcourt, 1983.

————, ed. *A Time of War: Air Force Diaries and Pentagon Memos*. Cambridge, MA: Harvard University Press, 1984.

Buck, Pearl S. *The Promise*. New York: Bartholomew House, 1946.

————. *The Promise: A Pearl Buck Reader, Vol. 2*. Pleasantville: Reader's Digest, 1985.

Buckley, William F. *Miles Gone By: A Literary Autobiography*. Washington, DC: Regnery, 2004.

Burns, Jennifer. *Goddess of the Market: Ayn Rand and the American Right*. New York and Oxford: Oxford University Press, 2009.

Burns, John Horne. *The Gallery*. 1947. New York: New York Review Books Classics, 2004.

Burt, John. *Robert Penn Warren and American Idealism*. New Haven, CT: Yale University Press, 1988.

Camus, Albert. *The Stranger* (1942). Cambridge: Cambridge University Press, 2004.

Capote, Truman. *Other Voices, Other Rooms*. 1948. Reprint, New York: Random House, Vintage, 1994.

Cash, Wilbur. *The Mind of the South*. 1941. Reprint, New York: Vintage, 1950.

Cassuto, Leonard. ed. *The Cambridge Companion to Baseball*. Cambridge: Cambridge University Press, 2011.

———. ed. *The Cambridge History of the American Novel*. Cambridge: Cambridge University Press, 2011.

———. *The Graduate School Mess: What Caused It and How We Can Fix It*. Cambridge, MA: Harvard University Press, 2015.

Cavett, Dick. *Talk Show: Confrontations, Pointed Commentary and Off-Screen Secrets*. New York: St. Martin's Press, 2011.

Chafe, William H. *The Unfinished Journey: America Since World War II*. 6th edition. New York and Oxford: Oxford University Press, 2007.

Chafee, Zechariah. *Free Speech in the United States*. Cambridge, MA: Harvard University Press, 1941. Reprint, New York: Atheneum, 1969.

Chambers, Whittaker. "Big Sister Is Watching You." *National Review*. December 28, 1957.

Chandler, Raymond. *The Big Sleep*. 1939. Reprint, New York: Vintage, 1988.

———. *Farewell, My Lovely*. 1940. Reprint, New York: Vintage Crime, 1988.

———. *Selected Letters*. New York: Columbia University Press, 1981.

Charney, Maurice. "James Baldwin's Quarrel with Richard Wright." *American Quarterly* 15 (Spring 1963), 65–75.

Cheever, John. *The Complete Novels*. New York: Library of America, 2009.

———. *The Short Stories of John Cheever*. New York: Alfred A. Knopf, 1978.

Chesnut, Mary Boykin. 1949. *Diary from Dixie*. Edited by Ben Ames Williams. Reprint, Cambridge, MA: Harvard University Press, 1980.

Clark, Septima. *Ready from Within*. Jackson, MS: Wild Tree Press, 1986.

Coates, Robert. *The Outlaw Years*. New York: Macauley, 1930.

Conlin, Joseph R. *The American Past*. Cengage Advantage, Wadsworth, 2012.

Costain, Thomas B. *The Black Rose*. Garden City: Doubleday, 1945.

Cowley, Malcolm, ed. *The Portable Hemingway*. New York: Viking, 1944.

Cowart, David. "Norman Mailer: Like a Wrecking Ball from Outer Space." *Critique* 51, no. 2 (Winter 2010): 159–67.

Coxe, Louis O. "The Complex World of *Guard of Honor*," *American Literature*, May 1955, 157.

Cozzens, James Gould. *Ask Me Tomorrow*. New York: Harcourt Brace, 1940.

———. *Guard of Honor*. New York: Harcourt Brace, 1948. Reprint, New York: Harvest, 1964.

———. *The Just and the Unjust*. New York: Harcourt Brace, 1942.

Davies, Norman. *Europe: A History*. Oxford: Oxford University Press, 1996.

———. *No Simple Victory: World War II in Europe, 1939–1945*. New York: Viking, 2006.

Dee, Jonathan. "John Hersey, The Art of Fiction No. 92." *Paris Review*, no. 100, Summer–Fall 1986, 211–49.

DeVoto, Bernard. "Genius Is Not Enough," *Saturday Review of Literature* 12 (April 25, 1936): 3–4.

Dewey, John. *The Public and Its Problems: An Essay in Political Inquiry*. 1927. Reprint, Chicago: Gateway, 1946.

Dickstein, Morris. *Dancing in the Dark: A Cultural History of the Great Depression*. New York: 2009.

Dobbs, Charles M. *The Marshall Plan Economic Corporation Act 1948*. New York: Macmillan, 2004.

Dos Passos, John. *Adventures of a Young Man*. New York: Harcourt Brace, 1939.

———. *The Big Money*. Introduction by Alfred Kazin. New York: Signet, 1969.

———. *The Grand Design*. New York: Houghton Mifflin, 1949.

———. *The Ground We Stand On: The History of a Political Creed*. New Brunswick: Transaction Press, 2010.

———. *The Prospect Before Us*. New York: Houghton Mifflin, 1950.

Douglas, Lloyd. *The Big Fisherman*. New York: Houghton Mifflin, 1949; London: Peter Davies, 1949.

―――. *The Magnificent Obsession*. New York: Grossett and Dunlap, 1929.

―――. *The Robe*. New York: Houghton Mifflin, 1942.

Dreiser, Theodore. *The Bulwark*. Garden City: Doubleday, 1946.

―――. *The Stoic*. Garden City: Doubleday, 1947.

Eisinger, Chester E. *Fiction of the Forties*. Chicago: University of Chicago Press, 1963.

Ellison, Ralph. *Flying Home: And Other Stories*. New York: Vintage 1998.

―――. *Invisible Man*. New York: Random House, 1952.

―――. "Richard Wright's Blues," *Antioch Review*, June 1945, 198–211.

―――. *Shadow and Act*. New York: Vintage, 1972.

―――. "The World and the Jug." *The Collected Essays of Ralph Ellison*. Ed. John F. Callahan. New York: Modern Library Classics, Random House, 2003.

Erenberg, Lewis A., and Susan E. Hirsch, eds. *The War in American Culture: Society and Consciousness During World War II*. Chicago: University of Chicago Press, 1996.

Fadiman, Clifton. *Party of One*. Cleveland: World Publishing, 1955.

Faulkner, William. *Light in August. Novels 1930–1935*. Ed. Noel Polk and Joseph Blother. New York: Library of America, 1994.

Novels: 1936–1940. Edited by Joseph Blotner and Noel Polk. New York: Library of America, 1990.

―――. *Novels, 1942–1954*. Edited by Joseph Blotner and Noel Polk. New York: Library of America, 1994.

Feenberg, Andrew. *Alternative Modernity: The Technical Turn in Philosophy and Social Theory*. Berkeley: University of California Press, 1995.

Ferrelly, John. Review of *Other Voices, Other Rooms New Republic*. January 26, 1948.

Fish, Hamilton. Comment from Representative Hamilton Fish, *The Congressional Record*. Vol. 87, Part 8 (December 19, 1941): 10051.

Fisher, Dorothy Canfield. "Introduction to the First Edition." In *Twentieth Century Interpretations of Native Son*, edited by Houston A. Baker, 121. Englewood Cliffs, NJ: Prentice Hall, 1972.

Frank, Richard B. *Downfall: The End of the Imperial Japanese Empire*. New York: Penguin, 1999.

French, Warren. *The Forties: Fiction, Poetry, Drama*. Deland, FL: Everett Edwards, 1969.

Friedman, Thomas L. *The World Is Flat: A Brief History of the Twenty-First Century*. New York: Farrar, Straus and Giroux, 2005.

Fussell, Paul. *Wartime: Understanding and Behavior in the Second World War*. New York and Oxford: Oxford University Press, 1990.

Gaddis, John L. *The United States and the Origins of the Cold War, 1941–1947*. New York: Oxford University Press, 1972.

―――. *Strategies of Containment: A Critical Appraisal of Postwar National Containment Policy*. 1982.

Gardner, John. *On Moral Fiction*. New York: Basic Books, 1978.

Gary, Brett. *The Nervous Liberals: Propaganda Anxieties from World War I to the Cold War*. New York: Columbia University Press, 1999.

Gates, Henry Louis, and Kenneth A. Appiah. eds. *Richard Wright: Critical Perspectives Past and Present*. New York: Amistad, Penguin, 1998.

Gellhorn, Martha. *Liana*. 1944. Reprint, New York: Picador, 1993.

Gilbert, Martin. *The Second World War*. New York: Henry Holt, 2004.

―――. *The Holocaust*. London: Folio, 2012.

Gioia, Dana. Preface, *"To Read or Not to Read: A Question of National Consequence."* Research Report no. 47, National Endowment for the Arts, 2007.

Girard, Rene. *The Girard Reader*. Edited by James G. Williams. New York: Crossroads, 1996.

Gordon, Caroline. *The Collected Stories of Caroline Gordon*. New York: Farrar, Straus, and Giroux, 2009.

―――. *Green Centuries* (1941). Chicago: J. S. Sanders, 1992.

————. *The Women on the Porch* (1944). Chicago: J. S. Sanders, 1993.

Gray, Larry A. "The Great Disconnect: Jack Burden and History in *All the King's Men*." In *Robert Penn Warren's All the King's Men*, edited by Michael J. Meyer and Hugh J. Ingrasci, 79–90. New York and Amsterdam: Rodopi, 2012.

Greenspan, Alan. *The Age of Turbulence: Adventures in a New World*. New York: Penguin, 2008, 53.

Grimes, Larry, and Bickford Sylvester. *Hemingway, Cuba, and the Cuban Works*. Kent, OH: Kent State University Press, 2014.

Gross, Beverly. "Our Leading Bitch Intellectual," *Twenty-Four Ways of Looking at Mary McCarthy*, edited by Eve Stwertka and Margot Viscusi, 27–34. Westport, CT: Greenwood Press, 1996.

Grumbach, Doris. *The Company She Kept*. New York: Coward McCann, 1967.

Gunn, James, and Michael Candelaria, eds. *Speculations on Speculation*. Lanham: Scarecrow Press, 2005.

Gwynne, Frederick, and Joseph Blotner, eds. *Faulkner in the University*. Charlottesville: University of Virginia, 1995.

Haines, William Wister. *Command Decision*. Boston: Little Brown, 1947.

Hammett, Dashiell. *The Maltese Falcon*. 1929. Reprint, New York, 1989.

————. *Novels and Stories*. 2 vols. New York: Library of America, 2013.

Hardwick, Elizabeth. Review of *Other Voices, Other Rooms*. *The Partisan Review*. March 1948.

Harris, Mark. *Five Came Back*. New York: Penguin, 2012.

Hartman, Susan. *The Homefront and Beyond: Women in the 1940s*. New York and Boston: Twayne, 1980.

Hauser, Marianne. "A Curtain of Green." *New York Times Book Review*, November 16, 1941, 6.

Heggens, Thomas. *Mister Roberts*. New York: Random House, 1948.

Heinlein, Robert. *Orphans of the Sky*. 1941. Reprint, Riverdale, NY: Baen, 2013.

————. *Rocket Ship Galileo*. New York: Charles Scribner's Sons, 1947.

————. *Sixth Column*. Riverdale, NY: Baen, 1988.

————. *Red Planet*. New York: Charles Scribner's Sons, 1949.

Hemingway, Ernest. *Across the River and Into the Trees*. New York: Charles Scribner's Sons, 1951.

————. *By Line: Ernest Hemingway*. Edited by William White. New York: Charles Scribner's, 1969.

————. *The Complete Short Stories of Ernest Hemingway*. Finca Vigia Edition. New York: Charles Scribner's, 1987.

————. *A Farewell to Arms*. New York: Charles Scribner's Sons, 1929.

————. *For Whom the Bell Tolls*. New York: Charles Scribner's Sons, 1940.

————. *Selected Letters*. Edited by Carlos Baker. New York: Charles Scribner's Sons, 1982.

Hemingway, Hilary, and Carlene Brenner. *Hemingway in Cuba*. Ruggedland, 2003.

Hersey, John. *A Bell for Adano*. 1944. Reprint, New York: Vintage, 1988.

————. *Hiroshima*. 1946. Reprint, New York: Bantam Books, 1968.

————. *Into the Valley*. Garden City: Sundial, 1944. Reprint Bison, 1990.

————. *Men on Bataan*. New York: Alfred A. Knopf, 1942.

————. *The Wall*. New York: Alfred A. Knopf, 1950.

Hicks, Granville. *James Gould Cozzens*. American Writers 58, University of Minnesota Pamphlets, 1966.

Himes, Chester. *If He Hollers Let Him Go*. 1945. Reprint, Chatham, NJ: Chatham Bookseller, 1973.

Howe, Irving. "Black Boys and Native Sons." *Dissent* 10 (Autumn 1963): 353–68.

————. "Faulkner and the Negroes." In *Faulkner: A Collection of Critical Essays*, edited by Richard Brodhead, 47–61. Englewood Cliffs, NJ: Prentice Hall, 1983.

Hughes, Langston. "Notes on a Native Son." *New York Times*, February 26, 1958.

Ickes, Harold. *The Secret Diary of Harold Ickes, Vol. 3: The Lowering Clouds, 1939–1941*. New York: Simon and Schuster, 1955.

Jackson, Esther Merle. "The American Negro and the Issue of the Absurd." In *Richard Wright, A Collection of Critical Essays*, edited by Richard Mackey and Frank E. Moore, 129–38. Englewood Cliffs, NJ: Prentice Hall, 1984.

Jones, James. *From Here to Eternity*. New York: Charles Scribner's Sons, 1951.

———. *World War II: A Chronicle of Soldiering*. 1975. Reprint, Chicago: University of Chicago Press, 2014.

Kaledin, Eugenia. *Daily Life in the United States, 1940–1959: Shifting Worlds*. Westport: Greenwood, 2000.

Kammen, Michael. *American Culture, American Tastes: Social Change in the Twentieth Century*. New York: Alfred A. Knopf, 1999.

Kazin, Alfred. *On Native Grounds: An Interpretation of Modern Prose Literature*. 1942. Reprint, New York: Mariner Books, 1995.

Keegan, John. *The Second World War*. London: Penguin, 1997.

Kennedy, Richard S. "Thomas Wolfe and the American Experience." In *Thomas Wolfe*, edited by Louis D. Rubin, 148–64. Englewood Cliffs: Prentice Hall, 1973.

Kerouac, Jack. *The Unknown Kerouac: Rare, Unpublished, and Newly Translated Writings*. Edited by Todd Tietchin. New York: Library of America, 2016.

Kershaw, Ian. *Fateful Choices: Ten Decisions That Changed the World, 1940–1941*. New York: Penguin, 2008.

Kert, Bernice. *The Hemingway Women: Those Who Loved Him—The Wives and Others*. New York: W. W. Norton, 1983.

Ketterer, David. *New Worlds for Old: The Apocalyptic Imagination, Science Fiction and American Literature*. Bloomington: Indiana University Press, 1975.

Keynes, John Meynard. *General Theory of Unemployment, Interest, and Money*. 1936. Reprint, New York: Palgrave Macmillan, 2007.

Kimbrough, Edward. *From Hell to Breakfast*. Philadelphia: J. B. Lippincott, 1941.

———. *Night Fire*. New York: Rinehart, 1946.

———. *Secret Pilgrim*. New York: Rinehart, 1949.

Kinder, John M. "The Good War's Raw Chunks: Norman Mailer's *The Naked and the Dead* and James Cozzens's *Guard of Honor*." *Midwest Quarterly*, January 2005: 187–202.

King, Richard. *A Southern Renaissance: The Cultural Awakening of the American South*. New York and Oxford: Oxford University Press, 1991.

Knight, Damon. "Not with a Bang." *Magazine of Fantasy and Science Fiction*. Winter 1949, n.p.

Knowles, A. S., Jr. "Carson McCullers in the Forties." In *The Forties: Fiction, Poetry, Drama*, edited by Warren French. Deland, FL: Everett Edwards, 1969.

Lennon, J. Michael. *Norman Mailer: A Double Life*. New York: Simon and Schuster, 2013.

———. "Norman Mailer, Journalist or Historian?" *Journal of Modern Literature* 30, no. 1 (Fall 2006), 91–103.

———. "Novelist, Journalist, or Historian?" Vol.30, No.1 (Fall 2006): 97–103.

Leong, Karen J. *The China Mystique: Pearl S. Buck, Anna Wong, May Ling Soon and the Transformation of American Orientalism*. Berkeley: University of California Press, 2015.

Leopold, Aldo. *Sand County Almanac*. 1949. Reprint, New York and Oxford: Oxford University Press, 1987.

Leuchtenberg, William E. *A Troubled Feast: American Society Since 1945*. Boston: Addison Wesley, 1982.

Lewis, R. W. B. *Trials of the Word*. New Haven: Yale University Press, 1965.

Ley, Willy. "Rockets: A Prelude to Space Travel." *Astounding Science Fiction*, July 1944, n.p.

Liebling, A. J. *World War II Writings*. New York: Library of America, 2008.

Lippmann, Walter. *Public Opinion*. 1922. Reprint, New York: Free Press, 1960.

Liptak, Andrew. "The Rise of the Paperback Novel." *Kirkus Reviews*, January 15, 2015. https://www.kirkusreviews.com/features/rise-paperback-novel/.

Loeb, Charles H. "Our Uncle Tomming Negro Artists: Our G.I.'s in the South Pacific Fiercely Resent 'Uncle Tom Roles.'" In *Reporting Civil Rights, Part One: American Journalism, 1941–1963*, edited by Clayborne Carson, David J. Garrow, Bill Kovach, and Carol Polsgrove, 71–73. New York: Library of America, 2003.

Luey, Beth. "The Organization of the Book Publishing Industry." In *The History of the Book in America*, edited by David Nord and Shelley Rubin, 29–54. Chapel Hill: University of North Carolina Press, 2009.

Lytle, Andrew. *At the Moon's Inn*. 1941. Reprint, Mobile: University of Alabama Press, 2010.

MacLuhan, Marshall. *Understanding Media: The Extensions of Man*. New York: McGraw-Hill, 1964.

MacShane, Frank. *The Life of John O'Hara*. New York: E.P. Dutton, 1981.

Mailer, Norman. *Advertisements for Myself*. New York, Putnam, 1959.

———. "The Case Against Mary McCarthy," *New York Review of Books*, October 13, 1963, 138–39.

———. "John Dos Passos" in *Dictionary of Literary Biography*, 173, cited by David Wyatt in *Secret Histories: Reading Twentieth Century American Literature*. Baltimore: Johns Hopkins University Press, 2000.

———. *The Naked and the Dead*. New York: Rinehart, 1947.

———. *Pieces and Pontifications*. Boston and New York: Little Brown, 1982.

Malamud, Bernard. *The Complete Stories*. New York: Noonday/Farrar, Straus and Giroux, 1997.

———. *Novels and Stories of the 1940s and 1950s*. Edited by Philip Davis. New York: Library of America, 2014.

Manning, Molly Guptil. *When Books Went to War*. New York: Mariner Books, 2014.

Mariani, Paul. *William Carlos Williams: New World Naked*. New York: W. W. Norton, 1990.

Marquand, John P. *B. F.'s Daughter*. Boston and New York: Little Brown, 1948.

———. *H. M. Pulham, Esquire*. Boston and New York: Little Brown, 1942.

———. *Last Laugh, Mr. Moto*. Boston and New York: Little Brown, 1942.

———. *The Late George Apley*. Boston and New York: Little Brown, 1937.

———. *Melville Goodwin, USA*. Boston and New York: Little Brown, 1951.

———. *Repent in Haste*. Boston and New York: Little Brown, 1945.

———. *So Little Time*. Boston and New York: Little Brown, 1943.

———. *Wickford Point*. Boston and New York: Little Brown, 1939.

Marshall, George C. Speech at Harvard University, June 5, 1947.

May, Charles E. "Why Sister Lives at the P.O." *Southern Humanities Review* 12 (1978), 243–49.

May, Rollo. *The Meaning of Anxiety*. 1950. Reprint, New York: W. W. Norton, 1977.

Mayer, Geoff, and Brian McDonell. *Encyclopedia of Film Noir*. Westport: Greenwood, 2003.

McAdam, Doug. *Freedom Summer*. Oxford University Press, 1988.

McCarthy, Mary. "America the Beautiful." *Commentary*, September 1, 1947, 116.

———. *The Company She Keeps*. 1942. Reprint, New York: Mariner, 1993.

———. *The Complete Fiction*. New York: Library of America, 2017.

———. "The Vita Activa." *New Yorker*, October 18, 1958, 156.

———. "The Weeds." *New Yorker*, September 1944, 25.

McCullers, Carson. *Complete Novels*. New York: Library of America, 2001.

———. *The Heart Is a Lonely Hunter*. Boston: Houghton Mifflin, 1940.

———. *The Member of the Wedding*. Boston: Houghton Mifflin, 1946.

———. *Reflections in a Golden Eye*. Boston: Houghton Mifflin, 1941.

———. *Stories, Plays, and Other Writings*. New York: Library of America, 2017.

McCullough, David. *Truman*. New York: Simon and Schuster, 1992.

———. "Truman." In *Character Above All: Ten Presidents from FDR to George W. Bush*. Edited by Robert A. Wilson, 39–47. New York: Simon and Schuster, 1995.

McDonnell, Thomas T., ed. "Meditatio Pauperis in Solitudine," *The Thomas Merton Reader*, New York: Harcourt, Brace, 1974, 513.

McHaney, Pearl, ed. *Eudora Welty: The Contemporary Reviews*. Cambridge: Cambridge University Press, 2005.

McMillan, George. "Race, Justice in Aiken." *The Nation*, November 23, 1946, *Reporting Civil Rights*. New York: The Library of America, 2013.

McMillen, Neal R., ed. *Remaking Dixie: The Impact of World War II on the American South*. Jackson: University Press of Mississippi, 1997.

Merton, Thomas. *Contemplation in a World of Action*. Garden City: Doubleday, 1971.

———. *The Hidden Ground of Love, Letters*. New York: Farrar, Straus and Giroux, 1985.

———. *The Seven Storey Mountain*. New York: Harcourt Brace, 1948.

Meyer, Michael J. "The Many Faces of God." In *Robert Penn Warren's All the King's Men*, edited by Michael J. Meyer and Hugh J. Ingrasci, 237–52. New York and Amsterdam: Rodopi, 2012.

Meyers, Jeffrey. "A Good Place to Work." *Commonweal*, February 7, 2015. https://www.commonwealmagazine.org/good-place-work.

———. *Hemingway: The Critical Heritage*, London: Routledge, 2009.

———. *Hemingway: A Biography*. New York: Harper and Row, 1985.

Michener, James. *Tales of the South Pacific*. New York: Macmillan, 1947.

Miller, Arthur. *Eight Plays*. Garden City: Nelson Doubleday, 1981.

———. *Focus*. New York: Penguin, 2001.

Mills, C. Wright. *The Power Elite*. 1956. Reprint, Oxford: Oxford University Press, 2000.

Milner, Lucille B. "Jim Crow in the Army," *New Republic* (March 13, 1944). In *Reporting Civil Rights Part One: American Journalism, 1941–1963*, edited by Clayborne Carson, David J. Garrow, Bill Kovach, and Carol Polsgrove. 339–42. New York: Library of America, 2003.

Mitchell, Margaret. *Gone with the Wind*. New York: Macmillan, 1936.

Naimark, Norman V. *The Russians in Germany: A History of the Soviet Zone of Occupation, 1945–1949*. Cambridge, MA: Harvard University Press, 1995.

The New Yorker Book of the 40s: Story of a Decade. New York: The New Yorker, 2014.

Niebuhr, Reinhold. *Major Writings on Religion and Politics*. New York: Library of America, 2015.

Nieves, Ellen. "Some Upset by Twist on Pearl Harbor," *New York Times,* May 28, 2001. http://www.nytimes.com/2001/05/28/us/some-upset-by-twist-on-pearl-harbor.html .

Nora, Pierre. *Realms of Memory*. 3 vols. New York: Columbia University Press, 1996–98.

O'Hara, John. *The New York Stories*. New York: Penguin, 2013.

———. *Pipe Night*. New York: Duell, Sloan and Pearse, 1942.

———. "Review of *Across the River and Into the Trees*." *New York Times Book Review*, September 10, 1950, 1, 30–31.

——— . *Stories*. New York: Library of America, 2016.

Ong, Walter J. *Orality and Literacy: The Technologizing of the Word*. New York: Routledge, 1982.

Orwell, George. *Homage to Catalonia*. London: Secker and Warburg, 1938.

———. *Orwell: The Lost Writings*. New York: Arbor House, 1985.

———. "Politics and the English Language," *George Orwell Reader: Fiction, Essays, Reportage*. New York: Mariner Books, 1961.

Osteen, Mark. *Nightmare Alley: Film Noir and the American Dream*. Baltimore: Johns Hopkins, 2012.

Packard, Vance. *The Hidden Persuaders*. New York: Penguin, 1957.

Patterson, James T. *Grand Expectations: The United States, 1945–1974*. 1996.

Patterson, William H., Jr. *Robert A. Heinlein: In Dialogue with His Century*. New York: TOR, Tom Doherty Associates, 2010.

"Pearl Harbor." *The Boston Globe*, September 6, 1941, 1.

Perkins, James. "Jack Burden: Successful Historian," In *Robert Penn Warren's All the King's Men*, edited by Michael J. Meyer and Hugh J. Ingrasci, 91–97. New York and Amsterdam: Rodopi, 2012.

Perloff, James. "Pearl Harbor Was Surprised, America Was Not." *New American,* December 7, 2016. https://www.thenewamerican.com/culture/history/item/4740-pearl-harbor-hawaii-was-surprised-fdr-was-not.

Perrin, Noel. *A Reader's Delight*. Lebanon, NH: University Press of New England, 1988.

Petry, Ann. *The Street*. Boston and New York: Houghton Mifflin, 1946.

Phelan, James. *Reading the American Novel, 1920–2010*. Hoboken, NJ: Wiley-Blackwell, 2013.

Pizer, Donald. "Norman Mailer, Theodore Dreiser, and the Politics of American Literary History," *Sewanee Review* 122, no. 3 (Summer 2014), 459–72.

Podoretz, Norman. *Making It*. New York: Random House, 1969.

Polk, Noel. *Faulkner and Welty and the Southern Literary Tradition*. Jackson: University of Mississippi Press, 2008.

Pollack, Jack. "Literacy Tests: Southern Style." *American Mercury*, June 1949. In *Reporting Civil Rights, Part One: American Journalism, 1941–1963*, edited by Clayborne Carson, David J. Garrow, Bill Kovach, and Carol Polsgrove, 85–91. New York: Library of America, 2003.

Porter, Katherine Anne. *Collected Short Stories*. New York: Harvest, Harcourt Brace Jovanovich, 1979.

———. "Introduction." In *Eudora Welty: Selected Stories*. New York: Modern Library, 1954, 3–16.

———. *Three Short Novels*. New York: Library of America, 2014.

Postman, Neil. *Amusing Ourselves to Death: Public Discourse in the Age of Show Business*. New York: Penguin, 1985.

Prange, Gordon W. *At Dawn We Slept: The Untold Story of Pearl Harbor*. Norwalk: Easton Press, 1988.

Prescott, Orville. "Outstanding Novels." *Yale Review* 38, no. 2 (December 1948), 380–84.

Putnam, Robert. *Bowling Alone: The Collapse and Revival of American Community*. New York: Touchstone, Simon and Schuster, 2000.

Railton, Ben. "The Awful Responsibility of Time." In *Robert Penn Warren's All the King's Men*, edited by Michael J. Meyer and Hugh J. Ingrasci, 103–20. New York and Amsterdam: Rodopi, 2012.

Rampersad, Arnold. *Ralph Ellison*. New York: Vintage, 2008.

Ramsey, Robert. *Fire in Summer*. New York: Viking, 1942.

Rand, Ayn. *The Fountainhead*. New York: Plume, 1994.

———. "Selfishness," *The Ayn Rand Reader*. Ed. Gary Hill and Leonard Peikoff. New York: Plume, 1999.

Reisman, David. *The Lonely Crowd* (1950). New Haven: Yale University Press, 2001.

Remnick, David. "*The New Yorker* in the Forties." *New Yorker*, April 28, 2014. http://www.newyorker.com/books/page-turner/the-new-yorker-in-the-forties.

Reynolds, Michael. *Hemingway: The 1930s Through the Final Years*. New York: Norton, 2012.

———. *Hemingway: The Paris Years*. Oxford: Blackwell, 1989.

———. *The Young Hemingway*. Oxford: Blackwell, 1986.

Rice, Elmer. *Flight to the West*. New York: Coward-McCann, 1940.

Roberts, Adam. *History of Science Fiction*. 2nd edition. New York: Palgrave, 2016.

Robinson, Douglas. *American Apocalypses: The Image of the End of the World in American Literature*. Baltimore: Johns Hopkins University Press, 1985.

Roosevelt, Franklin Delano. Message to Congress. January 4, 1939.

———. Message to Congress, Declaration of War. December 8, 1941.

———. Radio Address. September 4, 1939.

Rose, Jonathan. *The Holocaust and the Book: Destruction and Preservation*. Amherst: University of Massachusetts Press, 2008.

Rubin, Louis D., Jr. *A Gallery of Southerners*. Baton Rouge and London: Louisiana State University, 1982.

———. ed. *Thomas Wolfe*. Englewood Cliffs: Prentice Hall, 1973.

Rubin, Louis D., Jr., and Robert Jacobs, eds. *Southern Renascence: The Literature of the Modern South*. 1953. Reprint, Baltimore: Johns Hopkins University Press, 1966.

Rubin, Louis D., Jr., and James J. Kirkpatrick, eds. *The Lasting South: Fourteen Southerners Look at Their Home*. Chicago: H. Regnery, 1957.

Safire, William. *Lend Me Your Ears: Great Speeches in History*. New York: W. W. Norton, 2004.

Salinger, J. D. *The Catcher in the Rye*. New York: Grosset and Dunlap, 1951.

Sanders, David. *John Hersey*. New York: Twayne, 1967.

Schleuter, Paul. "The Dissection of Mary McCarthy." In *Contemporary American Novelists*, edited by Harry J. Moore, 61–64. Carbondale: Southern Illinois University Press, 1964.

Shaw, Irwin. *The Young Lions*. 1948. Reprint, Chicago: University of Chicago Press, 2000.

Shirer, William. *Berlin Diary: The Journal of a Foreign Correspondent*. New York: Alfred A. Knopf, 1941.

———. *The Rise and Fall of the Third Reich*. New York: Simon and Schuster, 1990.

Silverberg, Robert. "Science Fiction in the Fifties: The Real Golden Age." New York: Library of America, 2010.

Skaggs, Merrill. "Enchantment in 'Frontier Home' and *The Robber Bridegroom*." *Studies in American Humor* 3 (October 1976): 96–102.

———. *The Folk of Southern Fiction*. Athens: University of Georgia Press, 1972.

Sontag, Susan. "The Imagination of Disaster." *Commentary*, October 1, 1965, 42–48.

Spiller, Robert. *The Cycle of American Literature*. New York: Mentor Books, 1957.

Spock, Benjamin. *Pocket Book of Baby Care*. New York: Simon and Schuster, 1946.

Stafford, Jean. "The Empty Net." *Partisan Review* 11 (1944): 114–15.

Stein, Gertrude. "Reflections on the Atom Bomb." *Yale Poetry Review*, December 1947, 27.

Steinbeck, John. *Bombs Away: The Story of a Bomber Team*. New York: Viking, 1943.

———. *Cannery Row*. New York: Viking, 1945.

———. *The Grapes of Wrath*. New York: Viking, 1939.

———. *The Grapes of Wrath and Other Writings*. New York: Library of America, 1996.

———. *A Life in Letters*. Edited by Elaine Steinbeck and Robert Wallsten. New York: Viking, 1975.

———. *The Log from the Sea of Cortez*. New York: Viking, 1941.

———. *The Moon Is Down*. New York: Viking, 1942.

———. *Novels, 1942–1952*. New York: Library of America, 2002.

———. *Once There Was a War*. New York: Viking, 1958.

Stepto, Robert. *From Behind the Veil: A Study of Afro-American Narrative*. Urbana: University of Illinois Press, 1991.

Stinnett, Robert B. *Day of Deceit: The Truth About FDR and Pearl Harbor*. New York: Free Press, Touchstone, 2001.

Stock, Irving. *Mary McCarthy: Pamphlets on American Writers, 72*. Minneapolis: University of Minnesota Press, 1968.

Sturgeon, Theodore. *The Complete Stories of Theodore Sturgeon*. 4 vols. New York: North Atlantic Books, 2013.

Sundquist, Eric. *Faulkner: A House Divided*. Baltimore: Johns Hopkins, 1985.

Teachout, Terry. "Norman Mailer, Literary Hustler," *Commentary*, January 1, 2014, 57–59.

Thomas, Ronald R. *Detective Fiction and the Rise of Forensic Science*. Cambridge: Cambridge University Press, 1999.

Thompson, John B. *Merchants of Culture: The Publishing Business in the Twenty-First Century*. New York: Plume, 2012.

Tibbets, John C., and James M. Welsh. *Encyclopedia of Novels into Film*. New York: Infobase, 2005.

Toland, John. *Infamy: Pearl Harbor and Its Aftermath*. New York: Berkeley, 1986.

Trilling, Diana. "The Radical Moralism of Norman Mailer." In *Norman Mailer: A Selection of Critical Essays*, edited by Leo Braudy, 42–65. Englewood Cliffs: Prentice Hall, 1972.

———. "What Has Happened to Our Novels?" *Harper's*, May 1944, 533–34.

———. "The Wide Net and Other Stories: Fiction in Review," *The Nation* 157 (October 2, 1943): 386–87.

Trilling, Lionel. *The Liberal Imagination* (1950). New York: New York Review Books Classics, 2008.

Truman, Harry S. *Memoirs: The Year of Decisions, 1945*. Garden City: Doubleday, 1955.

———. *Memoirs: The Years of Trial and Hope, 1946–1952*. Garden City: Doubleday, 1955.

———. State of the Union Address, Washington, DC, January 6, 1947.

Ullman, James Ramsey. *The White Tower*. Philadelphia: J. B. Lippincott, 1948.

Vidal, Gore. *United States: Essays, 1952–1992*. New York: Random House, 1993.

———. *Williwaw* (1948). Reprint, London: Heinemann, 1986.

Warren, Robert Penn. *All the King's Men*. New York: Harcourt Brace, 1946.

———. *Band of Angels*. New York: Random House, 1955.

———. *Collected Essays*. New York: Random House, 1958. pp. 156–69.

———. "The Love and Separateness in Miss Welty's Fiction." *Kenyon Review* 6, no. 2 (Spring 1944), 246–59.

———. *Night Rider*. New York: Random House, 1939.

———. "A Note to All the King's Men." *Sewanee Review* 63, no. 3 (Summer 1953), 182–92.

———. *Selected Poems, 1923–1945*. New York: Random House, 1946.

Watkins, Floyd C., and John T. Hiers, eds. *Robert Penn Warren Talking: Interviews, 1950–1978*. New York: Random House, 1980.

Weinman, Sarah, ed. *Women Crime Writers: Eight Suspense Novels of the 1940s and 50s*. New York: Library of America, 2015.

Welty, Eudora. *A Curtain of Green*. New York: Doubleday, Doran, 1941.

———. *Delta Wedding*. New York: Harcourt Brace, 1946.

———. *The Golden Apples*. New York: Harcourt Brace, 1949.

———. *Losing Battles*. New York: Random House, 1970.

———. *The Optimist's Daughter*. New York: Random House, 1972.

———. *The Robber Bridegroom*. New York: Harcourt Brace, 1942.

———. *Selected Stories*. New York: Modern Library, 1954.

———. *Stories, Essays, and Memoir*. New York: Library of America, 1998.

———. *The Wide Net and Other Stories*. New York: Harcourt Brace, 1943.

Weyr, Thomas. *The Setting of the Pearl: Vienna Under Hitler*. New York: Oxford University Press, 2005.

White, Gleeson. *Strange Bodies: Gender and Identity in the Novels of Carson McCullers*. Tuscaloosa: University of Alabama Press, 2003.

Wilkinson, James D. *The Intellectual Resistance in Europe*. Cambridge: Harvard University Press, 1981.

Williams, Ben Ames. *All the Brothers Were Valiant*. New York: Macmillan, 1955.

———. *Amateurs at War: American Soldiers in Action*. Boston: Houghton Mifflin, 1943.

———. *House Divided*. Boston: Houghton Mifflin, 1947.

———. *Leave Her to Heaven*. Boston: Houghton Mifflin, 1944.

———. *The Strange Woman*. Boston: Houghton Mifflin, 1946.

———. *A Time of Peace: September 26, 1930 to December 7, 1941*. Boston: Houghton Mifflin, 1942.

Williams, Tennessee. *Complete Plays*. 2 vols. Edited by Kenneth Holditch and Mel Gussow. New York: Library of America, 2014.

Willis, Susan. "Aesthetics of the Rural Slum: Contradictions and Dependency in The Bear." In *William Faulkner: New Perspectives*, edited by Richard H. Brodhead, 174–94. Englewood Cliffs, NJ: Prentice Hall, 1983.

Wilson, Edmund. *Literary Essays and Reviews of the 1920s and 30s*. Edited by Lewis Dabney. New York: Library of America.

Winn, Marie. *The Plug-In Drug*. New York: Viking, 1977.

Winsor, Kathleen. *Forever Amber*. New York: Macmillan, 1945.

Wolfe, Thomas. *The Hills Beyond*. New York: Charles Scribner's Sons, 1941.

———. *Look Homeward, Angel*. New York: Charles Scribner's Sons, 1929.

———. *Of Time and the River*. New York: Charles Scribner's Sons, 1935.

———. *The Web and the Rock*. New York: Charles Scribner's Sons, 1939.

———. *You Can't Go Home Again*. New York: Charles Scribner's Sons, 1940.

Wolff, Tobias. *Collected Stories*. New York: Picador, 1988.

———. *Old School*. New York: Vintage, 2003.

Woods, Katherine. "The Wide Net," *Tomorrow* 3 (1943): 54.

Woodward, C. Vann. *The Future of the Past*. Oxford: Oxford University Press, 1989.

Woolrich, Cornell. *I Married a Dead Man*. 1948. Reprint, New York: Penguin, 1994.

Wright, Ellen, and Michael Fabre. *The Richard Wright Reader*. New York: Harper and Row, 1978.

Wright, Richard. *Black Boy: A Record of Childhood and Youth*. New York: Harper and Brothers, 1943.

———. "Blueprint for Negro Writing," *New Challenge*, Vol. 2, No. 1, fall 1937.

———. *Native Son*. New York: Harper, 1940. New York: Signet, 1969.

———. "How Bigger Was Born." In *Twentieth Century Interpretations of Native Son*, edited by Houston A. Baker, Jr., 20–29. Englewood Cliffs: Prentice Hall, 1972.

———. "Inner Landscape," *New Republic*, August 1941, 195.

———. "Introduction," *Native Son*. New York: Harper Perennial, 1993.

———. *The Outsider*. New York: Harper, 1953. Reprint. New York: Da Capo Press, 1997.

———. *12 Million Black Voices*. 1941. Reprint, New York: Arno Press, 1969.

Wyatt, David M. "Faulkner and the Burdens of the Past." In *Faulkner: A Collection of Critical Essays*, edited by Richard Brodhead, 92–116. Englewood Cliffs, NJ: Prentice Hall, 1983.

———. *Secret Histories: Reading Twentieth Century American Literature*. Baltimore: Johns Hopkins University Press, 2000.

Young, Philip. *Ernest Hemingway: A Reconsideration*. 1952. Reprint, University Park: Pennsylvania State Press, 1966.

Zinn, Howard. *A People's History of the United States*. New York: Harper and Row, 1980.

———. *Postwar America, 1945–1971*. Indianapolis: Bobbs-Merrill, 1973.

INDEX

ABC Radio, 108
Acheson, Dean, 160
Adams, John, 123
Agee, James, 152, 170
alienation, x, 26, 28, 59, 60, 61, 63, 72, 73, 168
American Jewish Congress, 156
American Mercury, 79
ancestral ghosts, 31
Anderson, Benedict, 183
anxiety, xxiii, 18, 20, 23, 26, 28, 87, 88–89, 108, 112, 159, 167, 168, 168–169, 183
Arendt, Hannah, 117, 173
Arguelles, Elicio, 7
Army Air Force, 18, 23, 88–89, 90
Arnold, Henry "Hap", 23, 83, 88–89, 90, 111
Asimov, Isaac, 166
Aswell, Edward C., 62
Atlantic Charter, xx
atomic bomb, xiv, 108, 111, 112, 155, 156, 167, 175
Atomic Energy Act, 109
Atomic Energy Commission, 154, 164
Auden, Wystan Hugh (W. H.), 169
Austria, 91

B-29 raids, 111
baby boom, xiv
Baker, Houston, 64
Baldwin, James, 66, 70–74

Ball, Lucille, 181
Ballantine Publishing, 176
Bantam Books, 174
Barkley, Alben, 157
Barlow, Joel, 123
baseball, 113–114
Batista, Fulgencio, 3
Bell, Daniel, 173
Bellah, Robert, xiv, 182
Bellow, Saul, xii, 115–117
Benet, Stephen Vincent, 167
Benchley, Robert, 130
Benedict, Ruth, 108
Benedictine Rule, 174
Berle, Milton, 181
Berlin, Germany, xviii, 13, 16, 93, 125, 137, 159, 162
Bettelheim, Bruno, 48
Beveridge, William H., 154
Bill of Rights, The, 60, 156
Bishop. John Peale, 148
Black, Hugo, 79
Blitz, The (London air raid bombings), 10, 13, 16
Bobbs-Merrill Publishing, 118
Bonn, Germany, 9
Book-of-the-Month Club, 3, 66, 76, 81, 99, 135, 137, 139, 141, 177, 179
books on radio, 177
bookstores, 171, 178, 179
Boston Globe, The, xxii

ABOUT THE AUTHOR

Robert McParland is professor of English and chair of the Department of English at Felician College. He has published numerous book chapters and articles, including essays on Herman Melville, Ernest Hemingway, and Robert Penn Warren. McParland is editor of *Music and Literary Modernism* (2008) and *Film and Literary Modernism* (2013), as well as author of *Charles Dickens's American Audience* (Lexington, 2010); *How to Write about Joseph Conrad* (2011); *Mark Twain's Audience: A Critical Analysis of Reader Responses to the Writings of Mark Twain* (Lexington, 2014); *Beyond Gatsby: How Fitzgerald, Hemingway, and Writers of the 1920s Shaped American Culture* (Rowman & Littlefield, 2015); and *Citizen Steinbeck: Giving Voice to the People* (Rowman & Littlefield, 2016).

CPSIA information can be obtained
at www.ICGtesting.com
Printed in the USA
BVOW08*1120281017
498765BV00003B/5/P